Peace Lessons

TIMOTHY BRAATZ

The Disproportionate Press

ISBN-13: 978-0692303757
ISBN-10: 0692303758

The Disproportionate Press

DP@lunycrab.com • www.lunycrab.com

PEACE LESSONS

TIMOTHY BRAATZ

A revised version of Chapter 4 of this book appears as "The Satyagraha of John Brown," *In Factis Pax* 8:1 (2014): 104-120, http://infactispax.org/journal.

Sections from Chapter 5 and Chapter 6 were condensed to create "The Limitations of Strategic Nonviolence," *Peace Review* 26:1 (2014): 4-11.

An excerpt from Chapter 9 appears as "Selma: A Gandhian Critique," TRANSCEND Media Services: Solutions-Oriented Peace Journalism, Jan. 26, 2015, https://www.transcend.org/tms/2015/01/selma-a-gandhian-critique/.

CONTENTS

NONVIOLENCE

This book is about nonviolence—not the absence of violence, but the presence of creative, nonviolent conflict resolution. Mohandas Gandhi called this *satyagraha*. The first purpose of this book is to identify and clarify nonviolence and other basic peace studies concepts, such as structural and cultural violence and integrative power. The early chapters address important questions like the nature of human goodness, the inevitability of war, and the problem of the ruthless opponent. The lessons offered here originated in college peace studies and history courses, and instructors may find this text useful as a curriculum guide or for assigned reading. Three appendices offer exercises, designed for the classroom, that dramatize some of the conceptual lessons presented in the early chapters.

The second purpose of this book is to apply peace studies concepts to select historical events to better understand the achievements and shortcomings of nonviolent campaigns. Unlike the social science fields, including history, which cling to the pretence of scholarly "detachment," peace studies admits to a specific social goal. The goal of peace studies is to understand and promote peace work, and the goal of peace work is to reduce current levels of violence and to make future violence less likely. To that end, this book looks at civilian resistance movements across the twentieth century, and offers a critique of strategic nonviolence as compared to Gandhi's principled nonviolence. Special attention is given to the US Civil Rights Movement, which has much to teach us about the importance of confronting all of a society's violent aspects.

Direct violence means actions that cause harm. *Structural violence* is the harm built into political and economic systems. Underlying these two types is *cultural violence*, which includes the beliefs, ideologies, cosmologies, and language that legitimize and justify other forms of violence. What we think, write, and say about peace and violence matters. However, as an academic field, US history has not fully recognized and appreciated the power of nonviolence. Economic exploitation and violent enforcement are pillars of the US ruling class—from early, slave-owning presidents to present-day bankers and oil executives—and historians, both as celebrators and critics, have reflected those interests. The tendency is to accept acts of violence as normal and inevitable, not requiring an explanation as to why infliction of suffering was chosen over other forms of conflict resolution. Not understanding or valuing integrative power, and unaware of peace theory, historians frequently overlook or discount historical nonviolence, and, thus, unwittingly perpetuate cultural violence.

The intended audience of this book is readers in the United States, particularly college students and teachers. If they find these lessons unfamiliar and surprising, it's for good reason. The US education system is primarily geared toward developing self-interested business managers and a compliant labor force—hence, the emphasis on grades and punctuality. Most teachers would probably agree that violence is a serious and urgent problem in the world today, yet surprisingly few are involved in preparing members of the next generation to be peacemakers. In a country where so many claim to be Christians, one might expect the ethic of peace taught by Jesus the Christ to prevail. On the contrary, the current US political economy is based on the capitalist ethic of greed and on massive amounts of military spending. Because this works against the basic material and spiritual interests of almost everyone, a steady stream of propaganda is required to convince the population that compassion is a sign of weakness and that militarism is necessary and desirable. Thus, students are far more likely to be taught that war brings positive outcomes and that acts of extreme violence are the only way to confront serious problems, rather than learn to employ nonviolence, including at the international level, to resolve conflicts without causing harm.

For example, US history students typically learn that, in the twentieth century, the United States became an economic and military "superpower." The positive language of that phrase, if left unexamined, is an affirmation of dominance and warfare: violence is super. A far less familiar lesson is the long line of nonviolence that runs through our past. Early American Quakers, most notably John Woolman, rejected war and slavery, and, along with Henry David Thoreau, author of "Civil Disobedience," influenced the Russian novelist Leo Tolstoy, who, taking seriously the Biblical commandment "Thou shall not kill," denounced the inherent violence of the state. Tolstoy's Christian anarchism influenced Gandhi, who was experimenting with nonviolence in South Africa. In the twentieth century, US civil rights organizations sent representatives to study Gandhi's resistance movement in India and invited Gandhian advocates to visit North America. The philosophy of nonviolence had come full circle: from Quakers to Tolstoy to Gandhi and back to the United States, where the Civil Rights Movement exposed the ugliness of the superpower and taught nonviolent resistance to the world. The civilian resistance movements that ended communist rule in east central Europe owe far more to Martin Luther King Jr.'s peace-building than to Ronald Reagan's war-making, but are often construed as an achievement of the superpower—i.e., "Reagan won the Cold War." Teaching the end of European totalitarianism as a victory for capitalism and US militarism, rather than as a triumph of nonviolence, is cultural violence.

This is correctable. Scholars and classroom instructors can make much-needed contributions to cultural peace—weakening, however slightly, faith in violence—by retrieving nonviolence from the historical record and showing what it can accomplish. When the story of the Birmingham "Children's March" is standard grade-school fare, when Mary Dyer's final testament is better known than George Custer's "Last Stand," and when Columbus Day is consigned to the dustbin, we'll be on the right track. US society, with all its energy, creativity, diversity, and openness, can become a superpower for peace. Hopefully, this book will contribute to that awakening.

GLOSSARY

ahimsa (ə-'him-sä): non-harming

ashram ('äsh-rəm): hermitage or spiritual retreat

civilian resistance: sustained, mass, nonviolent action directed against unwanted government

cultural peace: beliefs, language, ideologies, and cosmologies that legitimize and motivate direct and cultural peace

cultural violence: beliefs, language, ideologies, and cosmologies that legitimize and motivate direct and cultural violence

deep culture: underlying assumptions about the nature of the universe or cosmology

dehumanization: seeing others as means to an end; loss of compassion; denying one's own need for compassion and human connection

direct peace: nonviolent action

direct violence: physically or verbally causing harm; harmful events

historic trauma: massive, cumulative, intergenerational transfer of unresolved fear, anger, and grief

integrative power: ability to attract empathy, friendship, and concern

moral jujitsu: turning repressive energy against the oppressor; dynamic where violent repression leads to more, not less, resistance; also called political jujitsu

NAACP: National Association for the Advancement of Colored People

negative peace: absence or reduction of violence of all kinds

nonviolent interposition: unarmed third-party presence in conflict zones for the purpose of witnessing and mediating pacifism: rejection of violence

passivism: doing nothing

peace-building: creating an environment where future violence is less likely

peacekeeping: preventing violence from restarting

peacemaking: stopping violence

people power: civilian resistance

positive peace: creative, nonviolent conflict resolution

principled nonviolence: use of nonviolence out of conviction that violence is always wrong; nonviolence of the strong

reform: repair or alteration to a system; slow, gradual change

revolution: overthrow or replacement of an entire system; quick, dramatic change

satyagraha (sə-'tyä-grə-hə): holding firmly to Truth; refusal to cause harm in any way; active rejection of all forms of violence

satyagrahi (sə-'tyä-grə-hē): person committed to *satyagraha*

SCLC: Southern Christian Leadership Conference

shanti sainik (shən-tē shy-nik): member of a peace army

shanti sena (shən-tē sä-nä): peace army; organization of volunteers trained for large-scale, nonviolent interposition

SNCC: Student Nonviolent Coordinating Committee

strategic nonviolence: nonviolence as a strategic, rather than principled, choice; nonviolence of the weak; misleadingly called pragmatic nonviolence

structural peace: aspects of a political or economic system that provide for basic human needs structural violence: indirect violence; harm built into a political or economic system

violence: avoidable insult to basic human needs, which include survival, well-being, identity, and freedom

PEACE LESSONS

Chapter 1

- Humans have the capacity for violence and cruelty, but kindness is the prevalent characteristic.
- War is a disease, not a sporting event.

Chapter 2

- Direct violence, structural violence, and cultural violence constitute a mutually reinforcing triangle.
- Direct peace, structural peace, and cultural peace constitute a mutually reinforcing triangle.

Chapter 3

- Nonviolence is an active response and benefits from training.
- Integrative power draws people closer and builds upon itself.
- Principled nonviolence can be pragmatic—depending on the goal.

Chapter 4

- Satyagraha is active rejection of all forms of violence, and requires cultivation of fearlessness, self-reliance, and self-respect.

Chapter 5

- Mass, sustained, nonviolent resistance is more likely than violent rebellion to remove unwanted government because nonviolent resistance delegitimizes state violence, while violent resistance legitimizes state violence.

Chapter 6

- Nonviolent removal of a repressive regime is no guarantee of democracy, justice, equality of opportunity, and human rights protections if the many facets of structural and cultural violence are not addressed.

Chapter 7

- The best way to overcome extreme violence with nonviolence is to start early (now), before the violence becomes extreme.

Chapter 8

- To make society less violent, find like-minded people, identify a local problem, and together, using nonviolent means, try to fix it.
- For nonviolent resisters, imprisonment can bring freedom because they are no longer cooperating with or benefitting from a violent system in any way.
- In an oppressors-oppressed relationship, the oppressed have the better chance of emancipating both parties.

Chapter 9

- If you want a radically nonviolent society, be radically nonviolent.
- In destroying the legitimacy of a violent state, a nonviolent movement will awaken the oppressed masses, who may resort to violence, and that violence will restore the legitimacy of the violent state.
- Nonviolent revolution must be done outside a system built on violence.

PEACE LESSONS

TIMOTHY BRAATZ

1

THINKING ABOUT WAR

1

THINKING ABOUT WAR

A Fundamental Question

Morally speaking, are humans essentially good or bad? *Essentially* can mean biologically, genetically, inherently. It also means fundamentally, primarily, ultimately. Either way, the question is asking about the essence—the very core—of being human. Is human nature selfish or generous, mean or kind, hateful or loving?

For many in US society, the answer is that humans are essentially selfish, mean, and hateful. This notion is taught and reinforced in many ways. Biology students ponder natural selection and may come to think "survival of the fittest" rewards the worst of human behavior. Christian teaching emphasizes original sin and a fallen humanity that requires forgiveness and redemption. Capitalist dogma holds that humans are basically "rational," meaning selfish, and some claim this selfishness, this uninhibited drive for material acquisition, ennobles the hyper-capitalist US political economy. Indeed, the US political structure is supposedly based on "checks and balances," which means self-interested branches of government selfishly limiting each other's power. If these theoretical and theological arguments are not enough, concrete examples of hateful behavior are seemingly everywhere—in newspapers, news broadcasts, television shows, movies, comic books, bestselling novels. With all that killing, stealing, torturing, raping, assaulting, bullying, cheating, lying, hoarding, exploiting, and insulting, can anyone doubt that humans are vile creatures?

If human nature is essentially immoral, it seems to follow that humans are inherently violent. When people don't get their way—and even when they do—they are naturally inclined, perhaps biologically driven, to hurt each other, physically and otherwise. When a few of these violent creatures get together, war is inevitable. Again, the theoretical claims abound. Some biologists point to killing among chimpanzees as proof of the innate quality of human violence and war-making. Holy scriptures are filled with tales of slaughter, much of it divinely sanctioned. Humans even murdered Jesus, who Christians consider God in human form. In the current day, politicians loudly warn of the inevitability of attack by terrorists and foreign armies, and wars rage around the globe.

But is it true that humans are essentially hateful, inherently violent, and is war really inevitable? These are fundamental questions for the field of peace studies. If, on the one hand, the answer is simply *yes* on all counts, then studying nonviolence and working for a more peaceful world may be indulgent at best, foolish and suicidal at worst. It would be better to stockpile weapons, hone your warcraft, and prepare to defend yourself. On the other hand, if alternative answers are available and convincing, then peace study and peace work are legitimate. More than legitimate. If humans are *not* essentially hateful, violent, and warlike, then peace study and peace work are critical, if for no other reason than to counter the influence of those who continue to preach the primacy of human immorality. If you assume the worst about people, if you treat them as "bad"—attack them, lock them up, limit their options, seek to eliminate them—you are likely to evoke undesirable behavior—"badness"—in response. For example, take a teenager, label him a criminal, a "bad guy," deliver him to a violent, repressive prison, and see if he becomes a "good guy."

On the macro level, if a government builds a war machine to defend its population from potential attack, the supposed enemy will perceive this military buildup as a threat. What one government considers necessary defense, the other will interpret as an offensive act, and will prepare to defend itself accordingly. Thus begins an arms race. "If you wish for peace, prepare for war"—that tired, old dictum has it perfectly wrong.[1] If you prepare for war, one way or the other war is what you'll get. The belief in the inevitability of war, like the belief in human badness, is a self-fulfilling prophesy. So the first peace lesson must be to identify and explain human goodness.

Inclusive Fitness

A look at human evolution provides some clues to the evolutionary value and liability of both pacifism and violence, and suggests that humans have a strong biological drive to be good to each other. Almost all of human existence has been in nomadic foraging bands—all other forms of human social organization are relatively recent—so most of human evolution occurred in such bands. Like in other species, male aggression probably offered certain evolutionary advantages in the competition for females, and thus males evolved to be aggressive. But there were liabilities too. Early human bands likely expelled or executed a dangerous band member, and aggressive males who frequently provoked fights may have had a greater chance of being killed before siring or raising successful offspring.

While individual violence could get you expelled or killed, the inclination to cooperate within a group was an asset because early humans were mutually dependent group dwellers. Over the millennia, natural selection for human genes occurred in individuals, but those individuals lived, reproduced, and nurtured their offspring in nomadic foraging bands that included extended families with many shared genes. Intra-group cooperation—in hunting, babysitting, knowledge-sharing—was critical to the survival and success of the group and, thus, the genetic line; noncooperation was a liability. Individuals who didn't cooperate within the group, like individuals who didn't nurture their young, would have been at a disadvantage when it came to passing on their genes. Simply put, regarding "survival of the fittest," being the "fittest" included looking out for fellow band members—your own children, but also your siblings, cousins, nieces, and nephews—making sure they stayed alive and healthy enough to reproduce and to look out for you. This is known as *inclusive fitness*.

But if humans evolved to be nurturing, caring, and loving, how does one explain the biological basis, if one exists, for all the human violence in the world? The same way, actually. Just as the "fittest" nurtured their young, they also protected them and themselves from early death. True evolutionary fitness is the ability to produce offspring that survive long enough to reproduce. For humans, that means a relatively long period of feeding, teaching, and protecting their young, who are born helpless and totally dependent. Early humans—successful ones, anyway—figured out how to defend themselves and their young against attack by other creatures, possibly including other humans. Similarly, they defended fellow band members, meaning the extended family. Their defense strategies probably included running and hiding, but also fighting back by inflicting physical pain and death. A willingness to retaliate could serve as a deterrent to would-be attackers. Thus, the humans most likely to pass on their genes had a strong drive to care for their children and fellow band members—their in-group— and a strong drive to protect them, using physical force if necessary, from outside threats—the out-group. In-group cohesion, out-group hostility—but conditionally, because an in-group troublemaker might have to be expelled, and human outsiders, probably more often than not, offered beneficial cooperation and potential mates. So just as aggressiveness offered advantages and disadvantages, it seems humans evolved with the *capacity* to be both kind and hostile, cooperative and repulsive, toward other humans, but mostly they found ways to avoid violence. This is supported by behavior observed in nomadic foraging bands still in existence in the twentieth century. In the case of murder, family members might seek revenge, and the band as a group might agree to execute a repeat offender. In most instances, though, band members exercised restraint, employed nonviolent methods to resolve conflicts, and normally interacted in nonaggressive fashion. Human nature, it seems, is more cooperative than violent, more kind than cruel. In the language of morality, humans have the capacity to be bad, even "evil," but goodness is the essential or prevalent characteristic.[2]

It follows that to be human is to recognize the humanity of others, and part of that humanity is the need for interconnection. As the South African archbishop Desmond Tutu put it, "My humanity is bound up in yours for we can only be human together. We are different precisely in order to realize our need of one another."[3] Humans are social creatures by nature, being dependent on intraspecies cooperation for physical survival and emotional well-being. We may look different and speak different languages, but we all desire affiliation and empathy. Our human connections define our existence. A snake can thrive without social interaction—a human cannot (which is why solitary confinement is torture). Thus, to be human means to recognize the need for mutual support in others. To be fully human means, in the words of Jesus, to "love your neighbor as yourself."[4] *Dehumanization* means seeing people as objects, the means to an end, outsiders, enemies, unworthy of love, the Other. Dehumanization equals loss of compassion. If you dehumanize fellow humans, treat them as unworthy of your love, you dehumanize yourself because you are denying your own need for love and compassion.

Can this still be true today? Is the need for and tendency toward positive interaction really built into our DNA? Visit a news website or scan a newspaper, and you'll certainly find more examples of cruelty than kindness. The occasional generous donation or act of forgiveness is outnumbered and overwhelmed by all the murders, robberies, and bombings. At first glance, this appears to prove that human cruelty now outweighs kindness, but actually these are the exceptions that prove the rule, and the rule is that humans generally are more kind than cruel, more cooperative than hostile, more peaceable than violent. Humans are hardwired for eating, reproduction, and companionship. In all societies, no matter the culture or general situation, people seek food, sex, and friends. Dominance and aggression, by comparison, appear with great variability, depending on the milieu, and are often considered abnormal. If you assault your neighbor, this is news, and it will probably lead to a police report, perhaps a mention in the local paper, and undoubtedly word will spread around the neighborhood, because such an event is unexpected, alarming, outside the norm. If you help a friend move some stones or sweep the steps, or provide some flour when your neighbor runs short, it's hardly worth mentioning. Most humans, in all societies, go through most every day without committing direct acts of violence against other humans. Conversely, it is probably a rare day when they don't commit some act of kindness, which may be something as simple and normal as sharing food, allowing someone to step ahead in line, or helping someone stand up. For similar reasons, historians have given disproportionate attention to political conflicts, especially warfare. Wars are unusual, dramatic, noteworthy. The absence of warfare from the daily life of most humans is, for chroniclers, boringly normal.[5] Biologists, anthropologists, and philosophers can argue over how much of this normalizing of cooperation and kindness is cultural, how much is biological—the answer is probably unknowable—but a simple thought experiment may be useful for understanding the necessity of cooperation as the basis for society. Imagine a society where acts of cruelty and violence are the norm, and kindness and cooperation are so rare as to be noteworthy, a society where small acts of kindness make headlines:

Driver Allows Stranger to Merge on Freeway, Police Suspect Alcohol!
Father Makes Lunch for Children, Expects No Payment in Return!
No One Stabbed on Campus Yesterday!

Imagine trying to get through the day in an overwhelmingly "dog-eat-dog" world, where no one is generous, everyone hostile. Such a society could not last for long.[6]

The War Paradox of Civilization

If humans are basically good, if human society is based more on cooperation than competition, if most humans go through most days without committing violent acts, why is there so much warfare? The history books are filled with wars, historians consider the twentieth century the bloodiest one yet, and the twenty-first century is off to a belligerent start. Is it possible that, as humans evolved with the capacity for violence, especially retaliatory violence, war is a natural and inevitable human enterprise? Could it be that humans evolved to make war, that warfare has evolutionary value? Many people are quick to assume that warfare has occurred "since time immemorial" and will always be with us. As already stated, belief in the inevitability of war is a devastating, self-fulfilling prophesy.

Fortunately, it is not difficult to prove that war-making is a learned behavior, a cultural artifact, not an inherited genetic trait or a biological necessity. First, though, a definition of war is required. "Armed combat between political communities" is an elegant definition, but the vagueness of "armed combat" can be corrected with a more elaborate description:

> a group activity, carried on by members of one political community against members of another community, in which it is the primary purpose to inflict serious injury or death on multiple nonspecified members of that community, or in which the primary purpose makes it highly likely that serious injury or death will be inflicted on multiple nonspecified members of that community in the accomplishment of that primary purpose.[7]

Less concise but more discerning, the latter definition carefully excludes homicidal feuding, which targets specific individuals for vengeance killing, yet includes aerial bombardment which can be expected to cause many random casualties even though the primary target might be a specific individual.

The test for biological inevitability is simple: do *all* human societies make war? If war is natural and inevitable, a product of natural selection, if humans are hardwired for war, war should appear in all human societies. In fact, while most societies studied by anthropologists in the nineteenth and twentieth centuries did participate in warfare, *many did not*. Some non-warring societies did engage in homicidal feuding (e.g., you killed my brother, so I'm going to kill you), yet there were some with no known practice of either homicidal feuding or warfare. In the face of outside threat, such societies tended to employ avoidance and retreat rather than engage in defensive fighting. Not only is warfare not universal, archaeological study suggests that warfare is a relatively recent invention. According to the evidence, warfare became prevalent with the rise of complex states five to six thousand years ago. Before that—in other words, for ninety-nine percent of human existence—warfare was negligible or nonexistent, if for no other reason than nomadic foraging bands in sparsely populated territories had little to gain and much to lose from group combat.[8] That's the good news: War is a recent invention, a cultural development, not a biological imperative, so there is the possibility of its decrease or outright elimination. While an invention cannot be uninvented unless it completely slips from our collective memory, it can fall from favor, be rejected and replaced, like the rotary telephone or, in Margaret Mead's example, trial by ordeal.[9]

Eliminating war, of course, is no simple task. If warfare is not predetermined by human DNA, it may be built into human civilization. That's the bad news. Anthropological studies reveal a correlation between social organization and armed combat. Simply put, warfare is rare in egalitarian societies and common in hierarchical societies with strong leadership positions. In nomadic foraging bands, there is little motivation for individuals to engage in warfare, and leaders typically lack the power to compel participation in organized combat. Only when humans form more complex social structures does warfare become likely. In the shift from band to tribe to chiefdom to state, hierarchical classes replace egalitarian society; motivations for warfare emerge, such as internal political ambitions, territorial expansion, control of natural resources, and acquisition of slaves; and official leaders wield the power to require participation in battle. States can support standing armies led by professional bureaucracies, and preparing for war leads to war.[10] Indeed, some critics of the modern state insist that a hierarchical society necessitates warfare. Leo Tolstoy argued that the propertied elite require an army to protect their privileges from the impoverished masses, but the source of soldiers is those same masses, so elites must promote nationalist structures and identities, and cultivate foreign enemies, to justify and romanticize military service.[11] A king without an enemy has no army, and without an army has no throne.

As the shift to greater hierarchy created greater capacity for warfare, human societies developed more complex methods of suppressing *internal* homicide. Put another way, in chiefdoms and states, individuals lost the right to self-redress, especially the right to revenge killing. In foraging bands, individuals are free to take justice into their own hands, though third parties often act as mediators and peaceful conflict resolution is the norm. In tribes, violent conflict between two individuals might escalate into homicidal feuding between subgroups such as lineages or clans. In states, though, the government, with its police forces and courts, claims a monopoly on violent retribution.[12] Track down and kill your brother's murderer, and the police will come after you. Citizens of modern states generally consider such "law and order" a positive development, and thus often imagine themselves more "civilized," meaning less violent, than ancient "cavemen," who they wrongly assume pummeled each other at any opportunity.[13]

Therein lies a structural paradox for human societies. A "law and order" state with the centralized power to adjudicate disputes, enforce decisions, and ban civilian violence also has the power to conscript soldiers, fund standing armies, and declare wars. In a typical modern state, the government criminalizes and punishes vengeance killing among its citizens, yet claims for itself the right, indeed the duty, to pursue vengeance warfare against other states, and thus maintains a military in the name of self-defense. Does this mean warfare is inevitable so long as humans are organized into complex states—a kind of cultural, rather than biological, inevitability? Some countries, like Iceland, have gone centuries without participating in warfare. Some countries, like Costa Rica, have no army to speak of. However, Iceland is a unique case (isolated, tiny, homogenous population), and Costa Rica's disarmament may be a function of its submission to the war-making power of the US empire. Inevitable or not, warfare is likely among complex states with their military capacities and internal power struggles, that much is certain. Wars have persisted with the existence of states, and just as warfare cannot be uninvented, the state level of social organization probably cannot be dissolved, at least not without the precondition of massive global depopulation.

Complex states appear here to stay—at least in the short run—and, on the whole, may be beneficial, even necessary, on such a heavily populated planet, yet they also make war likely. Paradoxically, this paradox may contain its own solution, or partial solution anyway. If the authority of the state can make retaliatory murder among individuals unnecessary as a deterrent and generally unacceptable, it follows that international authorities—courts, unarmed peacekeeping forces, conflict mediators, and so forth—can make retaliatory warfare unnecessary and generally unacceptable. The development of such a peace system is underway, but is fraught with danger, because international authority, like state authority, can be abused. For example, the United Nations, in its current form, has some highly undemocratic features and is often used as a tool by aggressive, war-making states. However, a global peace system is a relatively new enterprise compared to nation-states and empires. So it remains an open question: Can humans imagine and create a more democratic and inclusive international system that significantly reduces the likelihood of armed combat, and will they do it before the expansion of high-tech warfare on a planet of diminishing natural resources brings extinction of the human species?

Another part of an imaginable solution to endemic warfare also emerges from the war paradox of civilization. The broadening of political structures has brought the broadening of group identities. In foraging bands and sedentary tribes, individuals identify themselves as members of kin and residential groups—the people they associate with on a daily basis. In states, the importance of kin and residential identity may decline with the adoption of political or national identity. Individuals identify themselves as members or citizens of large polities, and share that identity with hundreds, thousands, even millions of fellow citizens who they never encounter. But if they do encounter them, the shared political identity offers an immediate basis for friendly cooperation. This is the country or nation as in-group, and religious and ethnic identity can function similarly. Again, the paradox: National identity can unite millions in common cause (mass cooperation) and can unite millions in common cause *against* millions of others (typically, in war). Indeed, outside threat is a powerful unifying force within countries, no doubt an extension or distortion of the instinct to protect kin. And the solution: Just as popularly legitimized international authorities can outlaw war, international identity can make the in-group universal. *Species identity*, if promoted and reinforced, could trump national, ethnic, and religious identity. One species, no foreigners.[14]

In fact, the triumph of species identity could check the dangers of international authority and may be a necessary precondition for a successful global peace system. Empire builders and other cynical politicians typically encourage and appeal to divisions *within* a population, hoping that some other identity—race, religion, region, class, gender, age, sexuality—can overcome national identity and turn citizen against fellow citizen. The extreme result of internal division is genocide. For example, the slaughter in Rwanda, in 1994, was possible because powerful state authorities emphasized ethnic identities—Hutu and Tutsi—over shared Rwandan identity, and Hutu fear of the Tutsi "enemy," combined with class resentment, overwhelmed national unity.[15] The stronger the species identity, the less likely international leaders can abuse their power by turning one group against another. The more humans recognize our common humanity and see the global population as our in-group, the less toleration there is for intra-species war. US president Ronald Reagan, despite his embrace of militarism, seemed to understand this. He told the United Nations,

> I occasionally think how quickly our differences worldwide would vanish if we were facing an alien threat from outside this world. And yet I ask you, is not an alien force already among us? What could be more alien to the universal aspirations of our peoples than war and the threat of war?

Speaking of War

Changing the way people talk about war is another way to make war less likely. Frank public discourse about the nature of war, about the devastation it brings, diminishes public enthusiasm for militarism, and in the struggle to prevent wars, every little bit counts. However, in the United States today, with the possible exception of military families, war is easily discussed with a measure of indifference or ambivalence, without serious reflection on what war actually is. As currently used, the term *war* is an aspect of cultural violence, meaning the beliefs, ideas, and language that legitimize and encourage other forms of violence.

The word *war* itself is feeble, short and flat, so close to *wan*, so unlike *massacre*. Compared to *child molestation*, *human trafficking*, and *rape*, which register as vile acts and violations of taboo, *war* sounds benign; it doesn't hit the mind with the same moral weight. Most US citizens have not experienced firsthand the physical devastation of warfare, and without such personal context, the negative emotional resonance of *war* is minimal. Certainly among television pundits, comedians, and politicians, *war* can be the subject of light, unreflective banter. In the vernacular, *war* is often used to indicate an intense competition (e.g., "trade wars" and "ratings wars") or any large-scale effort to decrease or eliminate some unwanted phenomenon ("war on drugs" and "war on poverty"). Thus, when referring to armed combat, *war* is easily understood as the large-scale effort necessary for intense competition between nations, rather than the resultant human suffering—the strategizing, organizing, and mobilizing, not the killing and maiming.

Discussion of war typically mirrors discussion of a sporting event. US politicians understand that their constituents will quietly tolerate reports of significant US casualties so long as they believe their side is "winning." Promised a victorious end, the sacrifice is honorable. "Make no mistake," a congressman will bluster, "this is a war we will win"—though he will never clarify what winning looks like. For that, one must fall back on sports: winning means your opponents are losing. Reports of enemy combat casualties and conquered cities are received, then, as markers of success. And because the perception of eventual victory is critical for maintaining domestic cooperation with wartime measures, evidence of battlefield failures must be obscured. This is nothing new. During World War II, Polish Jews in the Lodz ghetto secretly listened to German radio reports boasting of victories over Soviet forces. But if you knew your geography, as one ghetto resident later recalled, you realized the Soviets were actually advancing and the Germans "were winning in the wrong direction."[16] In "unconventional" wars, where capturing and holding territory may be less critical, score is kept in body counts. The falsification of Vietnamese casualty statistics by the US Defense Department is well documented. When reports of the Tet Offensive, in 1968, undermined the official body-count narrative, beloved news anchorman Walter Cronkite publicly expressed dismay, but his famous line also betrayed a sportscaster's mentality: "What the hell is going on? I thought we were winning this war."

The sports analogy prevails today. In fact, the general population's role in "supporting our troops"—beyond federal taxation—has been largely reduced to applauding "our men and women in uniform" at professional sporting events.[17] The home crowd is the perfect audience for these carefully staged ceremonies, as the desire to belong—with minimal sacrifice—to a victorious institution is what draws many to the stadium in the first place. Just as the prospect of collective victory gives meaning to fan loyalty, it also contributes to the legitimization of war. After all, if a war, like a football game, can be won or lost, there must be great glory and reward in the winning, and losing can be viewed as noble failure. Furthermore, the win/lose dichotomy posits national unity on both "sides"—two opposing teams—thus obscuring internal conflicts on "our side," and demonizing "their side" as a monolithic enemy. To declare victory, or to suggest victory is even possible, is to frame war as a high-stakes game of capture-the-flag or Risk, where one side is all triumphant, the losers look forward to a rematch, and casualties, in the end, are beside the point. "This is a war we cannot win" is always a reasonable critique, except that it implies there are wars we can.

The first US congresswoman, Jeannette Rankin, the only member of Congress to vote against US entry into both World War I and World War II, rejected such sporting language, saying, "You can no more win a war than you can win an earthquake."[18] Her point was that in war everybody loses. Soldiers and civilians are wounded, traumatized, and killed. Infrastructure is destroyed, resources wasted, forests and farmland polluted. Our shared humanity is tortured. War, Rankin was suggesting, is better understood as a natural disaster rather than as a team sport. Does anyone declare victory over a city-leveling earthquake? Some people, such as the owners of construction companies, might see increased opportunity for profits. However, those lucky few are unlikely to celebrate loudly or wax triumphant. Such behavior in the face of human suffering and loss would generally be considered inappropriate, vulgar, and grotesque. Similarly, there are people who profit from wars: bellicose politicians, career military officers, weapons manufacturers. The difference, at least in the United States, is that claiming victory in war and celebrating loudly is socially acceptable and politically rewarded, even if almost all people touched by war experience loss.

Such exultant posturing is condoned, in part, because in US discourse, war is generally understood as something that happens in strange, foreign lands. The victims of US invasions are subhuman enemies who don't value life or suffer the way we do. They are threats to our safety, not innocent and deserving concern like earthquake victims. Overt invasions by US forces are remembered under the name of the invaded country—the Mexican War, Korean War, Vietnam War, and so forth. This emphasizes the foreignness of the event, both as location and experience, and reinforces the assumption that the conflict began elsewhere and, ultimately, is someone else's problem. As Robinson Jeffers observed in a poem equating war-makers to skunks, "Distance makes clean."[19]

In sum, war is easily thought of as an intense international competition, something briefly mentioned on the evening news but occurring overseas, like the Olympics, with flags unfurled and medals to the winners. In the years between 1945 and 1990, misleading phrases like "police action" and "military advisors" were needed to mollify war-weary voters and to temper Cold War panic, but no longer. The word *war* has lost its bite, has become a euphemism for itself, obscuring the ugly realities it should be indicating. To see how well the euphemism works, try the opposite: replace *war* in common phrases with a word that indicates the terrible human cost, such as *slaughter*. "Do you support the slaughter?" "The Vietnam Slaughter." "Just Slaughter Theory." *Bloodbath* and *mass killing* work equally well. When we emphasize the worst aspects of armed combat, when we call modern warfare precisely what it amounts to, the words don't glide so gently off the tongue or slip through the imagination, they bring pause. George W. Bush explained, "I'm a [slaughter] president. I make decisions here in the Oval Office in foreign policy matters with [slaughter] on my mind." Barak Obama accepted the Nobel Peace Prize by insisting, "So yes, the instruments of [slaughter] do have a role to play in preserving the peace." With *war* clarified, these presidential proclamations are more revealing, and human butchery is less easily mistaken for a sporting event.

World Slaughter II

While older wars fade from view, the perception of victory in World War II remains critical to the legitimacy of warfare in US political rhetoric. Pro-war pundits are quick to equate antiwar sentiment with European appeasement of German territorial demands in 1938: antiwar = pro-Hitler = evil. This simple device has rhetorical power because, in popular memory, the 1945 military conquest of Germany was the salvation of Europe: pro-war = anti-Hitler = good. US forces and their British allies liberated concentration camps, Hitler committed suicide, and the fascist German government surrendered. (The greater Soviet military contribution is conveniently forgotten.) Japan, too, surrendered after US bombers had destroyed most major cities there. "They" started it, and "we" finished it. Team USA suffered no destroyed cities, occupied western Europe and Japan, and emerged an unrivaled economic "superpower." The "good war" was an unambiguous triumph over evil, still beloved by US filmmakers and popular historians.

If we leave aside the team sports analogy, and define *winning* as personal or material gain and *losing* as human suffering, a different conclusion arises. Who won in the years 1940 to 1945? Communist Party elites secured a privileged existence for themselves as they solidified repressive rule in the Soviet Union and its European satellites. In the United States, the military-industrial complex—the weapons profiteers—became the federally subsidized, indispensible foundation for national economic stability. A very good war, indeed. Who lost? Millions of people in Europe, the Soviet Union, Japan, China, northern Africa, and on Pacific islands suffered death, injury, hunger, disease, emotional devastation, imprisonment, displacement, and loss of political self-determination—the numbers are staggering, the agony incalculable. American soldiers and their families also paid a high price, as did people of Japanese descent in the Americas.

Admitting that war brings enormous suffering, the righteousness of US participation in World War II is, for many, still "proven" by a simple fact: Allied forces liberated the concentration camps. That alone sounds like a win—even if ending the Holocaust was not an Allied war objective, even if the people who stumbled out of the camps were traumatized survivors, victims not victors. But by this thinking, we should celebrate as righteous the Japanese attack on US forces in Pearl Harbor, which led to formal US entry into the war, which led to German defeat. The Pearl Harbor attack also arguably saved millions in India, as the ensuing war in the Pacific hurried British departure from the subcontinent, thus removing the extractive and obstructive colonial dynamic that had allowed for frequent, devastating famines. War typically brings political upheaval, with all sorts of outcomes, a few predictable, many more unforeseen, some for the better, most for the worst. Framing a war as "won" means emphasizing what was gained, leaving aside or minimizing what was lost, and this includes privileging some lives over others. The Allied destruction of Germany ended the Holocaust, sparing the lives of many European Jews and others targeted for elimination by Hitler. This sounds like a net positive for the speculative body-count ledger in the "postwar" era, until weighed against other outcomes that followed from the expansion of US and Soviet militarism. The surrender of Nazi Germany saved many otherwise doomed lives, but US and Soviet ascendancy doomed many more.

A vision of victory is untenable when one evaluates the US war effort as an attempt at violence reduction. If the goal of the Allies (mainly Soviet, US, and British policymakers) was to extinguish the nascent German and Japanese empires and destroy their military capabilities, all-out warfare did the trick. If the goal was to reduce all forms of violence, make future wars unlikely, and promote all forms of peace, the armed response to German and Japanese militarism was counterproductive. If the goal was to transform conflict into opportunity for moral advancement, the military solution was a total failure. The Allied conquest of Germany and Japan did not defeat violence. The US and British leaders who condemned as immoral the bombing of civilian cities by the German and Japanese militaries were, a few years later, approving the systematic targeting of hundreds of thousands of civilians in Germany and Japan. After 1945, US and Soviet propaganda promoted ever more violence: military achievements were venerated, warfare was legitimized as the way to defeat bad regimes, and the ideological battle between the communist East and capitalist West led both sides to see bad regimes aligned against them. The Soviet Union established repressive control over eastern Europe and central Asia, and the extractive forces of US-dominated capitalism expanded across the rest of the globe, with a special focus on the oil-rich Persian Gulf region. Wartime suffering eased in western Europe, but soon intensified in China, Korea, and southeast Asia. Eastern Europe remained a place of misery. Stalin's reign of terror, in the Soviet Union, matched Hitler's for brutality and destruction—the mass killing just moved farther east. US military spending impoverished domestic social programs, and US soldiers and their families continued to bear the cost of combat in distant lands. Nuclear weapons programs poisoned the planet. One might express relief at the temporary cessation of widespread slaughter in 1945, but, in the face of such loss, it requires great narcissism to declare victory.

War as Disease

Rankin was right, war is about losing not winning, but her earthquake analogy can be interpreted to mean war is best understood as a natural disaster, an "act of God," a tragic event that comes with little warning and cannot be prevented or avoided. If war cannot be avoided, preparation for war is of utmost importance, for self-defense if nothing else. But traditional preparation for war—national military buildup—presents two obvious perils. First, given a commitment to militarism, national policymakers are quick to propose military solutions. In a most revealing example, in the aftermath of the catastrophic 2010 earthquake in Haiti, with tens of thousands killed, communications and medical infrastructure destroyed, and survivors in desperate need of food, water, medicine, and shelter, the official US relief response was to *send troops*. The focus of that particular invasion may have been humanitarian relief, but the point is that US officials turned to the military because that is where US resources, training, and manpower are concentrated; in a crisis—any crisis—send in the warriors. Second, foreign policymakers are likely to view the military buildup as a threat—even if labeled "defense," even if mobilized for "humanitarian" reasons—and will respond in kind, necessitating additional "defensive" buildup. The first leads to the second, and the second leads to more of the first. As previously stated, belief in the inevitability of war is a self-fulfilling prophesy.

Disease, then, is a better analogy. War is a disease, and a highly contagious one at that, spreading its own germs the same way a common cold causes its human host to sneeze. Thinking of war as disease affirms the wisdom of A.J. Muste's remark, "The problem after a war is with the victor. He thinks he has just proved that war and violence pay. Who will now teach him a lesson?"[20] You don't win a war, you catch the war germ, and the "victors," unaware of how sick they are, keep spreading it. A brief survey of the twentieth century shows World Slaughter I leading directly to World Slaughter II, which metastasized into the Cold Slaughter, which included the Korean Slaughter, the US Slaughter in Vietnam, and the Soviet Slaughter in Afghanistan. The Cold Slaughter eased around 1989, but the remission was short-lived. The Gulf Slaughter broke out in 1990, and continued into the next century. War is neither biological necessity nor natural disaster. A war is not a discrete episode that concludes with a full stop. No war will ever "end all wars." War is a disease, and humanity has it. War itself is the foreign threat. It emerged ten or twelve thousand years ago, and, with ever-greater human proficiency in destruction, may be getting worse.

If the natural disaster analogy encourages fatalism, the disease analogy clarifies the urgent task before us: find a cure. It may be more accurate to call war a *syndrome*, meaning a collection of associated symptoms with multiple causes. Either way, by changing our perception of war, use of medical terminology may itself be part of the cure. One way to confront a disease is to create an environment where the germ cannot thrive. As the UNESCO preamble tells us, "Since war begins in the minds of men, it is in the minds of men that the defences of peace must be constructed."[21] War ends in minds that are toxic to the war germ, that identify war as both slaughter and avoidable, not as sport and inevitable. But will the antiwar mindset overwhelm pro-war assumptions? Fifty years ago, Martin Luther King Jr. observed that "nonviolence can be as contagious as violence."[22] In recent decades, with advances in telecommunications, the likelihood of peace contagion—of a peace breakout—has increased. The planet is "shrinking," and interconnection brings greater awareness of antiwar sentiment and actions in distant lands. Such globalization undermines fear of foreign threats. People in the West no longer need to "hope the Russians love their children too," they can simply turn on their smartphones and verify that they do. Also, both confidence in the power of nonviolence and popular rejection of war appear to be spreading. Massive antiwar rallies—in Madrid, Rome, New York, London, Sydney, and hundreds of other cities—did not block the US assault on Baghdad in 2003, but the extent of protest *before* the killing began was unprecedented. That may be progress. Much more must be done. Not everyone can be organizer or leader, not everyone is prepared for street activism, but greater awareness of language, use of words to reveal rather than obscure, speaking with honesty and transparency—these can be aspects of cultural peace, and are universally available. The more the people of the world communicate across borders and discover their shared aversion to mass killing, the less likely human slaughter becomes. It is important that we speak clearly.

NOTES TO CHAPTER 1

---

[1] *"Si vis pacem, para bellum"* is attributed to Publius Flavius Vegetius Renatus, *De Re Militari* (ca. 390AD).

[2] Douglas Fry, *Beyond War: The Human Potential for Peace* (Oxford University Press, 2007), 148-165, 175-192.

[3] http://www.tutufoundationusa.org/2013/10/10-pieces-of-wisdom-from-desmond-tutu-on-his-birthday/. Tutu is deeply influenced by Ubuntu, the southern African worldview that understands "a person is only a person in the context of other persons."

[4] Matthew 22:39 and elsewhere.

[5] Gandhi wrote, "History, then, is a record of an interruption of the course of nature. Soul-Force, being natural, is not noted in history." Louis Fischer, ed., *The Essential Gandhi: An Anthology of His Writings on His Life, Work, and Ideas* (Vintage, 2002), 79.

[6] For more on human nature and violence, see Douglas Fry, ed., *War, Peace, and Human Nature: The Convergence of Evolutionary and Cultural Views* (Oxford University Press, 2013).

[7] These two definitions come from, respectively, Keith Otterbein, *The Evolution of War: A Cross-Cultural Study* (Human Relations Area Files Press, 1970), 3; and Roy Prosterman, *Surviving to 3000: An Introduction to the Study of Lethal Conflict* (Duxbury-Wadsworth, 1972), 140; as quoted in Fry, *Beyond War*, 14, 16.

[8] Fry, *Beyond War*, 2-20, 50-64.

[9] Margaret Mead, "Warfare Is Only an Invention—Not a Biological Necessity," *Asia* 40 (1940): 402-405.

[10] Fry, *Beyond War*, 65-80.

[11] Leo Tolstoy, *The Kingdom of God is Within You* (Wilder, 2009).

[12] Fry, *Beyond War*, 81-99.

[13] For a spectacular example of this misconception, see Steven Pinker, *The Better Angels of Our Nature: Why Violence Has Declined* (Viking, 2011), an 800-page argument that lacks a definition of violence and generally ignores structural violence because it would undermine Pinker's claim that late 20th-century Western "civilization" is the most peaceful of human societies ever. For a

systematic demolition of Pinker's thesis, see Edward Herman and David Peterson, "Reality Denial: Steven Pinker's Apologetics for Western-Imperial Violence," ZNet, July 25, 2012, http://zcomm.org/znetarticle/reality-denial-steven-pinkers-apologetics-for-western-imperial-volence-by-edward-s-herman-and-david-peterson-1.

[14] Jeremy Rifkin, *The Empathic Civilization: The Race to Global Consciousness in a World in Crisis* (Tarcher, 2009), 9-26.

[15] Scott Straus, *The Order of Genocide: Race, Power, and War in Rwanda* (Cornell University Press, 2006), 7-10.

[16] Anatol Chari and Timothy Braatz, *From Ghetto to Death Camp: A Memoir of Privilege and Luck* (Disproportionate Press, 2011), 72.

[17] Andrew Bacevich, "Ballpark Liturgy: America's New Civic Religion," TomDispatch.com, July 28, 2011, http://www.tomdispatch.com/blog/175423/andrew_bacevich_playing_ball_with_the_pentagon.

[18] James Lopach and Jean Luckowski, *Jeannette Rankin: A Political Woman* (University Press of Colorado, 2005).

[19] Tim Hunt, ed., *The Collected Poetry of Robinson Jeffers, 1939-1962* (Stanford University Press, 1991), 406.

[20] Howard Zinn, *A People's History of the United States, 1492-Present* (HarperCollins, 2001), 424.

[21] In 1946, twenty national governments, including the United States, ratified the Constitution of the United Nations Educational, Scientific, and Cultural Organization (UNESCO). The preamble avows "the purpose of advancing, through the educational and scientific and cultural relations of the peoples of the world, the objectives of international peace and of the common welfare of mankind for which the United Nations Organization was established and which its Charter proclaims."

[22] Taylor Branch, *At Canaan's Edge: America in the King Years 1965-1968* (Simon & Schuster, 2006), 738.

2

PEACE AND VIOLENCE AT
THE LITTLE BIGHORN

2

PEACE AND VIOLENCE AT THE LITTLE BIGHORN

Peace Theory

Peace and violence are opposites. Simply put, peace work means trying, through peaceful means, to reduce current levels of violence and to make future violence less likely. Peace is the goal and also the process. As postulated by Johan Galtung, the Norwegian polymath and founder of peace studies, one definition of peace, sometimes called *negative peace*, is the "absence or reduction of violence of all kinds." *Positive peace* is "nonviolent conflict transformation," understanding that conflict is inevitable but doesn't have to lead to violence. In fact, conflict can bring positive developments; conflict equals opportunity. Galtung has defined *violence* as "avoidable insult to basic human needs," those needs being survival, well-being, identity, and freedom. Violence comes in different forms. *Direct violence* is when one party physically or verbally causes harm. *Structural violence* (indirect violence) is built into a political or economic system, and the harm it causes may be unintentional. *Cultural violence* includes the beliefs, language, ideologies, and cosmologies that legitimize, motivate, and perpetuate direct and structural violence.[1]

To make these distinctions clear, imagine an unemployed man loses his house to bank foreclosure. In his anguish and despair, he takes his handgun to the bank and shoots several people. The shooting is direct violence. An economic system that puts property rights over human needs and allows the eviction of impoverished people from their homes is structural violence. Cultural violence is seen in a society that equates gunslinging with manliness and celebrates the physical punishment of opponents. The economic structure created the conflict, the popular culture normalized the use of violence to resolve a conflict, and the result is direct violence. Such a scenario is all too real in the United States, and how do people typically respond? The police arrive and shoot the gunman. Newscasters label them "heroes." Prominent opinion-makers call for "more cops on the streets," more armed citizens, and more frequent use of the death penalty as a deterrent. In other words, more violence. While a few people call for more gun restrictions, millions continue to watch titillating films and television dramas about bank shootouts and other violent crimes. The cultural violence is reinforced, the structural violence that created the conflict is ignored, and a repeat performance of the direct violence can be expected. Violence begets violence.

One can imagine three levels of violence. At the bottom is cultural violence, which is slow to change, seemingly permanent, and thus unnoticed. This provides the legitimizing base for structural violence, meaning economic and political systems or processes that seem to have evolved "naturally." At the top, breaking through the surface for all to see, are events of direct violence.

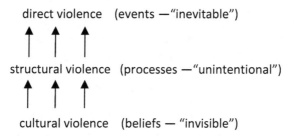

direct violence   (events —"inevitable")

↑ ↑ ↑

structural violence (processes —"unintentional")

↑ ↑ ↑

cultural violence   (beliefs — "invisible")

Without identifying the cultural violence, and without understanding the decision-making behind structural violence, the direct violence seems inevitable and unavoidable. Galtung believes "the major causal direction for violence is from cultural via structural to direct violence," but also acknowledges the arrows of causation can point in different directions, for example when the direct violence of war reinforces the cultural violence of belief in humans as inherently warlike. Hence, three layers of violence, but also a triangle of mutually reinforcing violence, with causation flowing in six different directions.

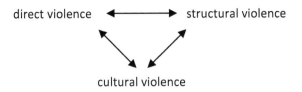

This unholy trinity has an opposite: *Direct peace* is nonviolent action, including acts of kindness and the refusal to cause harm. *Structural peace* is where political and economic systems provide for, rather than violate, basic human needs. A system of voting that gives all citizens, even the poorest, direct voice in the decisions that affect their ability to meet their basic needs, rather than a system where political influence flows from material wealth, is an example of structural peace. *Cultural peace*, in Galtung's thought, is "aspects of a culture that serve to justify and legitimize direct peace and structural peace." A public school instructor promoting empathy, critical thinking, and collaborative decision-making in her classroom, rather than obedience, authority, and bureaucracy, is teaching cultural peace. The diagrams are now familiar:

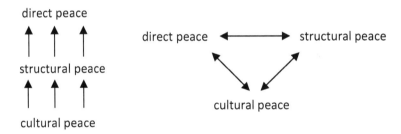

We return to the tragic scenario: An unemployed man who lost his house to bank foreclosure bursts into a bank and opens fire, then is shot down by a policeman. This time, though, a group of women decide that their community has had enough shootouts. They successfully lobby the city government to use the power of eminent domain to purchase foreclosed houses. Under the new arrangement, the city allows the occupants to remain, with affordable monthly payments, provided they also give hours of service to community programs, such as the anti-bullying seminars initiated by the same group of determined women. A government program that reduces homelessness and that tells people they are needed in the community is structural peace. Teaching compassion to counter intimidation—Bullying ain't cool, kindness is!—is cultural peace. A community with less anger, fear, and despair can expect fewer violent assaults, and, perhaps, fewer residents will feel the need to own a handgun, thus reducing the likelihood of accidental shootings. Peace begets peace.

Galtung's peace theory is more complex than these few diagrams, but his arrows of causation have explanatory power. They can help us understand why some societies experience more direct violence than other societies and how that violence is perpetuated. The diagrams can also help us understand the complexity of reducing violence and increasing peace. In fact, peace theory is an example of cultural peace because it legitimizes and directs efforts to reduce violence. With that in mind, why not apply it to one of the most celebrated violent events in US history?

Little Bighorn

On June 25, 1876, US soldiers and their Crow and Arikara scouts charged into an encampment of Lakota, Cheyenne, and Arapaho families along a river the Lakotas called the Greasy Grass, in what is now southeastern Montana. For over two decades, the US Army had been trying to conquer the Native peoples of the Great Plains and had found attacking villages more advantageous than facing off against highly skilled Native fighting men. In fact, eight days earlier, Lakota and Cheyenne fighters had repulsed US forces at the Rosebud battlefield. At the Greasy Grass, known to English-speakers as the Little Bighorn, the US attack was hurried, the blue-uniformed soldiers trying to reach the tipis before the women and children could escape. But, led by Crazy Horse, the Native defenders rallied quickly, drove the soldiers from the camp, and surrounded them on nearby hills. When the killing ended the following day, over 260 soldiers and at least 40 Natives were dead.

For many years, popular historical interpretation of the battle focused on identifying victims and victors, good guys and bad guys. The "heroic soldier" interpretation emphasized the suffering and death of Col. George Custer and his entire battalion—"Custer's Last Stand." This version, which depicted US soldiers as agents of "civilization" and Native peoples as "savage" obstacles, resonated in the US popular imagination because it struck a deep chord: white Americans as God's chosen people with a mission to save the world. Alternatively, the "doomed defender" interpretation identified Lakotas as the victims of US conquest who, despite victory at Little Bighorn, soon lost the war, and with it their territory, culture, and sovereignty. This version gained notice, beginning in the 1960s, as US military failures overseas and greater cultural awareness at home raised doubts about the divine ordination of US imperialism.[2] In the 1970s, the historic battlefield was again a place of conflict, as competing groups, sometimes characterized as "Custer buffs" and "Native American activists," vied for control of the symbolism of the site.[3]

These two interpretations have at least one thing in common, one aspect of cultural violence frequently on display in US public discourse: a tendency to glorify or romanticize warfare. The "heroic soldier" story transforms Custer's demise into noble sacrifice, surrounded and outnumbered but going down with guns blazing for the greater good. The "doomed defender" account is essentially the same, only now the Native warriors are surrounded and outnumbered—by the rapidly expanding US population and industrial capitalism. Lakotas and their allies fought valiantly to defend their families and their "traditional" way of life—who wouldn't do the same?—but in the long run their bows and arrows, rifles, and war ponies had little chance of success against steamboats, railroads, Gatling guns, and cannons. For Custer and Crazy Horse alike, there was dignity and virtue in a battling exit, dying for what you believe in, and when the fight is hopeless, when your death appears imminent, taking as many foes as possible with you. More recently, Little Bighorn chroniclers have tried to present a "balanced" account of the battle, trying to understand the motivations of all participants, rather than demonizing one side or the other.[4] But they do not condemn the violence itself as an illegitimate form of conflict resolution, and, thus, do not actively challenge the deep assumption, found in US culture, of warfare as noble and redemptive.

Peace theory offers a different way to interpret Little Bighorn—and war generally—not only to understand the past, but to see what lessons we can learn to help us create a less violent future. But why Little Bighorn? If the goal is to reduce violence, what can be accomplished by applying the triangles and arrows of peace theory to a battle fought well over a century ago? Why not let bygones be bygones and leave the dusty Montana battlefield to the military historians trying to deduce Custer's fateful maneuvers? Because, though Custer died in 1876, the violence on the northern Plains continues to this day, and, despite all the attention given the historic battle, the complicated connection between then and now is not fully appreciated. Reinterpreted from a peace perspective, the historic and historical battlefield, tragic yet compelling, can become a place of triumph over violence rather than violent triumph.

Violent Societies

Mid-19th-century Lakotas (western Sioux) were nomadic, horse-mounted hunters of bison, and violence played an important role in their society, as it did for most northern Plains tribes in that period.

Archaeological evidence, including remains of fortified villages, indicates that intertribal warfare went back centuries along the upper Missouri River, and historical accounts suggest an intensification of fighting sparked by the arrival of European trade goods in the seventeenth and eighteenth centuries and by the depletion of bison herds after 1800. The spread of guns, horses, and epidemic diseases changed the regional balance of power, and, by 1850, Lakotas were the dominant military force. Lakotas used warfare to drive neighboring tribes off valuable hunting and grazing lands, maintain access to trade networks, and subjugate farming villages.[5]

With group survival often dependent on martial prowess, Lakotas and other northern Plains communities held warriors in high esteem. Young men grew up training for violent combat, conducted small-scale raids on enemy villages, and gained status and leadership positions through battlefield displays of courage and skill. They took enemy scalps as trophies. They practiced ritual self-mutilation. Their exploits in battle and horse thievery were celebrated with dances, songs, and names. The death of kin in battle necessitated vengeance killing, which often disrupted attempts at peaceful relations. Indeed, if economic interest was the primary motivation for Lakota warfare, the warrior ethic contributed to a violent cycle of raiding and counter-raiding among rival tribes. In complex though understandable ways, direct violence encouraged cultural violence, and cultural violence perpetuated direct violence.[6]

With the elevation of individualistic hunting methods based on possession of horses, mid-19th-century northern Plains communities were becoming less egalitarian, less subsistence-oriented, less communal. Compared to other tribes, Lakotas were making this shift less rapidly, and had not reached an internal disparity of wealth and power that constituted structural violence. However, external structural violence emerged in the growing dependency of Plains tribes in general on foreign goods and horses, which led to the overhunting of bison for tradable hides, which contributed to food scarcity. The structural violence of this extractive and wealth-seeking economy was a motivation for the direct violence of warfare over territory, and the demand for guns and ammunition was a motivation for involvement in the extractive economy. All told, this triangle of mutually reinforcing direct, cultural, and structural violence meant the Lakotas and their neighbors lived under the shadow of violent death.[7]

Violence in the Lakota world, 1850

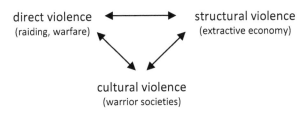

The mid-19th-century United States, too, was steeped in violence. The prevalent cosmology, or *deep culture*, included a belief in white male superiority with divine appointment.[8] The bigotry and sense of entitlement that flowed from this assumption underlay the structural and direct violence of expansionism, slavery, and male dominance. Simply put, US society was organized around the violent dispossession of Native communities, the enslavement of blacks, and the marginalization of women. By 1850, the older structures of economic inequality and exploitation—chattel slavery and feudalism—were giving way to a new one: industrial capitalism. The Civil War, 1861-65, revealed the depth and complexity of US violence, as members of the plantation-owning class sounded the call for southern secession to preserve slavery, northern politicians insisted on the legitimacy of federal rule over distant lands, and leaders on both sides employed industrialized warfare, with the poorer classes as cannon fodder, to resolve the sectional conflict. Soldiers on both sides sang "The Battle Cry of Freedom." The number of war-related deaths likely exceeded six hundred thousand, including an assassinated president.[9]

Violence in the United States, 1850

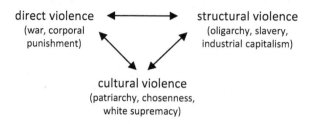

direct violence
(war, corporal
punishment)

structural violence
(oligarchy, slavery,
industrial capitalism)

cultural violence
(patriarchy, chosenness,
white supremacy)

The end of the Civil War slaughters and the abolition of slavery did not make US society less violent. In the South, former slave owners constructed a semi-feudal system (structural violence) based on the ideology of white supremacy (cultural violence) and shaped by racial segregation and terrorism (direct violence). In the West, US officers, hardened and emboldened by their "scorched earth" conquest of the South, turned their "total war" strategies against Plains tribes—slaughtering bison and pony herds, destroying whole villages, and capturing, raping, and killing noncombatants.[10] In the North, the structural violence of unregulated, industrial capitalism created misery and dependency for the urban poor, which intensified with the 1870s financial collapse, bringing cries for more confiscation of Indian lands, territorial expansion being the favored solution to class conflict. Custer and a few other professional soldiers may have constituted a warrior class, but they led an army of poorly paid and often inadequately trained volunteers, many of them recent immigrants from Europe.

After 1862, the primary conflict between US and Lakota societies was a dispute over use of the northern Plains.[11] Lakotas wanted to continue exploiting tribal hunting and grazing lands; US citizens wanted to transform the grasslands into privately owned farms and ranches and, beginning in 1874, to mine gold in the Black Hills. A conflict between two expansionistic, war-making societies—what was the likelihood of a nonviolent resolution? US and Lakota societies were in many ways different, but it was a similarity that made the conflict so devastating—as Lakotas clearly understood. In the oft-quoted words of Black Hawk, an Oglala Lakota, "These lands once belonged to the Kiowas and Crows, but we whipped those nations out of them, and in this we did what the white men do when they want the lands of the Indians."[12] Only now it was the Lakotas' turn to be "whipped." Within a few years of the Little Bighorn battle, continued attacks on their villages and the extermination of the bison herds forced Lakotas and their Cheyenne allies to surrender to US forces and accept sedentary life on significantly reduced territories. These "reservations," surrounded by the dominant US society and administered by a powerful, centralized state, functioned as internal colonies. The Native nations of the northern Plains had become subjects of the US empire.

Genocide

A Cheyenne named Wooden Leg, who fought at Little Bighorn, later said of reservation life, "It is pleasant to be situated where I can sleep soundly every night, without fear that my horses may be stolen or that myself or my friends may be crept upon and killed."[13] US dominance ended decades, if not centuries, of persistent warfare on the northern Plains—a Pax Americana. The powerful state claimed a monopoly on the right to employ direct violence, and essentially declared that intertribal warfare and raiding must cease. From this historical reality, apologists for empire argue that US rule brought peace, enlightenment, and progress to the Plains peoples, that US conquest was a blessing in disguise for the subjugated tribes.[14] This is a key tenet of the "heroic soldier" interpretation, with the US Army as the spearhead of "civilization," and it implies that Barack Obama was right, "The instruments of war do have a role in preserving the peace." But the absence of warfare should not be equated with the absence of violence, and the temporary absence of direct violence, known as negative peace, should not be confused with positive peace, meaning the presence of systems, processes, practices, and beliefs—structural peace and cultural peace—that make future direct violence less likely.

Jean-Paul Sartre's observation that imperialism is genocide certainly fit the newly created Sioux reservations.[15] Military conquest was only one step toward the US government's goal of eliminating Native peoples. Additional steps included the privatization of lands and the stamping out of Native leadership, languages, and religions. In most cases, reservation agents, teachers, and missionaries may not have intended the physical injury or biological death of Native individuals, but as an attack on the basic human need for identity and freedom, this "assimilation program" was violence. Indeed, the motto was "Kill the Indian, save the man"—in other words, eliminate Native tribes and Native identities—and the destruction of a group, even without mass murder, is the precise definition of genocide.[16]

A different aspect of the cultural violence of white supremacy—an obligation to enlighten "inferior" peoples—inspired the direct violence of boarding schools and state-enforced religion, with additional direct violence as an enforcement mechanism.[17] When reservation communities resisted assimilation, reservation officials and army officers organized the marginalization or elimination of Native leaders, kidnapping of Native children, and punishment of Native healers. In the most extreme example, thousands of US soldiers invaded the Sioux reservations, in 1890, to suppress the Ghost Dance, an elaborate ceremony some Lakotas believed would lead to restoration of their pre-reservation life. Over a decade had passed since Lakotas had given up military resistance to US empire, yet at Wounded Knee Creek, on the Pine Ridge Reservation, the US Seventh Cavalry—Custer's old regiment—killed over one hundred fifty Lakota men, women, and children.[18]

Federal policy not only condemned Lakota identity, it reinforced economic structures that kept Lakotas impoverished. With the bison gone, federal officials encouraged Lakotas to take up dry-land farming and ranching, even as US confiscations continued to reduce the Lakota land base. Cattle herding was a good match for formerly nomadic, equestrian bison-hunters on semi-arid lands. In the 1890s, ranching became a significant part of the reservation economy. In the early twentieth century, though, pressure from reservation agents and the lure of consumer goods convinced Lakotas to sell off livestock and land "allotments," leaving them without a self-sustaining economic base to withstand global depressions and years of drought on the Plains. Federal officials favored white-owned, corporate ranching interests on the reservation, while often failing to meet treaty obligations to provide for impoverished residents.[19] Boarding schools mostly prepared Native children for manual labor, and the emphasis on assimilation reinforced a sense of inferiority and self-hatred. For many Lakotas, survival depended on government checks and low wages from off-reservation work. Trapped in a psychology of dependency at the very bottom of the capitalist structure, they lacked the resources to move up. The result: Across the twentieth century, Sioux reservations were home to some of the worst quality-of-life indicators in the United States. Statistics for unemployment, illiteracy, poverty, disease, infant mortality, and life expectancy suggest Lakotas were caught in "third world" misery in the midst of what became "first world" affluence.[20]

US conquest may have ended the direct violence of intertribal fighting, but the intensified cultural and structural violence brought by US rule all but guaranteed that some new form of direct violence would emerge. With the sources of oppression seemingly unreachable or unknowable, reservation residents often directed their frustrations at fellow tribal members and themselves, a phenomenon known as *internalized oppression*.[21] Sioux communities suffered high rates of interpersonal violence (assault, rape) and intrapersonal violence (alcoholism, drug addiction, suicide). Much of this can be attributed to *historic trauma*, meaning the massive, cumulative, intergenerational transfer of unresolved fear, anger, and grief, which began with the carnage of military conquest and deepened with the experiences of forced assimilation. Restrictions on Native religion and medicine obstructed the healing process, and the boarding school onslaught of psychic degradation, corporal punishment, and sexual abuse created generations of abusers. Remnants of warrior society expectations may have increased the emotional burden on young Sioux men unable to match the individual achievements of storied ancestors—not as courageous battlers, not even as providers—and they often took out their misery on Sioux women. Poverty, self-hatred, unresolved trauma: the legacy of conquest is violence.[22]

Wounded Knee II

Without sufficient therapy at all three points of the triangle, Sioux communities were trapped in a cycle of violence. To outsiders, the situation might have appeared stable, but with human needs unmet, upheaval was likely. In the early 1970s, direct violence in and around the Pine Ridge Reservation expanded from individual acts—domestic abuse, suicide, and the like—to the group activity of riots, death squads, and shootouts. Why, eighty years after the Wounded Knee massacre, did gun battles return to the northern Plains? What had changed? For one thing, the Indian Reorganization Act (IRA) of 1934, a US law that allowed tribal members to establish federally approved tribal governments—following a non-Lakota model—often deepened political schisms between so-called "progressives," who were more willing to cooperate with the US Bureau of Indian Affairs (BIA), and "traditionalists," who put up greater resistance to federal paternalism. If nothing else, by creating elected offices with the authority to disperse reservation jobs and federal funds among an otherwise impoverished population, the IRA raised the stakes of intra-tribal politics. In 1972, the political tension at Pine Ridge was exacerbated by new tribal council president Dick Wilson, a petty tyrant who blatantly rewarded his "progressive" or "mixed blood" supporters, while his private police force intimidated political opposition.

A second political development began, in the 1950s, when the emergence of pan-tribal organizations and the empowerment of Native activists, many of them urbanites and college educated, brought more dynamic resistance to decades-old political dominance, economic exploitation, and cultural hegemony. Inspired in part by the Civil Rights Movement, Native activists drew national attention and sympathy with "fish-ins" and the occupation of Alcatraz. The most visible and controversial Native organization was the American Indian Movement (AIM), whose leaders, particularly Russell Means, an Oglala Lakota from Pine Ridge, had a genius for political symbolism. AIM members occupied Mount Rushmore, took over a replica *Mayflower* ship on Thanksgiving Day, and organized a "Trail of Broken Treaties" march to Washington, DC. But lacking nonviolent philosophy and training, their actions often disintegrated into violence, costing them the support of many otherwise sympathetic observers, and making it easier for federal authorities to characterize them as criminals.[23]

When AIM militancy entered the bitter tribal politics of Pine Ridge, the deeply rooted violence intensified. In 1972, hundreds of AIM members converged on nearby Gordon, Nebraska, and demanded tougher prosecution of local whites who had kidnapped and murdered an Oglala Lakota. The following year, after another off-reservation killing, AIM organized a caravan to the town of Custer, South Dakota, where a confrontation with the public prosecutor turned into a violent brawl with police.[24] By taking a stand against "white man's justice," AIM quickly gained new members and supporters on Pine Ridge, particularly among the "traditionalists" who formed the Oglala Sioux Civil Rights Organization (OSCRO) and tried to oust tribal president Wilson. Dozens of federal marshals from an elite paramilitary group soon arrived at Pine Ridge, not to investigate the murders, but to protect Wilson and the tribal headquarters from the AIM-OSCRO alliance of militant young activists and reservation opposition. Challenged by OSCRO leaders to become warriors again and defend their people, young Oglalas and their AIM allies, numbering around three hundred, went to the village of Wounded Knee, stole rifles from the local trading post, and detained its white owner, providing pretext for a federal military intervention. US marshals, BIA police, and FBI agents, equipped with automatic rifles, armored personnel carriers, and helicopters, and advised by army officers, surrounded the village and opened fire. Eighty-three years after the Wounded Knee slaughter, US officials had, once again, sent an army to crush a Native resistance movement. Despite two deaths from sniper fire, the protestors held out for 71 days, resurrected the Ghost Dance, then agreed to a negotiated surrender, only to face arrests and trials while their demands for federal investigation of reservation injustices were quickly dismissed. For some observers, the "Wounded Knee II" occupiers were making a heroic stand, shooting it out against overwhelming odds. For others, they were dangerous militants who deserved the violent response they received. The US government and the occupiers did agree on one thing: violent conflict resolution. And more was coming.

Over the next three years, Wilson functioned as a neocolonial strongman—dependent on US funds, weapons, and political support, while his "GOON" squad, tolerated if not encouraged by FBI agents, terrorized Pine Ridge. Federal officials saw Wilson as a useful counterweight against Lakotas who pushed for greater tribal sovereignty and treaty rights. FBI agents declined to investigate the deaths of Wilson opponents, choosing instead to employ a variety of "counterintelligence" tactics—surveillance, arrests, trumped-up charges, misinformation, falsified evidence—against AIM members. In 1975, after two FBI agents were killed in a shootout at an AIM camp, the FBI conducted a massive paramilitary crackdown on AIM members, leading to more arrests. The federal repression of AIM, and the election of a new tribal president, in 1976, eventually calmed the political atmosphere.[25]

The shootouts ceased, but reservation poverty and desperation remained, with little improvement over subsequent decades. Pine Ridge was too isolated to profit from the 1990s casino boom, and, despite treaty obligations to provide housing and medical care, federal agencies failed to meet reservation needs. Only a small, elite class of "mixed-blood" ranchers and tribal officials benefitted from reservation resources. In the early twenty-first century, Pine Ridge reports unemployment above eighty percent, almost the entire population living below the poverty line, an infant mortality rate three times the national average, a severe housing shortage, and extremely high rates of diabetes, alcoholism, and suicide. Hopelessness is pervasive. No surprise then that average life expectancy (around 50 years) is much lower than the US average (about 77). Perhaps also no surprise that Pine Ridge youths have formed street gangs modeled after the violent urban gangs celebrated in popular rap music. The one reliable source of employment for reservation youths is enlistment in the US military.[26] In 2000, a grassroots Lakota movement occupied the tribal headquarters in protest of tribal council corruption and neocolonialism, a resistance action invoking the spirit of Crazy Horse and the nonviolent philosophy of Martin Luther King Jr. However, with structural violence on Pine Ridge and other Sioux reservations intact, and with the cultural violence of US society frequently reinforced, it may just be matter of time before the next outbreak of armed combat on the northern Plains.[27]

Violence in the Lakota world, 2000

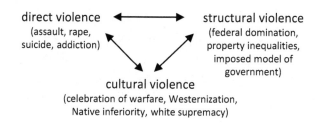

direct violence
(assault, rape,
suicide, addiction)

structural violence
(federal domination,
property inequalities,
imposed model of
government)

cultural violence
(celebration of warfare, Westernization,
Native inferiority, white supremacy)

The Monument

From a social sciences perspective, our work is done—we've investigated, albeit briefly, the connection between past and present.[28] The peace studies imperative asks us to apply that knowledge to reduce current and future violence. The reduction and prevention of direct violence in the region, particularly on impoverished reservations, requires transformation of cultural and structural violence. Much of this must come from within the tribal communities, but one imaginable first step toward structural peace is transfer of public lands in and around the Black Hills—sacred territory that the US Supreme Court has ruled was illegally taken—back to the Sioux tribes, as they have requested, along with compensation for well over a century of lost financial opportunity.[29] Properly managed—meaning with greater tribal participation, transparency, and shared benefit—Native repossession might provide a measure of economic security, reduce dependency, increase self-determination, and build self-esteem. However, a land transfer is unlikely without first reducing the cultural obstacles of "Manifest Destiny" entitlement and anti-Indian racism, mending old wounds, and addressing the fears of private landowners. In other words, a grand project of dialogue, negotiation, and conflict mediation is required, with a wide circle of participation, and with respect to differences in worldview and conflict resolution traditions.[30] Call it *peace-building*.

One place peace-building can begin—in fact, has already begun—is at Little Bighorn Battlefield National Monument, a historical site and interpretive center administered by the US National Park Service (NPS), which attracts hundreds of thousands of visitors each year. In the late twentieth century, following the general trend toward greater cultural inclusion, official park interpreters gradually reduced Custer worship, which for so long had contributed to the romanticization of the battle, and made room for alternative perspectives and Native voices, culminating in the construction of a Native memorial to complement a decades-old Custer memorial.[31] At present, the official interpretive program—museum, brochures, ranger talks—acknowledges that Little Bighorn means different things to different people, and no single perspective should be privileged. Inclusion not exclusion, dialogue not domination, participation not marginalization—this is peace-building.

Despite these positive developments, Little Bighorn remains a source of cultural violence. Rather than reduce the legitimacy of direct violence, practices in and around the national monument continue to perpetuate, by omission and commission, the perception that war is inevitable and acceptable. The official interpretive program at the park is marked by careful omission. In an understandable attempt to minimize offense, park personnel employ the phrase "a clash of cultures" as their interpretive theme, suggesting the awful killing in 1876 was the unavoidable result of cultural differences, and no individuals are accountable, no human decision-making is to blame—the historical equivalent of "shit happens."[32] Getting past blaming individuals may be commendable, but "clash of cultures" remains an empty phrase if the "cultures" are not investigated. Clash means conflict, but, at last check, the interpretive program avoids discussion of the root conflict between two expansionistic powers. Conflict—a contradiction of interests—does not necessarily lead to violence, still the interpretive program does not explain why Lakotas and US citizens chose armed combat to resolve their differences. In other words, the "Clash of Cultures" program leaves out the structural and cultural violence. Why? Because serious examination of warrior traditions, vengeance killing, and tribalism might raise discomforting questions. For example, if Sioux warrior societies were admirable institutions, why did Crazy Horse believe he needed to murder a woman to advance his spiritual development?[33] Also, honest discussion of the violence of imperialism, militarism, and capitalism might appear a pointed rebuke of current US policies—the sort of thing that can get a federal park superintendent fired. So, instead, the park program encourages visitors to focus on elements of the direct violence—troop movements, assorted weaponry—that occurred at the site, to ponder the unknowable details of Custer's last moments rather than the perfectly knowable phenomena that lead to such slaughters.

Two annual Little Bighorn battle reenactments, staged outside the park, constitute cultural violence by commission. Like action-packed war movies, the reenactments are unavoidably stirring and titillating—flags and feathers, thundering horses, resounding cries—except the reenactments cannot duplicate Hollywood representations of gore and suffering. The "dead" fighters arise in full view of the audience, vengeful Lakota women do not mutilate the soldiers' corpses, no children mourn their fathers' deaths, handshakes all around. Armed combat, it seems, is pageantry, fun and entertaining, a nice outing, something young children can happily anticipate. That such events are tolerated, in a way that reenactments of the rape of female captives or the funneling of prisoners into gas chambers wouldn't be, is measure of just how normalized, romanticized, and sanitized warfare is in US society. One wonders how a US marine, just returned from combat overseas, or the parent of one recently killed, might respond to the fake gunplay, or how military reenactments might be received in Croatia or Afghanistan or any other country recently scarred by internal warfare. Any redeeming social value such entertainments might contain must be weighed against the general effect of promoting violence by actively denying a basic fact: war is slaughter, not sport.[34]

The national monument, too, has contributed to cultural violence by hosting a celebration of warfare, though in somewhat ironic fashion. In 2003, the NPS officially dedicated the new Native memorial at Little Bighorn with a ceremony emphasizing reconciliation between former enemies—an important peace-building step.[35] However, a fundamental contradiction ran through the language and symbolism of the ceremony. The theme of the day was "Peace through Unity," the US Interior secretary declared the new memorial "another step together in seeking the peace that Black Elk spoke of," and the Montana governor reminded listeners that "Indian and non-Indian soldiers fought side by side" in the slaughter known as World War II. In other words, Natives and other US citizens should stop fighting old battles…and cooperate in new ones. The ceremony paid tribute to a Hopi woman, who had nothing to do with the northern Plains but was killed three months prior in the US invasion of Iraq, and two assault helicopters flew overhead to reinforce the message: peace through unity, and unity through warfare against common enemies.[36] War equals peace.

In a society where military prowess is so highly valued, calls for unity through cooperation in, say, community-building or environmental preservation would not carry the same weight. If nothing else, the ceremony's reference to the latest war—an invasion sold to the US public as a defense against "Islamic terrorism" and as necessary for delivering "democracy" and "freedom" to a distant land—is a reminder that the very cosmology that led to the Little Bighorn battle remains deeply embedded in US culture. A population that considers itself a superior people, views war as sport, and celebrates the power of warfare to unify "us" against "them," in contrast to a population that views war as slaughter and decries hostility between nations, is more likely to support calls for war-making.

The national monument does not have to be an exercise in cultural violence. Instead of "A Clash of Cultures," the park handouts might read "Little Bighorn: Confronting Violence" and describe the tragic battle as part of a larger confrontation between two violent, expansionistic societies. Ranger talks could explain how poor European men, propelled across the Atlantic Ocean by dreams of prosperity, ended up as mutilated corpses on Last Stand Hill, and also could help visitors understand the high rates of poverty, unemployment, and direct violence on the Crow reservation next door and on northern Plains reservations in general. The museum could exhibit photos from the Wounded Knee massacre and the Wounded Knee II shootout, outline the historical connections between 1890 and 1973, and display a map or two illustrating Native land claims and court decisions regarding the Black Hills. In sum, park personnel could address the history and ongoing reality of violence in the region.

Such a radical change in the monument's interpretive program would, like a Black Hills land transfer, require a grand project of dialogue and mediation. Paradigm shifts don't come easily, and imposing your own belief system on others is itself a form of violence. Thus, transformation of cultural violence into cultural peace, by definition, will require contributions from all groups with a stake in the matter. Undoubtedly, participants will come up with better solutions than the ones offered here. There will be conflict, of course—peace-building is controversial in a war-loving society—but conflict equals opportunity, and the opportunity is to use the controversial park as a place to confront violence.[37] If the cultural point on the triangle is the most deeply rooted, then making the Little Bighorn a place to teach peace would be no trivial accomplishment.

A (partial) peace prescription for Little Bighorn

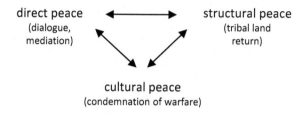

direct peace
(dialogue,
mediation)

structural peace
(tribal land
return)

cultural peace
(condemnation of warfare)

NOTES TO CHAPTER 2

[1] For peace theory, see Johan Galtung, *Peace by Peaceful Means: Peace and Conflict, Development and Civilization* (Sage Publications, 1996), especially 2, 9, 196-201 for definitions. Galtung first formulated his violence typology in "Violence, Peace, and Peace Research," *Journal of Peace Research* 6:3 (1969): 167-191. For Galtung's story, see Johan Galtung and Dietrich Fischer, *Johan Galtung: Pioneer of Peace Research* (Springer, 2013).

[2] This shift in popular interpretation can be seen in Hollywood films, for example, *They Died With Their Boots On* (1941) and *Little Big Man* (1970). Paul Hutton, "From Little Big Horn to Little Big Man: The Changing Image of a Western Hero in Popular Culture," in Hutton, ed., *The Custer Reader* (University of Nebraska Press, 1992), 395-423.

[3] Debra Buchholtz, *The Battle of the Greasy Grass/Little Bighorn: Custer's Last Stand in Memory, History, and Popular Culture* (Routledge, 2012), 114-115. Michael Elliott, *Custerology: The Enduring Legacy of the Indian Wars and George Armstrong Custer* (University of Chicago Press, 2007), 2-3, points out that "the picture of a two-sided debate with clear-cut, opposing sides oversimplifies the way that history is actually written, spoken about, and memorialized in the United States today." Still, it was the more strident voices that made the historic battlefield a focal point in the movement toward, and backlash against, increased cultural awareness.

[4] For examples, see Nathaniel Philbrick, *The Last Stand: Custer, Sitting Bull, and the Battle of the Little Bighorn* (Penguin, 2010); James Donovan, *A Terrible Glory: Custer and the Little Bighorn—the Last Great Battle of the American West* (Back Bay Books, 2008).

[5] Richard White, "The Winning of the West: The Expansion of the Western Sioux in the Eighteenth and Nineteenth Centuries," *Journal of American History* 65:2 (Sept. 1978): 319-343.

[6] Guy Gibbon, *The Sioux: The Dakota and Lakota Nations* (Blackwell Publishing, 2003), esp. 86-94.

[7] Pekka Hämäläinen, "The Rise and Fall of Plains Indian Horse Cultures," *Journal of American History* 90:3 (Dec. 2003): 848-862. Hämäläinen notes the rise of "horse-rich men who for all practical purposes had become protocapitalists" on the northern Plains, leading to "a relatively rigid rank society in which exchange and social relations of production benefited a selected few at the expense of the vast majority," but adds that the Lakotas were able to avoid this "destructive divisiveness."

[8] Reginald Horsman, *Race and Manifest Destiny: The Origins of American Racial Anglo-Saxonism* (Harvard University Press, 1981), 1-2, explains that "By 1850 the emphasis was on the American Anglo-Saxons as a separate, innately superior people who were destined to bring good government, commercial prosperity, and Christianity to the American continents and to the world." Early Massachusetts colonial governor John Winthrop, in 1630, famously equated divine appointment with a "city upon a hill." A New York journalist named John O'Sullivan, in 1845, reconfigured it as "manifest destiny." This notion of "chosenness" persists today, and can be heard in the frequent expressions of American exceptionalism and indispensability made by US politicians and pundits.

[9] Drew Gilpin Faust, *This Republic of Suffering: Death and the American Civil War* (Vintage, 2009), xi-xiii.

[10] For evidence of US soldiers raping Native women, see Philbrick, *The Last Stand*, 138-139.

[11] Lakota-US conflict has always been rooted in US claims to continental sovereignty, but in the 1850s, the immediate conflict was more about US citizens crossing Lakota territory on their way to lands west of the Continental Divide rather than white settlement on the northern Plains. Jeffrey Ostler, *The Plains Sioux and U.S. Colonialism from Lewis and Clark to Wounded Knee* (Cambridge University Press, 2004), 34-42.

[12] Quoted in White, "The Winning of the West," 341.

[13] Thomas Marquis, *Wooden Leg: A Warrior Who Fought Custer* (University of Nebraska Press, 2003), 383-384.

[14] For an example of this thinking, see Steven Pinker, *The Better Angels of Our Nature: Why Violence Has Declined* (Viking, 2011), 47-56, 102-106. Without carefully defining violence, Pinker argues that "states are far less violent than traditional bands and tribes" and that while "imperial conquest and rule can themselves be brutal, they do reduce endemic violence among the conquered." It follows that "the Civilizing Process in the American West" eventually cured the "anarchy" and "mayhem" that preceded it.

[15] Jean-Paul Sartre, "Vietnam: Imperialism and Genocide," in Sartre, *Between Existentialism and Marxism* (Verso Books, 2008), 67-83.

[16] Dominik Schaller and Jürgen Zimmerer, eds., *The Origins of Genocide: Raphael Lemkin as a Historian of Mass Violence* (Routledge, 2009), 5.

[17] Brian Dippie, *The Vanishing American: White Attitudes and U.S. Indian Policy* (University Press of Kansas, 1982), 111-121, 185-188.

[18] Ostler, *The Plains Sioux and U.S. Colonialism*; William Coleman, *Voices of Wounded Knee* (University of Nebraska Press, 2000).

[19] Paul Robertson, *The Power of the Land: Identity, Ethnicity, and Class Among the Oglala Lakotas* (Routledge, 2002), esp. 49-58, 123-132.

[20] Gibbon, *The Sioux*, 134-148.

[21] Paolo Friere, *Pegagogy of the Oppressed* (Continuum, 2006), 46-48; Lisa Poupart, "The Familiar Face of Genocide: Internalized Oppression Among American Indians," *Hypatia* 18:2 (Spring 2003): 86-100.

[22] Maria Yellow Horse Brave Heart, "The Historical Trauma Response among Natives and Its Relationship to Substance Abuse: A Lakota Illustration," in Ethan Nebelkopf and Mary Phillips, eds., *Healing and Mental Health for Native Americans: Speaking in Red* (AltaMira Press, 2004), 7-18. For an autobiographical example, see Mary Crow Dog, *Lakota Woman* (HarperPerennial, 1991).

[23] Paul Smith and Robert Warrior, *Like a Hurricane: The Indian Movement from Alcatraz to Wounded Knee* (New Press, 1996); Sherry Smith, *Hippies, Indians, and the Fight for Red Power* (Oxford University Press, 2010).

[24] Stew Magnuson, *The Death of Raymond Yellow Thunder and Other True Stories from the Nebraska-Pine Ridge Border Towns* (Texas Tech University Press, 2008), esp. 19-24, 47-48, 138-141.

[25] Akim Reinhardt, *Ruling Pine Ridge: Oglala Lakota Politics from the IRA to Wounded Knee* (Texas Tech University Press, 2007), 146-208; Steve Hendricks, *The Unquiet Grave: The FBI and the Struggle for the Soul of Indian Country* (Thunder's Mouth Press, 2006), 62-80, 206-209; Magnuson, *The Death of Raymond Yellow Thunder*, 227-237; Peter Matthiessen, *In the Spirit of Crazy Horse* (Penguin, 1992).

[26] Contemporary reservation conditions are summarized in Chris McGreal, "Obama's Indian Problem," *The Guardian*, January 10, 2010, http://www.theguardian.com/global/2010/jan/11/native-americans-reservations-poverty-obama. See also Pine Ridge CDP, South Dakota, US Census Bureau, 2010.

[27] Robertson, *The Power of the Land*, 241-249.

[28] One example of the ambivalence of many academics toward applied peace theory is a reader who insisted that an American Indian studies journal is not an "appropriate vehicle" for "advocacy for peace at the Little Bighorn," even if such

advocacy is a "valuable perspective." (Peer review in author's possession.) While the current content of the journal in question is overtly anti-colonial on a variety of levels (i.e., outspokenly critical of certain categories of structural and cultural violence), suggestions for a paradigm shift beyond the printed page seem to violate, for some, expectations of scholarly "detachment." This raises two open questions: Does scholarly detachment mean advocating ways to think but remaining silent on ways to act? (The dividing line is perhaps fuzzier and more arbitrary than some realize.) If the twin towers of environmental destruction and global militarism threaten species survival, if the crisis is urgent, and if a profound cultural transformation is required to avoid a tragic end, how much detachment should one indulge?

[29] Jeffrey Ostler, *The Lakotas and the Black Hills: The Struggle for Sacred Ground* (Viking, 2010), 167-192.

[30] Polly Walker, "Decolonizing Conflict Resolution: Addressing the Ontological Violence of Westernization," *American Indian Quarterly* 28:3-4 (Summer-Autumn 2004): 527-549; Paul Robertson, Miriam Jorgensen, and Carrie Garrow, "Indigenizing Evaluation Research: How Lakota Methodologies are Helping 'Raise the Tipi' in the Oglala Sioux Nation," *American Indian Quarterly* 28:3-4 (Summer-Autumn 2004): 499-526.

[31] Buchholtz, *The Battle of the Greasy Grass/Little Bighorn*, 114-130; Elliott, *Custerology*, 1-58; Edward Linenthal, *Sacred Ground: Americans and Their Battlefields* (University of Illinois Press, 1991), 127-172. The symbolism and meaning of Little Bighorn, its significance in Euroamerican and Native American memory, is nuanced and complex, but it is perhaps most valued as a place where non-Native citizens can simultaneously celebrate national expansion and acknowledge Native suffering, and do so without guilt, because US soldiers suffered too—an irony captured in Lakota writer Vine Deloria Jr.'s famous phrase, "Custer died for your sins."

[32] For more thorough deconstruction of the interpretive program, see Timothy Braatz, "'Clash of Cultures' as Euphemism: Avoiding History at the Little Bighorn," *American Indian Culture and Research Journal* 28:4 (2004): 107-130.

[33] Kingsley Bray, *Crazy Horse: A Lakota Life* (University of Oklahoma Press, 2006), 45-49.

[34] For more thorough discussion of Little Bighorn reenactments, see Elliott, *Custerology*, 224-272; Buchholtz, *The Battle of the Greasy Grass/Little Bighorn*, 106-107, 138-143.

[35] Jerome Greene, *Stricken Field: The Little Bighorn since 1876* (University of Oklahoma Press, 2008), 234-238.

[36] Braatz, "'Clash of Cultures' as Euphemism."

[37] One example of resistance to peace-building at Little Bighorn is the complaint of a military historian and Civil War reenactor who derided as "leftist" and dismissed as an "exercise in futility" what he characterized as a proposal to "convert a military park dedicated to interpreting the most famous Indian fight in U.S. history into an institute for peace studies." (Peer review of Braatz, "'Clash of Cultures' as Euphemism," in author's possession.) But why not interpret that tragic battle through the prism of peace studies rather than military studies, comparative anthropology, and international relations? Why assume tourists will not tolerate moral challenges—don't the Vietnam Veterans Memorial and the Holocaust Memorial Museum attract their share of visitors? If asked, most people will say they deplore direct violence, but don't know what more can be done to reduce it; they accept it as "the human condition." So, assuming violence reduction is a legitimate and urgent goal, then a new way of thinking is required, and the NPS has a role to play. Just as NPS interpreters at other parks unapologetically teach ecological concepts and environmental preservation, Little Bighorn personnel could promote human preservation. In fact, the US law authorizing creation of the Native memorial directed it be used "to provide visitors with improved understanding of the events leading up to and the consequences of the fateful battle, and to encourage peace among people of all races." (US Public Law 102-201, 102nd Congress, Dec. 10, 1991.)

3

WHAT'S THE GOAL?

3

WHAT'S THE GOAL?

The Crazed Gunman

If you advocate nonviolence, or at least claim to reject violence, eventually someone will confront you with a question like this: What would you do if a crazed gunman broke into your house and tried to rape your grandmother? Naturally, you want to protect the old woman, but because her attacker is "crazed"—lacks moral conscience, has no concern for his own well-being, cannot listen to reason—there is nothing you can say to dissuade him, no way to appeal to his better nature. In some renditions, he is "on PCP," giving him superhuman strength. But you're in luck. Despite your adherence to nonviolence, you possess a gun and know how to use it. That's part of the presented scenario. You've got a gun, and here comes Mr. Insane, wild-eyed and bursting through the front door, an Uzi in his right hand, his left hand now around Grandma's frail neck. Well, what would you do?

The point of the Crazed Gunman question, of course, is to discredit nonviolence. Your interrogator is not seeking edification. The question is a rhetorical trap. In the given scenario, you appear to have only two options, and one is doomed to fail. If you were to intercede nonviolently, perhaps shielding Grandma with your body, then you'd be killed and she'd still be raped. Nonviolence doesn't work! If you were to choose the only "viable" option—shoot the attacker—then you have "proved" your interrogator's point. Violence works!

Short of ending the conversation, the way to avoid a rhetorical trap is through redirection; don't let your opponent dictate the terms of debate. For example, rather than take the setup seriously, give a hypothetical answer—it's a hypothetical question after all. "If he had my grandmother by the neck, I would dodge his bullets, take my own hit of PCP, and use my superhuman strength to wrap him in a bear hug and whisper 'I love you,' over and over, until he calms down, and maybe have Grandma give him a foot massage." Such a response—call it the Crazed Grandchild—shifts focus from the rigid polarity of the original scenario to its absurdity, and everybody can have a nice laugh. Folksinger and peace activist Joan Baez said she would "yell 'Three cheers for Grandma!' and leave the room."[1]

One can also redirect the conversation by responding with questions, not answers. Rather than try to argue your way out of a hopeless situation, ask about motivations. Why are you trying to trap me with an imaginary scenario? Why are you so eager to discredit nonviolence? Maybe follow up with a more realistic problem: Forget my imaginary grandmother, how can we reduce handgun violence, knowing that keeping a handgun for protection greatly increases the chances of someone in the house being shot? Rather than defend imaginary nonviolence, shift attention to the mutually reinforcing cycle of real violence. In other words, respond to the intent behind the Crazed Gunman scenario, rather than to the scenario itself.

But these, too, are rhetorical devices, and do not adequately address the important questions raised by the Crazed Gunman. Will a nonviolent response always succeed against violence? Doesn't nonviolence leave you vulnerable against a violent attacker? Are there situations where violent defense is a better option? Can someone who espouses nonviolence on principle still use violence if necessary? Those who pose the Crazed Gunman problem typically don't understand what nonviolence is or how it functions. They may mistake *pacifism* (rejection of violence) for *passivism*, meaning doing nothing, sitting quietly while Grandma is brutalized, "turning the other cheek" to be hit again. Pacific means peaceful; passive means submitting. And they may not *want* to understand, preferring to discredit nonviolence in order to justify their embrace of violence or their failure to confront violence—itself a form of violence. Nevertheless, they have a point. It is not enough simply to insist nonviolence is right, even if Jesus seemed to agree. People want proof.

Two Guys in a Bar

There's an old joke: A guy walks into a bar and says "ouch." Here's a new one: Two guys walk into each other in a bar; one takes offense and says, "I'm gonna kick your ass." It's a joke because fighting over an unintentional and harmless collision is laughable, but this scenario, unfortunately, is easily imagined and believable—more so than the Crazed Gunman. So what happens next? Guy A (Mr. Aggressive) has threatened Guy B (Mr. Bumper)—how does Guy B respond? Actually, the punch line is up to you. Imagine that Guy B, through the magic of theoretical physics or Hollywood special effects, freezes the action, whips out his cell phone, and dials your number. "Hey, I accidentally bumped this guy, and he says he's gonna kick my ass. What should I do?" What do you tell Guy B, what advice can you offer? Take a few moments and give this some thought. Go ahead—no one in the bar is moving, Guy B has stepped out of time, so there's no rush.

Unlike the Crazed Gunman, the bar fight scenario doesn't ask you to choose one of two unappealing options. How to advise Guy B is a more open question, but responses typically fit into one or more of the following categories:

Avoidance:	Walk away, leave the immediate area, leave the bar.
Appeasement:	Apologize for the bump, offer to buy a drink for Guy A.
Passivity:	Stand still, curl up in a ball, say "please don't hurt me."
Distraction:	Commence odd behavior, sing loudly, undress, play the fool.
Violent Resistance:	Get ready to fight, look for a weapon, mock Guy A, strike the first blow.

Another category of advice is often overlooked:

Direct Nonviolence:	Look Guy A in the eyes and tell him that if he needs to hit you that's his business, but you reject violence and won't fight back, you won't hurt another human.

Notice how a nonviolent response differs from passivity. More than merely refraining from violence (pacifism) or essentially doing nothing (passivism), *nonviolence is an active response*—"proactive" in today's parlance—that directly addresses violence. But will it protect you from harm?

A chart can be drawn to outline the likelihood of someone getting physically hurt with each potential response employed by Guy B, assuming he employs no other response. For example, if Guy B attempts to hit Guy A (Violent Resistance), there is a good chance one or both of them will get hurt. If, instead, Guy B walks away and leaves the bar (Avoidance), Guy A won't get hurt, and it's unlikely Guy B will get hurt, though Guy A could throw something at Guy B or follow him out the door and hit him over the head. In fact, any response could lead to Guy B getting hurt. When confronted with a violent threat, there are no guarantees of physical safety.

	Guy A hurt?	Guy B hurt?
Avoidance	No	Unlikely
Appeasement	No	Unlikely
Passivity	No	Maybe
Distraction	No	Maybe
Violent Resistance	Probably	Probably
Direct Nonviolence	No	Maybe

The value of this chart is that it reveals how little value it has. With the exception of Violent Resistance, the possible responses seem to offer similar results, suggesting that the potential for injury to Guy B may not be the key determinant in advising a course of action. Since there may be other considerations, an important question must be asked—perhaps the fundamental question in any decision-making: *What's the goal?* When Guy B calls on his cell phone and requests guidance, your advice is more likely to be useful if you first ask him, "What is your goal in this situation?" Guy B's primary concern might be to avoid physical injury, or maybe he's more worried about injury to his pride and doesn't want to appear cowardly, or perhaps most of all he wants to teach Guy A a lesson by punishing him for being a bully.

If Guy B just wants to avoid physical injury, the best advice may be walk away and leave the bar. If he's concerned about his pride and thinks a hasty retreat will be shameful, you might recommend he offer to buy a beer for Guy A—no shame in that, and they might become friends. However, such appeasement, like avoidance, probably won't dissuade Guy A from future bullying, as his boorish behavior earned him a free drink. So how about teaching him a lesson? If Guy B feels up to it, he could punch Guy A in the mouth, knock him down, kick him in the ribs. That'll teach him! It's a high-risk strategy because Guy A might be armed, or be a more skilled fighter, or have five friends with him, and Guy B might end up on the ground. Also, if Guy B does give Guy A a beating, what lesson will Guy A learn? Guy B is hoping Guy A will conclude that bullying is unhealthy behavior as it gets you hurt, but a more likely message is that Guy A needs to get better at fighting or carry a weapon so that next time he comes out on top. This suggests a more extensive chart might be useful.

	Damage to Guy B's self-esteem?	Best likely outcome	Worst likely outcome	Lesson on violence
Avoidance	Maybe	Nobody hurt	B hurt	Bullying rewarded
Appeasement	Unlikely	Nobody hurt, mutual respect	B hurt	Bullying rewarded
Passivity	Probably	Nobody hurt	B hurt	Bullying rewarded
Distraction	Maybe	Nobody hurt	B hurt	Bullying rewarded
Violence	Maybe	Nobody seriously hurt, mutual respect	Serious injury to A/B, escalation into brawl	Be a skilled fighter

What about nonviolence—what can it accomplish that avoidance and appeasement cannot? If Guy B stands up to Guy A, but with compassion not hostility—if he says, "I won't fight you because I don't believe in violence, and I'd rather we were friends"—how will Guy A respond? You can imagine for yourself how the scenario plays out, but consider a few possibilities. Guy A may realize that Guy B is not a threat and leave him alone, maybe even shake his hand. If so, Guy B has avoided injury, rejected violence, and boosted his self-esteem. Alternatively, Guy A might physically attack Guy B, maybe punch him in the mouth. If Guy B resists the urge to run or hit back, if instead he wipes the blood off his lip and says, "I still won't fight you because I care about you as a human being," what then? Onlookers in the bar are likely to view Guy A's violence as inappropriate and disgraceful. Female onlookers especially, due to gender differences in socialization, are likely to think, "What a jerk!" Guy B's nonviolence exposes Guy A's violence as illegitimate. If, by comparison, Guy B fights back with violence, Guy A's violence is less likely delegitimized in the eyes of onlookers because both participants agreed to use violence. Yet another result may develop if Guy B responds with nonviolence and Guy A still assaults him. It may take some time, but Guy A, unless he is deeply dehumanized, is likely to experience some remorse for having hurt someone who was trying to help him. This is the power of nonviolence: to reach a would-be opponent at a deeper level, to touch his heart. How Guy A responds to this—perhaps seeking self-esteem through similar acts of compassion rather than more attempts at domination—is up to him.

	Damage to Guy B's self-esteem?	Best likely outcome	Worst likely outcome	Lesson on violence
Nonviolence	Self-esteem boosted	Mutual respect, A/B transformed	B hurt	Violence delegitimized

While probably not the safest choice in the short term, only a direct nonviolence response to direct violence carries a real possibility of interrupting the mutually reinforcing triangle of violence. The other tactics either avoid violence without challenging it or lead to increased violence. They offer little hope of transforming the cultural violence, whatever it might be, which caused Guy A to think that inviting combat is an appropriate, perhaps necessary, response to incidental contact. In this sense, Guy A has presented Guy B with an opportunity—conflict equals opportunity—to reduce, however slightly, the level of cultural violence in his world. With a few brief words and some courage, he may be able to show Guy A, and any onlookers, that physical violence is unacceptable and unnecessary, and that direct nonviolence can be an effective antidote. That's a lesson worth teaching! The entire chart looks like this:

	Guy A hurt?	Guy B hurt?	Damage to Guy B's self-esteem?	Best likely outcome	worst likely outcome	Lesson on violence
Avoidance	No	Unlikely	Maybe	Nobody hurt	B hurt	Bullying rewarded
Appeasement	No	Unlikely	Unlikely	Nobody hurt, mutual respect	B hurt	Bullying rewarded
Passivity	No	Maybe	Probably	Nobody hurt	B hurt	Bullying rewarded
Distraction	No	Maybe	Maybe	Nobody hurt	B hurt	Bullying rewarded
Violence	Probably	Probably	Maybe	Nobody seriously hurt, mutual respect	Serious injury to A/B, escalation into brawl	Be a skilled fighter
Nonviolence	No	Maybe	Self-esteem boosted	Mutual respect, A/B transformed	B hurt	Violence delegitimized

But before you go advising Guy B, or anyone else, to respond to direct violence with direct nonviolence rather than with avoidance, you may want to inquire if he has the discipline to stay nonviolent and the will to risk physical injury. Remember, reducing cultural violence may not be his immediate goal. Guy B may mean well, but doubt that standing up to a barroom bully will have much effect in the grand scheme of things. "Thanks for the advice, I see your point, but is it really worth the trouble?"

One answer to the preceding question is that with violence so pervasive, every tiny bit of active nonviolence helps. A big peace is made up of lots of little pieces. A second answer is that the person most affected by a nonviolent act usually is the nonviolent actor. If, when threatened by Guy A, Guy B responds with nonviolence, imagine the boost to his self-esteem. He didn't back down, didn't resort to violence, didn't give in to a desire to punish Guy A, and likely discovered courage and strength he didn't know he had. Even if he comes away with a bloody mouth, even if he never finds out what effect he had on Guy A and any onlookers, he will know he did the right thing.

Integrative Power

In patriarchal cultures, where aggression and dominance are honored, nonviolent action is typically dismissed as evidence of weakness. The assumption is that nonviolent actors are motivated by fear; they are cowardly avoiding suffering. A second common assumption is that nonviolence is ineffective, in part because nonviolence often takes time to achieve its goals and doesn't offer the immediate gratification of violent intimidation. The refusal to meet violence with violence may appear meek, but *meek* has two meanings: (1) submissive, especially when under provocation, or (2) humbly patient. The latter definition fits with the spirit of nonviolence, and, in that sense, "meek ain't weak."[2]

In fact, nonviolent action is remarkably powerful. There are many ways to define *power*, but political and economic thinkers who dominate public discourse tend to view power as the way to produce desirable behavior in others, to get them to do what you want them to do—a perspective that reflects the interests and social standing of such thinkers. As such, power is a relationship between Self and Other. The groundbreaking economic theorist Kenneth Boulding identified three such types of power. The first, *threat power*, says, "Do this or else!" This is the power of direct violence, it functions on fear, and its weakness is that without frequent reinforcement it will wither away. The threat must be maintained because Other is likely to resent the coercion and will discontinue cooperation at the first opportunity. The second type, *exchange power*, says, "Do this for me and I'll do this for you." This is economic power, it functions on material desire, and its weakness is that it requires the continued possession of desirable items of exchange. You have to be able to supply what Other wants. Threat and exchange power both tend to heighten the distinction between Self and Other by identifying Other as the means to an end. (Johan Galtung added an additional type, *persuasive power*, which functions on cultural insecurity, saying, "Do this because it's a really good idea.")[3]

Boulding's third type of power, *integrative power*, takes the opposite approach, saying, "I'll do this for you because I care about you." This is, yes, the power of love, and it means the ability to attract empathy, concern, and friendship. Integrative power functions on the human need for interconnection, and its strength is the universality of that need. Humans are mutually dependent, social creatures—from Day One. When an infant cries to be fed and a mother responds affirmatively, that's integrative power at work, and it brings the two of them closer together, it builds upon itself. When Guy B says to Guy A, "I won't fight you because I care about you," he is appealing to Guy A's need for human connection, to his very humanity. To be human is to embrace that need for connection and to recognize it in others—to see *their* humanity. To be *fully human* is to see no meaningful separation between Self and Other. Whoever truly believes "it is better to be feared than loved" is deeply dehumanized and is choosing, like a slave owner, to live in fear of the Other losing fear.[4] Being feared may be the means to an end; being loved is an end in itself.

The weakness of integrative power, at least for personal self-defense, is that it requires direct interpersonal communication. In the case of assault, the potential victim must be able to express concern for the attacker *to* the attacker. This is why the proverbial gunman must be "crazed"—so you cannot communicate with him in any meaningful way. This also shapes one of the more devastating realities of modern technological warfare: the more removed one is from a targeted human, the easier it is, psychologically, to pull the trigger, push the button, click on FIRE, and the more difficult it is for the targeted human to appeal to the killer's heart.[5] But if an attacker is staring you in the face, there may be hope. Maybe. A group of students were quizzing a gung fu master on how to use martial arts in particular situations. "What about if you're on your back," one student asked, "and the guy has his knees on your chest and a gun at your forehead?" The master replied, "Then it's Jesus time." Like gung fu, and all other forms of self-defense, direct nonviolence is no guarantee of physical safety. It's a rough world. Can a political prisoner use direct nonviolence to escape from a torture table? Can a woman pinned down by a rapist appeal to his heart? An attacker may be so dehumanized, the space for communication may be so limited, there's nothing left to do but pray for a miracle.

Yet some people have experienced the effectiveness of integrative power in a seemingly hopeless situation. Conflict resolution specialist Marshall Rosenberg has written about such encounters, including the time a drug addict at a detoxification center threw the night clerk to the ground, sat on her chest, and put a knife to her throat after she told him there was no room in the inn that night. Rather than focus on her own peril, rather than pray for a miracle, she "concentrated on listening for his feelings and needs" and reflected them back to him, showing she understood. Rosenberg calls this "receiving empathically." The woman discovered that what her attacker wanted most was not a room for the night, but respect, and he wanted his need for respect to be heard. The woman recalled, "The more I was able to focus my attention on his feelings and needs, the more I saw him as a person full of despair whose needs weren't being met. I was confident that if I held my attention there, I wouldn't be hurt. After he'd received the empathy he needed, he got off me, put the knife away, and I helped him find a room at another center."[6] A.T. Ariyaratne, the founder of the Sarvodaya Movement, in Sri Lanka, has described two different occasions in which he was approached by an angry man. Both times, Ariyaratne said, he was so focused on responding to the man's need for empathy—he only saw a person asking for help—that he didn't realize, until later, the man was holding a gun.[7] Empathy can defuse anger and transform violent intentions.

Again, be careful about advising Guy B to "just listen with empathy, you'll be fine." Some people may, in a flash of inspiration or intuition, perhaps out of desperation, find an empathic response in the heat of a perilous moment—women more likely than men in US society, as women tend to receive more encouragement as caregivers. Generally, though, if the primary goal is to escape physical harm, it's probably better to choose avoidance, if possible, than attempt a technique you don't know. The night clerk at the detox center may have been desperate when she tuned in to her attacker's needs—"What choice did I have?"—but she had previously attended one of Rosenberg's Nonviolent Communication workshops where she received instruction in empathic listening. An important point: Nonviolence benefits from training—you cannot resist with weapons you don't have or don't know how to use. Fortunately, nonviolent techniques are available to all, no special equipment, muscular fitness, or financial assets required, and just as soldiers spend hours honing the finer arts of violence, peacemakers can study and refine their own methods. One simple way to practice is by responding to rudeness with empathy. If someone snaps at you or says something unkind, don't walk away (avoidance) or snap back. Rather, express concern for the person, and observe what ensues.

But technique alone may not be enough. You can suggest that Guy B tell Guy A that he's concerned for him, and Rosenberg offers precise formulas for communicating without alienating, but the right language must be backed by genuine concern. Appealing to the heart means communicating at the emotional level or deeper, and while translating feelings into words is problematic, humans are geniuses at reading each other's facial expressions, body language, and speaking tones—and less skilled at disguising their own. You cannot fake compassion under hateful circumstances. If you honestly care about an attacker and can access that concern under stress, if you can focus on the attacker's emotional needs rather than your physical well-being—big if's, indeed—your eyes and voice will convey that message. Similarly, lack of genuine concern will also show. Half-hearted empathy from Guy B might forestall half-hearted bullying from Guy A, but when your life is on the line, when your attacker is deeply dehumanized and prepared to kill, your survival may depend on how deeply humanized you are. There's training for this too. The work of therapeutic emotional processing can reduce your own deep-rooted fear and anger, allowing you to respond compassionately, rather than react emotionally, to a verbal or physical assailant. Meditation empowers the areas of the brain associated with calmness and empathy. Indeed, there is a growing awareness that humans connect and communicate on the cellular level, in the vibrational or spiritual dimension, and this may be the realm of purest nonviolence, laughable to those absorbed in material identity, but accessible to those who observe deep within. Years of meditating on compassion for others prepared Ariyaratne for his powerful responses to potential assassins.[8]

Ariyaratne's example contradicts those who dismiss nonviolence as evidence of weakness. However, Mohandas Gandhi criticized his fellow Indians for indulging in "nonviolence of the weak," meaning they used nonviolent methods against British colonial rule only because violent methods appeared doomed to fail—the British occupiers were more skilled at and better prepared for violence. For Gandhi, "nonviolence of the strong" was based on a willingness to suffer, even die, before intentionally harming others.[9] These two approaches are often categorized separately as *pragmatic nonviolence*, used because it appears the most effective method available under the circumstances, and *principled nonviolence*, whose practitioners reject violence under any conditions. The desperate night clerk believed empathic listening was her only option—which sounds like pragmatic nonviolence—but her empathy was genuine. Would she have resisted with violence if that option were available? If an iron pipe were within reach, would she have attempted to smash her assailant's skull? Even she may not know. With Ariyaratne there is little doubt: principled nonviolence is his life's work.[10]

But as the example of the night clerk suggests, the either/or of these two characterizations can be misleading. *Pragmatic* means attention to results. A pragmatic choice is practical, sensible, nothing fancy; as simply as possible it gets the job done. Does this mean principled nonviolence is impractical and idealistic, requiring more effort or commitment than necessary? Is pragmatic nonviolence really more practical than principled nonviolence? Again, the key question: What's the goal? A deeply principled commitment may not be necessary to avoid a bar fight while preserving self-esteem, but if the goal is to transform fundamentally the cultural or structural violence of a society, principled nonviolence may be the only possible way and, therefore, the only pragmatic choice. If so, then believing otherwise, believing you can transform society at the deepest level without principled commitment, is unrealistic and, in that sense, idealistic. As typically defined, principled nonviolence might actually be pragmatic, and pragmatic nonviolence might be unrealistic—*depending on the goal.* Thus, rather than an either/or distinction, a *continuum* of commitment to nonviolence may be more appropriate.

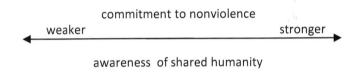

The important question is not is your nonviolence principled or pragmatic, but how strong is your empathy and humanity, how aware are you of the deep interconnection between all humans. (Does *commitment to nonviolence* equate with *awareness of shared humanity*? Try it.)

Compared to the night clerk, Ariyaratne would probably be farther to the right on the continuum, the direction where nonviolence means strength, fearlessness, and refusal to harm another person, even in self-defense, preferring instead to absorb suffering. The more dehumanized the attacker, the greater humanity required to respond with compassion and humble patience. In extreme cases like the Crazed Gunman, the ultimate sacrifice might be necessary. Gandhi, who was assassinated at very close range, called this commitment to nonviolence *satyagraha*—holding firmly to Truth.

NOTES TO CHAPTER 3

[1] Joan Baez, *Daybreak* (Dial Press, 1968), 131-138, offers a marvelous response to the Crazed Gunman scenario.

[2] Tom Hastings, *Meek Ain't Weak: Nonviolent Power and People of Color* (University Press of America, 2002).

[3] Kenneth Boulding, *Three Faces of Power* (Sage Publications, 1989). Johan Galtung, *Peace by Peaceful Means: Peace and Conflict, Development and Civilization* (Sage Publications, 1996), 2, identifies four power types: military (threat), economic (exchange), cultural (persuasion), and political (decision-making).

[4] Niccolo Machiavelli, *The Prince* (Penguin Classics, 2003), 54, posits that "it is far better to be feared than loved if you cannot be both."

[5] See Dave Grossman, *On Killing: The Psychological Cost of Learning to Kill in War and Society* (Back Bay Books, 1995), 97-137, for the "direct relationship between the empathic and physical proximity of the victim, and the resultant difficulty and trauma of the kill." Quote on 97.

[6] Marshall Rosenberg, *Nonviolent Communication: A Language of Life* (PuddleDancer Press, 2003), 119-120. For a similar story, see Michael Nagler, *The Search for a Nonviolent Future: A Promise of Peace for Ourselves, Our Families, and Our World* (Inner Ocean Publishing, 2004), 75-76.

[7] "The Power of Love," speech by A.T. Ariyaratne, Ahimsa Center, California Polytechnic University, Pomona, Oct. 27, 2007.

[8] Articles summarizing the growing body of neurological research on meditation and the mind-body connection are easily found online. For related perspectives, see Eckhart Tolle, *A New Earth: Awakening to Your Life's Purpose* (Penguin, 2008); Nagler, *The Search for a Nonviolent Future*. Those prepared for deep emotional cleansing may consider Michael Brown, *The Presence Process: A Journey into Present Moment Awareness*, rev. ed. (Namaste Publishing, 2010).

[9] Louis Fischer, ed., *The Essential Gandhi: An Anthology of His Writings on His Life, Work, and Ideas* (Vintage, 2002), 300.

[10] Gunadasa Liyanage, *Revolution Under the Breadfruit Tree: The Story of Sarvodaya Shramadana Movement and Its Founder Dr. A.T. Ariyaratne* (Sinha Publishers, 1988); George Bond, *Buddhism at Work: Community Development, Social Empowerment and the Sarvodaya Movement* (Kumarian Press, 2004).

4

THE SATYAGRAHA OF JOHN BROWN

4

THE SATYAGRAHA OF JOHN BROWN

Satyagraha

What did Mohandas Gandhi mean by *satyagraha*? The term is a combination of two Sanskrit words: *satya* (ultimate Truth) and *graha* (holding). For Gandhi, Truth meant *ahimsa* (without harm or coercion), and universal Truth is God. Put another way, the interconnectedness of all living things is ultimate reality. Christians can easily understand this as "God is love," and members of all three Abrahamic faiths may see similarities between "holding firmly to Truth" and the admonition to "love your neighbor as yourself."[1] For those in tune with a universal consciousness or the unity of life, no further explanation is required.

$$ahimsa = non\text{-}harming = love = Truth = God$$

A *satyagrahi* is a person committed to Truth, both as a goal (the integration of all humankind) and a means to that goal (non-harming).[2] In A.J. Muste's perfect phrase, "There is no way to peace—peace is the way."[3] In renouncing violence and embracing human interconnection, satyagrahis are nurturing their deepest humanity. Satyagraha—persistence in Truth—is a way of life, one that rejects all forms of violence—but not one that ignores conflict.

Conflict, in Gandhian thought, is an opportunity to bring the conflicted parties, Self and Other, closer together by correcting a bad relation. Other is not the enemy, but, rather, a partner in the conflict, and is invited to join Self in transforming their conflicted connection. However, there is much Self can do without Other's cooperation. To break away from dehumanizing relations, a satyagrahi seeks to develop power over Self, or *autonomy*. This includes fearlessness, to neutralize threat power; self-reliance, to eliminate vulnerability to exchange power; and self-respect, to rise above the power of persuasion.[4] Autonomy works on either side of a bad relation: power over Self rather than *submission to* Other, and power over Self rather than *power over* Other. A fearless person won't be intimidated by threat of harm and also won't need to intimidate; bullies are motivated by deep-seated insecurity. A truly self-reliant person isn't vulnerable to exploitation and has no need to exploit others. True self-confidence means holding firmly to your truth, not submitting to Other's truth, but without the need to force your truth onto Other; evangelists may be seeking affirmation.

Autonomy is an antidote for the three types of violence: fearlessness versus direct violence, self-reliance versus structural violence, and self-respect versus cultural violence (which normalizes fear and dependency).

AUTONOMY	resistance to:	no desire to:	antidote to violence
fearlessness	intimidation	Dominate	direct
self-reliance	dependency	Exploit	structural
self-respect	persuasion	manipulate	cultural

Conflict, then, is also an opportunity to test and strengthen Self's commitment to nonviolence, an opportunity to rid oneself of fear, dependency, and submissiveness. The presence of conflict is an announcement: There is room here for improvement! Ultimately, this requires reducing ego, releasing attachment to the material world, and locating Self in the spiritual dimension: Self-purification and Self-realization. By holding firmly to Truth, by being willing to absorb suffering but refusing to inflict it, by showing respect and concern for Other, Self employs integrative power, hoping this will inspire Other to move in a similar direction. Gandhi called this "soul force." So satyagraha is a method of nonviolent conflict resolution that approaches conflicts as opportunities to reduce violence of all types and also as opportunities for transformation of all parties involved.

Gandhi applied satyagraha in his attempt to resolve the conflict known as British colonial rule over India—a dehumanizing relation that kept the British imperialists dependent on exploitation of Indians, Indians submissive before British demands, and all sides persuaded of British superiority. But when Gandhi spoke of *Hind swaraj* (Indian self-rule), his was not the late 20th-century Western notion of freedom as license or "freedom to."[5] Rather, Gandhi was concerned with "freedom from." True freedom meant liberation from passions and desires. "The outward freedom therefore that we shall attain will only be in exact proportion to the inward freedom to which we may have grown at any given moment."[6] For example, the attachment to material existence, the desire for physical satisfaction, will bring fear of physical suffering and death, and thus submission before superior threat force. Gandhi asserted that, "You cannot be ruled without your consent." You can be tortured and killed without your consent, but giving into demands in order to avoid suffering—however coerced and unfair the choice may seem—is to cooperate in your subjugation. So Indian independence would come when Indians developed fearlessness in the face of British direct violence; self-reliance, rather than colonial dependency, to dismantle structural violence; and self-confidence to end the cultural violence that taught British superiority and Indian inferiority. Gandhi viewed the British as partners in this enterprise because the ultimate goal was integration of humankind—a planet of friends, no enemies; freedom from domination, not freedom to dominate.

The problem, Gandhi argued, was not British individuals, but British "civilization." The remedy was to develop an indigenous Indian society, based on autonomy, which the British would be unable to exploit, but were welcome to join. In 1920, Gandhi predicted that if Indians practiced complete noncooperation with British rule—if they boycotted British goods, withheld taxes, refused to serve as lawyers, policemen, government officials— independence would come within a year.[7] The prediction seems rash, and the Indian National Congress was unable to organize and sustain sufficient noncooperation, but Gandhi's claim was almost tautological. Total Indian noncooperation would end British rule—it had to—because Indian cooperation *was* British rule. What's the point in ruling over a population that refuses to submit? You can brutalize them, but you can't exploit them.

Gandhi's satyagraha campaigns were less concerned with forcing British withdrawal, and more concerned with transforming all partners in the conflict, especially the people of India. The salt satyagraha campaign, in 1930, which included the celebrated Salt March and the nonviolent invasion of the Dharasana Salt Works, was an attempt at such transformation. Gandhi encouraged the unlawful making of salt, openly violating a British monopoly. The obvious goal was to end the salt tax, one of many British tools for extracting wealth from the colony. Gandhi also hoped to reveal the nature of the colonial relationship; British and Indian alike had been taught that British rule benefitted Indians. If Indians employed mass, sustained, nonviolent civil disobedience and noncooperation, the British would have to concede to Indian demands or employ arrests and physical attacks to crush the resistance. If the British conceded, Indians would be empowered, knowing that mass noncooperation with British laws could end British rule. If colonial forces assaulted nonviolent protestors, British rule would be revealed as tyrannous. All parties would then see that British rule was built on violence, not on British benevolence. The Indian protestors would have the opportunity for self-purification, developing fearlessness and self-confidence, and the British would be encouraged to substitute self-reliance for their dependency on colonial exploitation. But the campaigns usually left Gandhi disappointed, as passionate but untrained Indian protestors indulged in direct violence, which undermined the nonviolent dynamic.

The dramatic undertakings—the salt satyagraha, general strikes and boycotts, the near-fatal fasts—usually receive the most attention from casual observers, but far more of Gandhi's effort went into what he called the "Constructive Programme"—putting into action his vision of Indian "civilization." In his own words:

> I am not interested in freeing India merely from the English yoke. I am bent upon freeing India from any yoke whatsoever....Work of social reform or self-purification of this nature is a hundred times dearer to me than what is called purely political work.[8]

Gandhi established small, communal villages called *ashrams*, where he experimented with a simple, sustainable, subsistence-oriented lifestyle. He worked against illiteracy, ignorance, and unsanitary living conditions, and he encouraged daily, universal "spinning"—Indians producing their own cotton thread to make homespun cloth as an alternative to dependency on imported British textiles. He promoted Muslim-Hindu unity, women's rights, and the elimination of "Untouchability." Regarding the so-called "Untouchables," Gandhi renamed them *Harijan* (children of God) and invited them into his communities. Full integration was Gandhi's vision, and he also knew that British rule was impossible over a united India of three hundred million people in autonomous yet cooperative communities; the British could join or depart. Scholars looking for Gandhi's successes often point to the satyagraha campaigns, arguing that he awakened Indians to the realities of British minority rule and made British control of India no longer worth the trouble. Indian independence came in 1947, but Gandhi himself saw failures. Personally, he doubted he had "purification enough to realize peace or nonviolence."[9] When he criticized "nonviolence of the weak," he meant Indians were using nonviolence as a strategy to *defeat* the British, not as a way to build a better society *with* the British.[10] Even as the British withdrew, even as Gandhi undertook his most remarkable personal campaigns against direct violence, the Hindu-Muslim rivalry devolved into mass killings and a divided subcontinent. Gandhi's unparalleled accomplishment was not as a nation-builder, but, rather, his systematic investigation into the potential of a human society based on "nonviolence of the strong." Through his teaching, writings, and personal example, his "experiments with Truth" showed the way forward.

Compassionate Warriors

How does any of this apply to John Brown, a renowned man of violence?[11] In 1859, Brown led eighteen heavily armed men in an audacious invasion of the US arsenal at Harpers Ferry, Virginia. He hoped to outfit a guerrilla army of escaped slaves that would terrify southern plantation owners into abandoning slavery. The violent plan failed at the outset; Brown was captured at the arsenal by federal troops, tried for treason, and executed by the Virginia government. This sensational event, which presaged the Civil War, made Brown a household name and a polarizing symbol of the national slavery debate. Over one hundred fifty years later, Brown remains an iconic figure. In popular memory, Brown is known for taking an unwavering stand against the evil of slavery, to the point of killing civilians who stood in his way, and his example typically serves as a centerpiece in discussions regarding the use of direct violence for moral ends.[12] As such, the John Brown story can easily become an aspect of cultural violence. Beyond a few recent Brown biographies that depict a complex personage, the tendency is still to view him *only* as a man of violence.[13] The Pottawatomie Massacre of 1856, which Brown directed, was so outrageous, and Brown's career ended so dramatically, that it's easy to interpret his life as one long, increasingly violent journey to Harpers Ferry. But to focus on Brown's violence is to miss his remarkable work *against* violence. Indeed, in his final hour—his finest hour—

Brown appealed to integrative power, to the human need for interconnection that invigorates nonviolence, and may have done more to undermine US slavery than his violence did. Reframing the narrative, placing Brown in the context of Gandhian thought, can be a way to teach the power of nonviolence.

The story of John Brown may seem an unlikely place to observe integrative power at work. Born in Connecticut in 1800 to parents who taught him the Calvinist doctrine of predestination and helplessness in the face of divine sovereignty, Brown was, in religious conviction, an old-style New England Puritan. The Puritan search for evidence of individual salvation may have promoted personal humility, but notions of predestination could easily become justifications for rather vile behavior: in a word, divinely ordained violence. The Puritan ministers who led the 17th-century colonization of the Massachusetts Bay region claimed that represented the new "chosen people," replacing the "chosen" Hebrews of the Old Testament and charged with a special mission to create the "true Christian community." In the minds of Puritan leaders, "chosenness" justified the destruction of Native communities, with methods that included the slaughter and burning of entire towns and enslavement of the few survivors; religious certainty, expansionism, and militarism make a dangerous brew.[14]

Brown grew from a rather militant branch of Christianity—both of his grandfathers participated in the Independence War—but the tree had more than one root. New England also had a tradition of antinomianism—literally, "against the law"—which held that God spoke directly to the individual and one's conscience trumped socially established moral precepts. Anne Hutchinson is New England's best-known early antinomian; Massachusetts officials exiled her to Rhode Island, in 1637, for believing she could interpret scripture for herself. However, her friend, Mary Dyer, eventually presented a more powerful challenge to Puritan orthodoxy. Back in England from 1652 to 1657, Dyer converted to Quakerism, joining a new and rapidly growing sect whose beliefs threatened religious and political authorities. Quakers believed that all individuals had access to a divine "inner light," and, thus, there was no need for seminaries and clergy, no need to obey unjust secular laws. Quakers also rejected violence. Faced with brutal persecution, Quakers were learning that "patient suffering" not only met the biblical admonition to "resist not evil," but it could "purchase peace." They were discovering the potency of integrative power. When Quakers who were sentenced to public flogging vocally forgave their tormentors, onlookers often expressed empathy, were moved to tears; some became Quakers. According to Quaker belief, awakening the world to the "inner light" would bring about the kingdom of heaven on earth, so suffering for faith was not simply individual martyrdom, it was also a tactic for fulfilling God's covenant.[15]

In 1657, Mary Dyer sailed back to Massachusetts Bay, and was soon expelled for preaching Quakerism.[16] Twenty years earlier, Dyer had gone quietly into exile with Hutchinson, but this time she was prepared for a campaign of "patient suffering." When Dyer reappeared in Massachusetts, in 1659, to protest the arrest and flogging of fellow Quakers, the governor ordered her and two men, William Robinson and Marmaduke Stephenson, banished "upon pain of death." A month later, the trio returned, ready to "lay down their lives." The exasperated governor ordered their execution. As they walked to the gallows, Dyer called it "an hour of the greatest joy I can enjoy in this world." Robinson forgave the assembled crowd. Stephenson whispered to the hangman, "I suffer for Christ." After the two Quaker men were killed, Dyer received a prearranged pardon, but she objected, insisting, "I am willing to die as my brethren did unless you nullify this law." Despite the presence of a large detachment of soldiers, the crowd refused to allow another killing—"patient suffering" had moved them. They surged on the gallows to pull Dyer to safety. Soldiers physically removed Dyer from the colony, and she rejoined her family in Rhode Island. But seven months later, she was back before a Massachusetts court, demanding repeal of anti-Quaker laws.

The eloquence of Dyer's next and final visit to the gallows is a revelation. Onlookers begged her to accept banishment rather than be killed. She declined and was hanged, but not before explaining herself.

> I came to keep Blood-guiltiness from you, desiring you to repeal the unrighteous and unjust Law of Banishment upon Pain of Death, made against the innocent Servants of the Lord; therefore my Blood will be required at your Hands who willfully do it: But for those that do it in the simplicity of their Hearts, I desire the Lord to forgive them. I came to do the Will of my Father, and in Obedience to his Will, I stand even unto death.[17]

Recalling Johan Galtung's definition of violence—"avoidable insult to basic human needs"—it's safe to say that violation of the human need for life is usually more obvious and dramatic than violation of the need for identity. With her bold civil disobedience, Dyer was dramatizing the violence of religious intolerance, equating religious identity with life, thereby confronting Massachusetts residents with the ugly implication of anti-Quaker laws: actively oppose religious intolerance or tacitly support murder. The Massachusetts governor did not want to kill Quakers, he just wanted them gone, but Dyer, Stephenson, and Robinson would not let him off so easily. They were directing their "patient suffering" at the cultural violence of religious exclusivism, which was reinforced by the structural violence of Puritan theocracy—government by churchmen—and which led to the direct violence of floggings and hangings. Peace theory aside, Dyer's words and actions made her intentions clear; a tearful onlooker reportedly said, "She hangs there as a flag for others to take example by."[18]

What did the deaths of Dyer and her friends accomplish? The governor was employing threat power—do this or else!—to keep out Quaker influence, but integrative power—I do this because I care about you—reversed the effect. Puritans continued to become Quakers, among them a soldier guarding the gallows when Dyer was killed. When the king of England was informed of the events, he ordered Massachusetts to cease torturing and killing Quakers, and, under popular pressure, the governor halted even the jailing of Quakers—the beginning of the end of official religious intolerance in the colony. Longer-term results are more difficult to track, and the influence of these stunning demonstrations of "patient suffering" may be impossible to measure, but Dyer and other Quakers planted a seed of nonviolence in New England, and such powerful acts are not easily expunged from emotional memory. Just as an abusive parent teaches a child to abuse, lessons of tolerance and nonviolence were certainly passed through generations of New Englanders, knowingly and unknowingly, by word and example. Indeed, Quaker thought and experience were the original impetus for the US peace societies and the slowly emerging abolitionist movement.[19]

The life of Owen Brown provides an instructive example of transgenerational integrative power. As a boy in Connecticut, Owen played with a neighbor's Guinean slave and was deeply affected when the man died. The kindness of an enslaved African humanized Owen, prevented him from seeing blacks as less than human, despite the dehumanizing culture of white supremacy. As an adult, Owen Brown became an abolitionist, but went beyond most white abolitionists in rejecting racial prejudice altogether, and taught his children to respect people of all races.[20] When the family moved to Ohio, Owen's son John befriended local Natives, whose lingering presence other settlers resented. After he observed a white master abuse a black boy,

John became, at age twelve, a committed abolitionist.[21] Like father, like son. In the ensuing decades, Owen and John participated in the Underground Railroad, assisting runaway slaves on their northward flight. The ideas of abolitionist Quakers, including John Woolman and Lucretia Mott, also influenced John Brown's thinking, and the rude behavior of US soldiers during the War of 1812 disgusted him so that, as he explained in his curious syntax, "he would neither train, *or drill*, but paid fines & got along like a Quaker until his age finally has cleared him of military duty."[22] One acquaintance reported that Brown was a committed nonresistant.[23] In 1837, though, in response to the murder of defiant antislavery editor Elijah Lovejoy by a proslavery mob, John Brown stood up at a prayer meeting, with his father at his side, and declared, "I pledge myself, with God's help, that I will devote my life to increasing hostility to slavery."[24] His father had taught him colorblindness, but the abused boy, the desperation of fugitive slaves, Lovejoy's courageous death on their behalf—these reached Brown's heart. He felt their suffering and knew their humanity.

After his public vow, Brown emerged a Puritan warrior certain of his divine mission. William Lloyd Garrison and other prominent abolitionists rejected violence; they were Christian "perfectionists," believing that by achieving a sinless existence they could provide a righteous model that would persuade slave owners to cease their sinful ways.[25] In contrast, Brown's old-school Calvinism led him to believe that he was chosen by God to end slavery and that God, not human efforts to rise above sin, determined who was saved and who was damned. Inspired by accounts of violent slave revolts throughout the Americas, and by the example of Oliver Cromwell, a 17th-century English Puritan who believed he had been chosen by God to wage war against monarchy, Brown declared a war of arms, not words and piety, against slavery.

The conflict over the expansion of slavery into Kansas Territory provided Brown with a theater to begin his holy war. After "border ruffians" sacked Lawrence, an antislavery town, in 1856, Brown organized the brutal murder of five proslavery settlers. The Pottawatomie Massacre, as it was called, escalated hostilities from threats and property damage to pitched battles—"Bleeding Kansas"—with "Captain" Brown leading antislavery forces. In late 1858, Brown directed a raid on two Missouri farms, liberated eleven slaves, and delivered them over one thousand miles to permanent freedom in Canada. Next came the spectacular takeover and shootout at the Harpers Ferry arsenal, which brought death to ten of Brown's men, one federal soldier, and four townsmen, including a slave. Brown and six others were subsequently hanged—live by the sword, die by the sword—and Brown's plan to "carry the war into Africa," meaning into southern states, appeared a complete failure.

The John Brown Problem

Brown's antislavery violence created a problem for white Americans opposed to slavery.[26] For the pacifist abolitionists, the question Brown raised was should they abandon their nonresistance principles. Garrison, for example, had rejected moderation and gradualism in the fight for abolition, but, after Harpers Ferry, Brown appeared the one man fully committed to destroying slavery *immediately*. By comparison to Brown's method, perfectionism could seem hesitant, even cowardly. In a public address on the day Brown was killed, Garrison invoked "the spirit of '76" and equated Brown with George Washington and other "revolutionary fathers" who struck "a blow for freedom." The rhetoric of the Independence War— patriotic killing in the name of "liberty"—had great resonance, even for a self-described "ultra peace man." "I am trying him by the American standard," Garrison said, and characterized that standard as violent resistance to despotism. Garrison affirmed his own rejection of violence, but insisted that violent resistance by the oppressed was better than submission. "Rather than see men wear their chains in a cowardly and servile spirit, I would, as an advocate of peace, much rather see them breaking the head of the tyrant with their chains."[27] When they were the foremost abolitionists, the pacifists' claim to moral superiority had been secure. But when violent abolitionism took the lead, the pacifists had to decide whether or not to support killing that might bring liberty to the enslaved, and, indeed, all but a few dedicated pacifists eventually embraced Union efforts in the Civil War.[28]

For others, the problem was *non-state* direct violence. As the "paradox of civilization" suggests, governments claim a monopoly on violent redress; officeholders and courts get to decide when killing is just; blood feuds and vigilantism are circumscribed. (See Ch. 1.) The Pottawatomie murders made Brown a federal outlaw, and the Harpers Ferry action was a blatant attack on federal property, so expression of support for Brown could easily be construed as promoting vigilantism, anarchy, and treason. Immediately after Brown's capture, public opinion in the North generally condemned the raid, and presidential candidate Abraham Lincoln, even as he spoke against slavery, took pains to deny any connection between his Republican Party and Brown's "peculiar" and "absurd" enterprise.[29] But the demise of slavery at the end of the Civil War complicated the issue. Lincoln issued his Emancipation Proclamation as a wartime maneuver, and Union victory led to ratification of the Thirteenth Amendment by southern states. The simple equation that follows—the Civil War ended slavery—implies that antislavery slaughter was appropriate or served a higher purpose. In that sense, as W.E.B. Du Bois insisted, "John Brown was right."[30] He was fighting the good war before it was officially declared, while federal laws were still protecting slavery, while Lincoln was repeating his promise not to "meddle" with the South. Brown was a premature antislaveryist.[31] But lauding Brown's antislavery raids is to honor unsanctioned direct violence—unsanctioned by the state—which mainstream opinion usually deems illegitimate. Approval of Brown sets a dangerous precedent, as it suggests violent enforcement by private citizens is acceptable if their cause is righteous, or if they simply believe it is.[32]

In the early twenty-first century, the US political class's nervous obsession with "terrorism" made the John Brown problem even more awkward.[33] Scholars who label Brown a "terrorist" may be referring to a category of violent action, but in current parlance, this term is an indictment.[34] It says that extralegal killing defines the historic figure—defines him as "evil"—with no room for nuance. But how could he be evil if he was trying to end the evil of slavery? One way around the John Brown problem is to dismiss the old man as insane—a strategy originally attempted by Brown's lawyers and roundly rejected by Brown and recent scholarship. Heroic or dastardly, misguided or treasonous, good or evil—what to do with "Osawatomie" Brown?

Radical Egalitarianism

Peace theory offers a different perspective on John Brown's career. Brown characterized slavery as "war," and believed that God had chosen him to end it. That was Brown's stated goal: the elimination of slavery in the United States, the liberation of the slaves. He declared war on a war. Direct violence to stop direct violence—the contradiction is clear. Yet Brown had other methods, and while it would be wrong to equate him with Gandhi and other advocates of nonviolence, looking beyond his violence reveals surprising parallels to Gandhi's approach to conflict resolution.

Like Gandhi, Brown believed he served a higher power, desired to liberate an exploited people, and was willing to die for his cause, but Brown wholeheartedly embraced direct violence as the means to his goal. Brown's solution to the direct violence of slavery was greater direct violence—a guerrilla army of escaped slaves terrorizing slave owners—violence of the strong. In this, he succeeded. The Kansas slavery war and the Harpers Ferry raid hurried secession by the South, leading to the warfare of 1861-65, which created the circumstances of slavery's demise, most critical being the willingness of slaves to become Union soldiers—mass, state-sanctioned slave revolt. (Hence, the John Brown problem.) If Gandhi's goal had been simply the end of British rule over India, we could say he, too, succeeded. Yet just as Gandhi failed to create a nonviolent, unified subcontinent, Brown's war against slavery, even with the federal government taking up his crusade and then outlawing slavery, did not end the subjugation, exploitation, and marginalization of black Americans by white Americans. Brown's antislavery efforts, though, amounted to more than a war of arms, albeit without the benefit of Gandhi's philosophical analysis, profound insight, formal education, and international influences. A hide tanner by trade, remarkably unsuccessful as a businessman, seemingly only skilled at producing children— nineteen by two wives—and starting wars, John Brown still managed to develop a "constructive program" of his own.

As peace theory predicts, structural and cultural violence supported the direct violence of US slavery. The structural violence included an economic system based in part on private, concentrated ownership of land and other means of production, and on the exploitation of the laboring masses by ownership. In the North, industrialization brought "wage slavery"; in the South it was worse yet. The US political system was an anemic version of representative government, with participation usually limited to white adult males and filtered by two-party dominance of the electoral process. Dissenting voices were excluded, co-opted, or drowned out. The most obvious cultural violence was the ideological partnership of patriarchy and white supremacy. The Gandhian approach to resolving the conflict known as US slavery would likely have included the creation of communal, interracial, self-sustaining, gender-cooperative, agrarian villages, with former slave owners welcomed as friends. The John Brown approach too. In his own home, Brown taught racial tolerance, sheltered fugitive slaves, insisted on gender cooperation rather than task differentiation, supported women's rights including suffrage, promoted education for blacks, and tried to establish a cooperative warehousing system to protect wool producers from corporate buyers. His son, John Jr., later recalled, "Father's favorite theme was that of the *Community plan of cooperative industry*, in which all should labor for the common good; 'having all things in common' as did the disciples of Jesus in his day."[35]

Again similar to Gandhi, though perhaps more intuitively than philosophically, Brown understood that to overcome the divisiveness of racism, blacks and whites would have to live and work together as equals. To understand the uniqueness of Brown's radicalism, consider that many antislavery activists supported deportation of freed slaves, believing blacks and whites could never, in Lincoln's words, "live together upon the footing of perfect equality." In 1848, Gerrit Smith, an immensely wealthy abolitionist, designated 120,000 acres in far northeastern New York for distribution to black families; they would be free and self-supporting and *isolated*. Brown convinced Smith to sell him a farm in the same mountainous region, promising to provide farming instruction and assistance to his black neighbors.[36] There Brown lived among blacks as equals, cooperating at work, socializing, even seeking their advice and approval as he plotted his next move. He imagined a free state farther south, in the Appalachian Mountains, and he wrote a political blueprint modeled after the US Constitution, then organized a biracial convention to ratify his document. In a clear rebuke of US slavocracy, Brown's "Provisional Constitution and Ordinances for the People of the United States" would guarantee protection of all citizens regardless of race and gender, institute communal ownership of property, and require all "to labor in some way for the general good." Males and females alike would be encouraged to carry arms for defense of the community, and slave owners who voluntarily freed their slaves would be "treated as friends." In brief, Brown's "Provisional Constitution"—like his personal life—challenged the cultural violence of racism and patriarchy by providing for an interracial, gender-cooperative community, and addressed the structural violence of capitalism by proposing economic communalism.[37]

Of course, the contradictory commitment to direct violence remained; the Provisional Constitution wouldn't go into effect without a violent uprising. But even Brown's war plan incorporated his vision of radical egalitarianism. More than simply abolish slavery, Brown wanted to empower blacks, and he surmised that arming them for battle would do both. In 1851, he issued a call to arms urging free blacks in the North to organize and fight back against slave catchers.

> Be firm, determined, and cool; but let it be understood that you
> are not to be driven to desperation without making it an awful
> dear job to others as well as you. Give them to know distinctly
> that those who live in wooden houses should not throw fire, and
> that you are just as able to suffer as your white neighbors.[38]

At Brown's encouragement, 44 black men and women formed the United States League of Gileadites to do just that. Brown believed that antislavery whites would be inspired by courageous blacks and compelled to take their side. "Nothing so charms the American people as personal bravery," he wrote, an argument later echoed by Frederick Douglass's call for blacks to join the Union Army to prove their worth, and by Gandhi's encouragement of Indians to fight in World War I to prove their manhood; Gandhi, like Brown, preferred brave men of violence to pacifist cowards.[39] Brown wanted a black president for his biracial state, and he recruited black leaders for his invasion of the South. Douglass, who thought the plan hopeless and who had no desire to return to Virginia, declined the leadership role offered by Brown. Harriet Tubman, legendary "Moses" of the Underground Railroad, responded more positively to Brown's overtures—he dubbed her "General Tubman"—but she missed the adventure, perhaps due to illness. (Brown recruited a sickly black woman to lead white and black men—sound absurd? In 1863, while serving the Union Army as nurse, spy, and recruiter, Tubman led Union forces up a river to liberate hundreds of slaves from South Carolina plantations, the first woman to direct a US combat operation.[40])

All told, Brown had a plan to cultivate fearlessness, self-reliance, and self-respect among blacks and their white allies. The comparison to Gandhi's Constructive Programme may be unconvincing or unfair—Gandhi laid out a far more comprehensive and holistic philosophy, Brown's approach was marred by advocacy of direct violence—but whereas Gandhi worked at it for over forty years before he was killed, Brown was just getting started.

The Sword of the Spirit

The raid on Harpers Ferry began smoothly enough. In short order, Brown's men seized the weapons stockpiles, taking townspeople hostage in the process. All that remained was for slaves to flee nearby farms en masse and take up arms with the raiders. That did not happen, due to fear, mistrust, and lack of communication. (One can speculate on a different outcome had "General Tubman" been present.[41]) When Brown realized only a few slaves were bold enough to answer his call, he still had time to attempt a withdrawal; some of his men suggested it, and a few did escape capture. Shortly after surrendering to US troops, Brown explained it was out of concern for his prisoners that he had erred in not fleeing—perhaps he had imagined more townspeople being killed in a fighting retreat. But Brown seems to have been weighing both the power of personal sacrifice and a desire for national attention when at the chaotic point of no return—run or die—he stayed put. At least a year earlier, according to one of his confidantes, Brown had concluded that only the deaths of white men could awaken people in the North from their apathy toward slavery.[42]

More certain is how Brown, in prison for six weeks awaiting execution, viewed his failure at Harpers Ferry and his impending death. He believed it was all part of God's plan to end slavery, and thus he would go joyfully to the gallows. His many letters and interviews are consistent on that point. He rejected talk of a rescue attempt, insisting, "I am worth now infinitely more to die than to live."[43] With two days to go, he wrote to his family, "I have now no doubt that our seeming *disaster* will ultimately result in the most *glorious success*."[44] He didn't explain just how his death would bring change, but there are clues as to what he anticipated. His "Words of Advice to the United States League of Gileadites," written eight years earlier, begins with reference to the *Amistad* trial, but reads like instructions to himself:

> The trial for life of one bold and to some extent successful man, for defending his rights in good earnest, would arouse more sympathy throughout the nation than the accumulated wrongs and sufferings of more than three millions of our submissive colored population.[45]

Brown knew, too, how the fighting death of Elijah Lovejoy had inspired his own commitment to ending slavery. Brown held the Puritan belief that the innocent must suffer for the sins of the guilty, but, in his talk of joyful sacrifice, the Puritan warrior was sounding more and more like Mary Dyer and her comrades in "patient suffering."

> To me it is given in behalf of Christ, not only to believe in him, but also to *suffer* for his sake....I think I feel as happy as Paul did when he lay in prison. He knew if they killed him it would greatly advance the cause of Christ....Let them hang me; I forgive them, and may God forgive them, for they know not what they do. I have no regret for the transaction for which I am condemned. I went against the laws of men, it is true; but "whether it be right to obey *God* or *men*, judge ye."[46]

When the threat power of armed struggle could take him no further, Brown had turned to integrative power, dying to win sympathy for his cause. Or, as he put it, "Christ...*saw fit* to take from me a sword of steel after I had carried it for a time but he has put another in my hand ('The sword of the Spirit;')."[47]

What did Brown accomplish? The Harpers Ferry raid unleashed a wave of violence across the South that became the Civil War. In the North, thanks to the storm of publicity surrounding his trial and execution, particularly the exultant pronouncements of Garrison, Henry David Thoreau, and Ralph Waldo Emerson, Brown became the symbol of the war, the rallying cry, and the meaning.[48] The Union Army's wildly popular marching song, "John Brown's Body"—the source of "The Battle Hymn of the Republic"—ended with the refrain "His soul goes marching on." And his "soul" imbued antislavery with a greater moral authority.[49] Brown is often labeled a "martyr," but this term implies a kind of passivity—at best, refusing to betray one's beliefs, trying to maintain personal purity; at worst, choosing to play the self-pitying victim—and does not adequately capture the proactive nature and social dimension of "patient suffering" and integrative power. A Bible-quoting white man, undeniably courageous and sincere, who proclaimed his joy in forfeiting his life for slaves, who demonstrated that such people are worth fighting and dying for, was rehumanizing blacks in the eyes of whites. His eloquent words reached minds, and, like Mary Dyer, his eloquent deed touched hearts.[50] In so doing, he was also rehumanizing whites, teaching them to recognize the humanity in blacks, and dramatizing the violence of slavery in a fashion they could not ignore, undoing what Douglass called the "benumbed...moral sense of the nation."[51]

Brown's influence worked in remarkable ways. For example, his death inspired Tubman to be bolder in her antislavery efforts. A few months later, in Troy, New York, Tubman transformed a biracial crowd of onlookers, including prominent white townsfolk, into a rescue party that liberated a fugitive slave in broad daylight. A reporter concluded that the rescue "has developed a more intense Anti-Slavery spirit here, than was ever known before."[52] Just as Gandhi expanded the notion of freedom, Brown's "soul" was liberating *whites* from enslavement—enslavement to racist indifference. This was the power of Brown's soul force: From the outset, Lincoln's political war for the Union was becoming a righteous war against slavery; even white Union soldiers understood they were killing and dying for black freedom.

Yet one courageous death was not enough to transform the most deeply dehumanized individuals in a deeply dehumanized society. The greater the dehumanization, the greater the sacrifice required for rehabilitation, and it did not help that Brown's soul force was compromised by his earlier violence. The integrative power of his sacrifice may have moved northern whites, but southern whites responded more to the threat force of his raids. Brown's last scribbled note was predictive:

> I John Brown am not quite *certain* that the crimes of this *guilty, land: will* never be purged *away*; but with Blood. I had *as I now think: vainly* flattered myself that without *very much* bloodshed; it might be done.[53]

Understood in traditional terms, Brown was anticipating the Civil War catastrophe—US society would pay for its sins at the price of over six hundred thousand corpses. But mutual slaughter is not how a society overcomes violence. This is where the Brown approach falls well short of the Gandhian. Wars dehumanize, they widen the gap between Self and a "foreign" Other. Slavery plus war does not equal peace. If southern whites viewed black slaves as subhumans, they now imagined black soldiers as subhuman enemies coming to rape and kill. After the war, the presence of the Union Army in the South—threat power—allowed former slaves the space to practice citizenry and improve their condition, but the weakness of threat power is that it requires frequent reinforcement. When federal soldiers departed, southern whites remade black subjugation into racial segregation and de facto slavery. The cultural violence of white supremacy not only lingered, but intensified—across the entire country—in the late nineteenth and early twentieth centuries.[54] Slavery was outlawed; racial harmony was hard to find. A century after Brown's death, the integrative power of the Civil Rights Movement, organized around Gandhian principles, finally put a dent in US racism. The suffering and deaths of those who nonviolently absorbed the violence of police batons, Klan bombs, assassins' bullets, attack dogs, and fire hoses gave new meaning to Brown's final prediction. From Mary Dyer to John Brown to Martin Luther King Jr.—when you open your eyes to integrative power, you start to see connections everywhere.

There are, indeed, strong ties between Brown and the Civil Rights Movement. Well into the twentieth century, Brown remained an inspiration to those who worked for black liberation. One of the founders of the NAACP, the most important early civil rights organization, acknowledged it was "a direct descendant of the old League of Gileadites founded by John Brown."[55] King's masterful speech at the Alabama state capitol, in 1965, concluded with words from "The Battle Hymn of the Republic"—a tribute, in effect, to John Brown on the scaffold: "His truth is marching on!" The Gandhian influence behind the Civil Rights Movement actually reaches back to the early Quakers who learned, through painful trial, the integrative power of "patient suffering." Quakerism influenced the nonviolence of US abolitionists, including Adin Ballou, who influenced the Russian writer Leo Tolstoy's radical Christian anarchism, which in turn influenced Gandhi's satyagraha. Thoreau is also part of this tradition, not for nonviolence, but for other principles—individual conscience, asceticism, the integrity of labor—shared with Tolstoy and Gandhi.[56] Good company to be in, and John Brown is there too. Perhaps more than any other contemporary white observer, Thoreau immediately understood the power of Brown's sacrifice. In his lecture, "A Plea for Captain John Brown," Thoreau noted, "When a man stands up serenely against the condemnation of mankind, rising above them literally *by a whole body*...the spectacle is a sublime one...and we become criminal in comparison."[57] Brown's Puritan militarism took him away from the nonviolent tradition, but, in the end, "the sword of the spirit" brought him back: an accidental satyagrahi.

As interpreters of our past, we can choose the John Brown we want. The popular framing of Brown as a man *only* of violence, while other aspects of his life and work are largely disregarded, is an aspect of cultural violence as it emerges from, and reinforces, the thinking that legitimizes direct violence. The emphasis on Brown's violence fits the mindset that believes direct violence "works," without careful consideration of what the maiming and killing of others actually accomplishes. This follows from the belief that threat power, which functions on fear, is more potent than integrative power, which functions on the universal human need for interconnection.[58] From this perspective, Brown's violence was more effective and remains more noteworthy than his attempts at biracial community, and his attack on a federal arsenal deserves more attention than his radical revision of the federal constitution. But if the goal is to decrease violence of all types, then integrative power, especially in the form of "patient suffering," is what works. The Harpers Ferry raid may have sped the demise of southern slavery, but it didn't bring any lasting reduction in the violence of white supremacy and exploitation of southern blacks. That shift came a century later with the "patient suffering" of Civil Rights Movement activists. Therein lies a solution to the John Brown problem. Rather than debating whether or not his resort to vigilante murder was legitimate, justified, and righteous, it is more fruitful to investigate the dynamic that made his death so powerful and to consider how his positive peace efforts, throughout his life, challenged a violent status quo. Consider this a prescription for cultural peace: less discussion about when killing might be justified, more discussion about how to address all violent aspects of society.

NOTES TO CHAPTER 4

[1] Bible quotes: 1 John 4:16 and Leviticus 19:18.

[2] Raghaven Iyer, ed., *The Essential Writings of Mahatma Gandhi* (Oxford University Press, 1991), 244.

[3] Quoted in Ira Chernus, *American Nonviolence: The History of an Idea* (Orbis Books, 2004), 133. An excellent summary of Gandhi's philosophy is found on 91-110.

[4] Gandhi's conflict resolution is summarized in Johan Galtung, *Peace by Peaceful Means: Peace and Conflict, Development and Civilization* (Sage Publications, 1996), 114-126.

[5] Eric Foner, *The Story of American Freedom* (Norton, 1999), 262-274, 307-332, discusses the notions of "consumer freedom" and "free market" that prevailed in the United States after World War II.

[6] Dennis Dalton, ed., *Mahatma Gandhi: Nonviolent Power in Action* (Columbia University Press, 1993), 100.

[7] Judith Brown, *Gandhi: Prisoner of Hope* (Yale University Press, 1989), 147-148.

[8] Dalton, *Mahatma Gandhi*, 120.

[9] Iyer, *The Essential Writings of Mahatma Gandhi*, 257.

[10] Brown, *Gandhi*, 372-376.

[11] A revision of this chapter appears in *In Factis Pax* 8:1 (2014): 104-120, http//infactispax.org/journal.

[12] Blakeslee Gilpin, *John Brown Still Lives!: America's Long Reckoning with Violence, Equality, and Change* (University of North Carolina Press, 2014), 1; Bruce Lesh, "Interpreting John Brown: Infusing Historical Thinking into the Classroom," *OAH Magazine of History* 25:2 (Apr. 2011): 46-50.

[13] David Reynolds, *John Brown, Abolitionist: The Man who Killed Slavery, Sparked the Civil War, and Seeded Civil Rights* (Alfred Knopf, 2005); Evan Carton, *Patriotic Treason: John Brown and the Soul of America* (Free Press, 2006); Louis DeCaro Jr., *"Fire from the Midst of You": A Religious Life of John Brown* (New York University Press, 2002); Robert McGlone, *John Brown's War Against Slavery* (Cambridge University Press, 2009). For an example of the prevailing emphasis, see Barack Obama, *The Audacity of Hope: Thoughts on Reclaiming the American Dream* (Crown, 2006), 97, which says, "It was the wild-

eyed prophecies of John Brown, his willingness to spill blood and not just words on behalf of his visions, that helped force the issue of a nation half slave and half free. I'm reminded…that it has sometimes been the cranks, the zealots, the prophets, the agitators, and the unreasonable…that have fought for a new order." Tony Horwitz, *Midnight Rising: John Brown and the Raid that Sparked the Civil War* (Henry Holt, 2011), 7, calls Brown's early life and career "The Road to Harpers Ferry."

[14] David Chichester, *Patterns of Power: Religion and Politics in American Culture* (Prentice-Hall, 1988), 18-27; Francis Jennings, *The Invasion of America: Indians, Colonialism, and the Cant of Conquest* (Norton, 1976), 202-227.

[15] Meredith Weddle, *Walking in the Way of Peace: Quaker Pacifism in the Seventeenth Century* (Oxford University Press, 2001).

[16] This section on Mary Dyer is drawn in part from the research and conclusions of Casey McEachern, "Through Blood We Purchase Peace: Mary Dyer, Patient Suffering, and Puritan Persecution in Massachusetts Bay, 1656-1661," MA thesis, University of California, Berkeley, 2007. A summary of this paper can be found in McEachern, "The Quaker Martyr Mary Dyer and the Principles of Nonviolence at Work," *Peace Power* (Summer 2006): 26-28, www.calpeacepower.org.

[17] The words of Robinson, Stephenson, and Dyer come from William Sewel, *The History of the Rise, Increase, and Progress of the Christian People Called Quakers* (1728), 222-229, as quoted in McEachern, "Through Blood We Purchase Peace," 27-32.

[18] Horatio Rogers, *The Quaker Martyr that was Hanged on Boston Common* (Preston and Rounds, 1896), 62, quoted in McEachern, "Through Blood We Purchase Peace," 32.

[19] Gerda Lerner, "Nonviolent Resistance: The History of an Idea," in Lerner, *Why History Matters: Life and Thought* (Oxford University Press, 1997), 60-66.

[20] DeCaro Jr., *"Fire from the Midst of You,"* 23-24.

[21] Brown's account of the beating is likely stylized, but it accurately presents his view of blacks as peers. DeCaro Jr., *"Fire from the Midst of You,"* 53-56; McGlone, *John Brown's War Against Slavery*, 53-55.

[22] Quoted in Reynolds, *John Brown*, 33.

[23] McGlone, *John Brown's War Against Slavery*, 54, 237; DeCaro Jr., *"Fire from the Midst of You,"* 72.

[24] Quoted in Carton, *Patriotic Treason*, 82.

[25] Henry Mayer, *All on Fire: William Lloyd Garrison and the Abolition of Slavery* (Norton, 2008), 223-226, 236-237.

[26] Black Americans generally had little quarrel with Brown's antislavery violence. Benjamin Quarles, *Allies for Freedom: Blacks and John Brown* (Oxford University Press, 1974).

[27] Garrison's eulogy for John Brown was printed in *The Liberator*, Dec. 16, 1859. John Stauffer and Zoe Trodd, eds., *The Tribunal: Responses to John Brown and the Harpers Ferry Raid* (Belknap, 2012), 160-165.

[28] Mayer, *All on Fire*, 518-526. In explaining Garrison's decision to support the Union war effort, Mayer wrote, "The wound dealt to his pacifism by John Brown had now proved fatal." (520)

[29] Eric Foner, *The Fiery Trial: Abraham Lincoln and American Slavery* (Norton, 2010), 137; Stauffer and Trodd, eds., *The Tribunal*, 2012, 206-209.

[30] W.E.B. Du Bois, *John Brown* (Kraus-Thomson, 1973, originally published 1909), 338.

[31] Milton Wolff, an American citizen who fought with the International Brigade against Spanish fascists while the US government claimed "neutrality," discovered during his World War II service that the US Army had labeled him a "premature anti-fascist"—a very dangerous creature. Studs Terkel, *"The Good War": An Oral History of World War II* (New Press, 1984), 480.

[32] Robert E. Lee, the US officer who captured John Brown at Harper's Ferry, and who later committed unambiguous treason by going to war against the United States, isn't nearly as problematic as Brown, because the treasonous Lee was a professional soldier dutifully serving a government—directing state-sanctioned killing—even if that government was the Confederate States of America (CSA) slavocracy. Lee and CSA president Jefferson Davis received US presidential pardons in the 1970s. Brown has not been pardoned.

[33] US opinion-makers use the term "terrorism" to indicate direct violence they condemn and "counter-terrorism" to mean direct violence they condone. A US Army manual's more technical definition of terrorism—"the calculated use of violence or threat of violence to attain goals that are political, religious or ideological in nature"—would include most US war-making, and thus cannot be employed. Noam Chomksy, *Hegemony or Survival: America's Quest for Global Empire* (Metropolitan Books, 2003), 188-189.

[34] Tony Horwitz, "Why John Brown Still Scares Us," *American History* 46:5 (Nov.-Dec. 2011): 38-45. Michael Fellman, *In the Name of God and Country: Reconsidering Terrorism in American History* (Yale University Press, 2010), 14-56, 237-244, places Brown within an American tradition of terrorism, and concludes with an insightful essay about the term. Reynolds, *John Brown*, 500-506, is careful to distinguish Brown from less tolerant "modern terrorists": "He was an *American* terrorist in the amplest sense of the word, because he believed in the American ideal of equal rights for all, regardless of creed or race." (503) In other words, Reynolds believes Brown's terrorism was for a worthy cause. DeCaro Jr., *"Fire from the Midst of You,"* 268, believes that Brown's concern for his hostages proves he wasn't a terrorist.

[35] Quoted in Reynolds, *John Brown*, 82.

[36] Fergus Bordewich, *Bound for Canaan: The Underground Railroad and the War for the Soul of America* (HarperCollins, 2005), 397-400.

[37] Tony Horwitz, *Midnight Rising*, 80-82, 113; Stauffer and Trodd, eds., *The Tribunal*, 26-37.

[38] "Words of Advice to the United States League of Gileadites," in Jonathan Earle, *John Brown's Raid on Harpers Ferry: A Brief History with Documents* (Bedford/St.Martins, 2008), 45.

[39] Brown, *Gandhi*, 125-126.

[40] Catherine Clinton, *Harriet Tubman: The Road to Freedom* (Little Brown, 2004), 124-136, 163-168.

[41] Horwitz, *Midnight Rising*, 136, 145; McGlone, *John Brown's War Against Slavery*, 268-274. Brown chose a Sunday night for his raid, not realizing that slaves would be out visiting, away from their homes, and hard to locate. Tubman probably wouldn't have made that mistake. Also, she probably would have been more successful than John Cook, Brown's point man, in communicating with local slaves ahead of time, as she did before her South Carolina raid.

[42] McGlone, *John Brown's War Against Slavery*, 249, 304-306; Horwitz, *Midnight Rising*, 236-240; DeCaro Jr., *"Fire from the Midst of You,"* 251. Garrison wondered if Brown's intent at Harpers Ferry was "a desperate self-sacrifice for the purpose of giving an earthquake shock to the slave system." Quoted in Mayer, *All on Fire*, 496.

[43] Quoted in Reynolds, *John Brown*, 388.

[44] Earle, *John Brown's Raid*, 101.

[45] Earle, *John Brown's Raid*, 44.

[46] Earle, *John Brown's Raid*, 97. Quaker influence can be seen in Brown's last days: in court he quoted John Woolman, and from prison he corresponded with Quaker friends.

[47] Earle, *John Brown's Raid*, 93.

[48] Mayer, *All on Fire*, 495-507. Mayer's comment—"Brown's act…irrevocably moved the slavery controversy from the sphere of constitutional and moral abstraction to the visceral realm of feelings intensified beyond measure or reason" (495)—identifies the emotional power of Brown's sacrifice.

[49] Franny Nudelman, "'The Blood of Millions': John Brown's Body, Public Violence, and Political Community," *American Literary History* 13:4 (Winter 2001): 639-670, discusses how proponents of wartime nationalism used Brown's sacrifice as a model for the suffering of soldiers, transforming Brown's attack on a federal installation into a basis for greater state authority.

[50] According to a New York reporter, Brown's testimony in a hostile courtroom "touched the hearts of many who had come only to rejoice at the heaviest blow their victim was to suffer." Quoted in Merrill Peterson, *John Brown: The Legend Revisited* (University of Virginia Press, 2002), 14.

[51] Quoted in Horwitz, *Midnight Rising*, 287,

[52] Clinton, *Harriet Tubman*, 136-138.

[53] Quoted in Reynolds, *John Brown*, 395.

[54] James Loewen, *Sundown Towns: A Hidden Dimension of American Racism* (New Press, 2005).

[55] Quoted in Reynolds, *John Brown*, 496. After the Civil War, a Maine businessman funded a school in Harpers Ferry with the stipulation that it would uphold Brown's commitment to racial and gender equality. Storer College trained African Americans to be teachers, and, in 1906, hosted the Second Niagara Movement conference, whose members later formed the National Association for the Advancement of Colored People (NAACP). Reynolds, *John Brown*, 491-496.

[56] Chernus, *American Nonviolence*, esp. 1-25; Lerner, *Why History Matters*, 59-73.

[57] Stauffer and Trodd, eds., *The Tribunal*, 105-109.

---

[58] DeCaro Jr., *"Fire from the Midst of You,"* 39, for example, argues that "fear of escalating violence is a far greater catalyst for change within an indifferent majority than 'moral suasion' or appeals to the conscience of a society." DeCaro, a Christian minister who seems to see God at work in human history, has done a fine job of describing Brown's religious life without getting caught up in the sensationalism of Brown's violence. He calls Brown a "saint," but his apparent skepticism of integrative power may prevent him from understanding the power of Brown's death. See pages 4-7, 283-284.

5

TOPPLING DICTATORS

5

TOPPLING DICTATORS

People Power

One of the great human achievements of the twentieth century was the discovery and refinement of "people power," also known as *civil* or *civilian resistance*.[1] As generally understood, this means the organization of mass, sustained, nonviolent actions—protest, noncooperation, disobedience, and intervention—to force political change, usually at the national level. In some remarkable cases, campaigns of noncooperation and civil disobedience ousted entrenched and repressive dictatorships in a matter of days. Other nonviolent resistance movements succeeded after years of struggle, and some failed in their attempts to depose unwanted regimes. The achievement, though, was cumulative, as activists and scholars learned from the successes and failures of previous movements so that, by century's end, a body of knowledge regarding the dynamics of nonviolence was available to resistance leaders who no longer had to "reinvent the wheel"; nonviolent campaigns now included careful strategizing and training, not simply spontaneous uprisings.[2]

The narrative of people power often begins in 1905 in Russia, where two great lessons were demonstrated.[3] The first was that a widespread general strike could force concessions from a repressive government. When factory and railroad workers across Russia walked out en masse and began to organize politically, Tsar Nicholas II reluctantly agreed to democratic reforms—a noteworthy event in a deeply rooted autocracy. This was, in some ways, a function of industrialization. Work stoppages were less effective for agrarian laborers. In systems of chattel slavery, slaveholders typically had little tolerance for expressions of discontent and often inflicted brutal punishment, so resistance was usually secretive (slowdowns, sabotage) or all-out revolt. With feudalism, peasant farmers who didn't work now, didn't eat later, as their toil produced the necessities of life. Urban industrialization, by comparison, allowed wage workers more negotiating space and opportunity to withhold labor. There was already a long history of nonviolent labor actions in the industrializing nineteenth century, and, in fact, examples of nonviolent resistance against unwanted laws date to the first century AD and earlier.[4] But the 1905 Russian uprising represents an early example of a nonviolent movement challenging the very *existence* of an autocratic regime. Faced with growing rejection of his authority, the tsar decided he had two options: compromise or violent repression.

The second lesson from 1905 has to do with the role of violence in a people's movement. In January, on what became "Bloody Sunday," soldiers attacked and killed unarmed marchers who were converging on the Winter Palace, in St. Petersburg, to demand political changes. The direct violence of the soldiers made clear the repressive nature of tsarist rule, undermined Nicholas's assertion of love for his people, and transformed a local political action into a widening resistance movement. The violent response was intended to weaken the uprising, but it had the opposite effect. Social philosopher Richard Gregg later identified this dynamic as "moral jujitsu."[5] Government assaults on nonviolent protestors can actually work against the regime's interests by producing sympathy for the victims and contempt for the perpetrators, and the greater the brutality, the greater potential for such reversal. In the eyes of a great many Russians, the attack on nonviolent protestors weakened the moral authority of the tsar, who had always claimed divine mandate and benevolent intentions, and strengthened the moral legitimacy of resistance. As nonviolent resistance spread across the country, the tsar's dilemma worsened: concede the freedom and representation demanded by protestors or, as Nicholas himself put it, "crush the rebellion with all available force" leading to "rivers of blood."[6] Either way, his legitimacy as autocrat was in jeopardy. The willingness of soldiers to shoot unarmed civilians was increasingly in doubt, and Grand Duke Nikolai, a military commander, threatened suicide rather than direct the crackdown, so an unhappy Nicholas signed the "October Manifesto," promising democratic reforms.

Protestors celebrated in the streets of Moscow and St. Petersburg, but the Marxist revolutionaries among them were not satisfied. They agitated for armed insurrection, believing a violent uprising was necessary to erase completely the old regime. In December, soldiers moved against armed strikers in Moscow, gun battles ensued, and the clear moral line between a ruthless regime and nonviolent resisters became a fuzzier distinction between a heavy handed tsar who had conceded some demands and revolutionaries who had shown their own willingness to shed blood. The earlier assault on peaceful protestors may have been wrong, but many Russians, especially in the military, accepted the government's prerogative to put down armed revolt, to enforce "order," which it did harshly. Soldiers who might have hesitated to attack unarmed protestors could now understand a crackdown as self-defense. They executed hundreds of civilians, many of them armed, and arrested thousands more. The resistance divided over the question of violent tactics, the successful dynamic of a nonviolent general strike disappeared, and the movement for greater reform stopped in its tracks. Still, the lesson of *moral jujitsu*—nonviolent resistance delegitimizes state violence while violent resistance legitimizes it—was now available to observers, including the great Russian novelist Leo Tolstoy, who wrote, "The violence of the old regime will only be destroyed by non-participation in violence, and not at all by the new and foolish acts of violence which are now being committed."[7]

In faraway South Africa, Mohandas Gandhi followed reports of the dramatic happenings in Russia. He also learned of a boycott of British goods in the Indian province of Bengal, which had been inspired by a Chinese boycott of US products that same year. From these disparate events, Gandhi concluded that nonviolent noncooperation could be effective against British imperialism. "Even the most powerful," he wrote, "cannot rule without the cooperation of the ruled." He was thinking of his homeland: "The governance of India is possible only because there exist people who serve."[8] Years later, from 1920 to 1922, Gandhi and the Indian National Congress (INC) led a mass noncooperation campaign against British rule in India, but this, too, was weakened by protestor violence. Gandhi's later use of trained satyagrahis in the salt campaign was more promising. The British colonial government—the raj—enforced a monopoly on salt production and taxed its sale. In 1930, Gandhi announced he would walk 240 miles to the seashore and illegally gather salt unless the raj met eleven demands, including abolition of the salt tax, a decrease in taxes on farmland, and placement of a tariff on foreign cloth. At the outset, Gandhi limited his entourage to eighty disciplined men—products of his Constructive Programme—who he trusted to remain nonviolent. In villages along the way, he preached civil disobedience against corrupt government and pressured local officials to quit their posts. Gandhi's purpose was to undermine British authority and to promote unity, strength, and fearlessness among Indians.

The dramatic, three-week march put the British viceroy, Lord Irwin, in a bind similar to what Tsar Nicholas had faced. Arresting Gandhi before he broke the salt law would appear unduly repressive and strengthen Gandhi's position, yet the Indian press, film crews, and foreign journalists were reporting his every step and generating sympathetic publicity across India and around the globe. British officials figured that Gandhi was trying to provoke them into using violence against nonviolent Indians, which would destroy the fiction of benign British rule and weaken their hold on the colony. They refrained from arresting Gandhi after he had reached the coast and led a crowd of twelve thousand in making salt, but finally jailed him a month later to prevent him from directing a nonviolent raid on the government salt works at Dharasana.

The raid went forward without Gandhi, and produced the desired effect: moral outrage over government violence. Day after day, for several weeks, unarmed satyagrahis tried to occupy the salt works, and policemen beat them back with bone-cracking clubs. Intentionally courting state violence may seem to violate the principles of a nonviolent movement, but governments typically rule with some degree of threat force—pay taxes or else!—and civil disobedience brings that underlying and often internalized threat into the open. In the case of the salt campaign, violence was already present in the form of imperial rule, and the nonviolent intervention at the salt works simply transformed it from structural ("unintentional") and cultural ("invisible") violence into the more obvious and easily understood direct violence of police brutality. The raj had showed its fangs, hundreds of satyagrahis were hospitalized with broken skulls, and eyewitness reports of the beatings were widely read, including on the floor of the US Senate.

A civil disobedience movement, promoted by the INC, spread to most every region of India, with millions making salt, boycotting foreign cloth, withholding taxes, and ostracizing government servants. The raj lost administrative authority over large areas, including the city of Bombay, and resorted to mass arrests, police violence, and land seizures to restore control. In early 1931, Irwin released Gandhi, and the two began negotiating. The pact they agreed on—which included release of political prisoners and restoration of some confiscated property, but little change to salt laws— seemed to many Indians like return to status quo, with nothing gained. But Gandhi understood that protestors were exhausted, the campaign was waning, and great things had been achieved: Indians had discovered their political strength, the raj had lost moral authority, the INC now spoke for an Indian majority, Irwin and Gandhi were meeting essentially as equals, the days of British rule appeared numbered.

An old canard holds that British imperialists believed in "fair play" and that Gandhi's nonviolence would have been less effective against a more ruthless opponent.[9] In fact, the 1920 Jallianwalla Bagh massacre, where British soldiers shot down hundreds of Indians in an enclosed plaza, may have created the greatest Indian unity in the Gandhi era. Had Irwin been more ruthless in 1930, he would have played into Gandhi's hands. The British skill at exploiting divisions among the Indian people made British rule possible, and the civil disobedience campaign did not bring sufficient Indian unity to end British domination. The campaign drew little Muslim support—Muslims were always skeptical of the Hindu-controlled INC—and the Hindu-Muslim schism was a major factor in the delay of Indian independence until 1947.[10]

Three years before the British finally quit India, nonviolent movements in Central America did put ruthless regimes out of business. In 1931, Gen. Maximiliano Hernández Martínez became president of El Salvador through military coup, then approved *La Matanza*—the indiscriminant slaughter of thousands of *campesinos*, mostly from indigenous communities—as collective punishment for an armed rebellion led by communists. For over a decade, Hernández Martínez headed a one-party police state. After a military coup against the regime failed, in 1944, the state repression intensified, with more arrests, torture, and executions. The brutality undermined popular tolerance of the dictatorship. In San Salvador, the capital city, university students called for a general strike.[11] Student organizers realized a violent uprising would be futile and feared peaceful marchers would be gunned down, but perceived that the forces of repression would have difficulty targeting people who simply stayed home from work and school. The strike spread quickly, business in the capital city ceased, and the dictator, seeing students, urban professionals, financial elites and some army officers aligned against him, resigned and exited the country. He had not hesitated to quash armed rebellion with a vengeance, but balked at ordering a slaughter to end mass, nonviolent noncooperation. Hernández Martínez's departure inspired university students, teachers, and lawyers in neighboring Guatemala, three weeks later, to begin challenging the rule of Gen. Jorge Ubico y Castañeda, whose harsh dictatorship was also thirteen years old. Police in Guatemala

City responded to the nascent public demonstrations of discontent with the usual arrests and beatings. Opposition leaders called for a general strike, and outrage over the police killing of a teacher the day before brought almost total participation. The capital city shut down, repressive forces had no demonstrators to fire on—Ubico's threat force was made suddenly irrelevant—and five days later he resigned. In El Salvador, the noncooperation campaign had taken three weeks to topple a dictator; in Guatemala it took four. However, after Ubico resigned, general strike organizers failed to oust heads of state in Honduras and Nicaragua.[12]

The 1944 Central American uprisings fit within a remarkable Latin American tradition: urban shutdowns forced out rulers in Chile (1931), Cuba (1933), Haiti (1946, 1956, 1957), Panama (1951), Colombia (1957), and the Dominican Republic (1961). But the wave of general strikes did not reach beyond the region. The Cold War inhibited the emergence of people power, as the two belligerent superpowers were willing to arm resistance movements that met their ideological criteria and were just as quick to crush resistance movements that rejected their hegemony. The Soviet and US militaries were the culmination of centuries of research, experimentation, institutionalization, and state employment of direct violence, while the viability of civilian resistance was only starting to become known. Communist ideology held that violent revolution was necessary to erase capitalist structures, and the Russian (1917) and Chinese (1949) revolutions seemed to bear this out. A violent uprising in Hungary (1956) and nonviolent resistance to Soviet invasion in Czechoslovakia (1968) were put down by Soviet troops, who may have believed they were crushing counter-revolution and whose foreign origin kept them from seeing resisters as fellow countrymen. The violent uprising in Cuba that overthrew the Batista dictatorship, in 1959, inspired revolutionaries throughout Latin America to employ violent tactics against repressive regimes in the following decades. Aside from the Sandinista revolt in Nicaragua, in the late 1970s, these violent rebellions had little success against government forces, which were usually trained and funded by the US government. Also, the violent resistance made it difficult for nonviolent movements to gain traction, as government propagandists could easily demonize and delegitimize any opposition as "communists" intent on violent, destructive revolution that would usher in Soviet-style, anti-church totalitarianism.

In Iran, though, sixteen months of street demonstrations culminated in the exit of the US-supported Shah, a dictatorial monarch, in January 1979. This might have become the global breakthrough for people power, except it was marred by violent slogans, stone-throwing, and frequent burning and looting, and demonstrators fought street battles against loyalist soldiers after the Shah's departure.[13] In the West, the focus quickly turned to the takeover of the US embassy in Tehran and the ensuing "hostage crisis." US opinion-makers condemned the new Islamic Republic as "anti-American," and the accomplishment of the mostly nonviolent Iranian masses was forgotten.

The real coming-out party for people power came courtesy of the Philippines. In 1972, an elected but corrupt president, Ferdinand Marcos, declared martial law and suppressed political freedom. He blamed the crisis on a violent communist insurgency, and counted on backing from the US government, which wanted anticommunist allies in the region. Among the noncommunist opposition, former senator Benigno Aquino Jr. emerged as the symbol of democracy. From exile in the United States, he called for open elections, and, influenced by Gandhi's example, promoted nonviolent struggle as an alternative to communist revolution. In 1983, Aquino flew back to the Philippines, and was shot dead on the airport tarmac by military personnel— the beginning of the end for the Marcos regime. The assassination led to growing demands for democratic reforms and to greater nonviolent resistance. Richard Attenborough's influential film *Gandhi* was already known in the capital city of Manila, and Catholic churchmen sponsored nonviolent training sessions led by the International Fellowship of Reconciliation. Mass demonstrations, strikes, and sit-ins put pressure on the Marcos regime, as did capital flight and complaints from the Filipino business class and even from Marcos's US patrons. Marcos called for a quick election in early 1986, hoping to catch his opposition unprepared and divided. When his opponents rallied around a single candidate—Aquino's widow, Corazon—Marcos attempted to steal the election. Clear evidence of electoral fraud and intimidation, including the murder of opposition supporters, further delegitimized the Marcos regime; many believed Aquino had won. Prominent church leaders called for continued nonviolent protest, and Aquino supporters organized a boycott of banks and other loyalist businesses. They called their campaign "Triumph of the People." Several army generals declared their allegiance to Aquino and took refuge at two adjacent bases outside Manila.

The events of February 22-25, 1986, in the Philippines were breathtaking. With loyalist generals threatening an assault on the defecting battalions, opposition leaders issued radio announcements requesting civilians to the rescue. Thousands responded and formed a human barricade around the rebel soldiers. The party had begun. The situation was dangerous, but the crowd was dancing and blowing horns, and priests and nuns kept the masses organized and nonviolent. The next day, two armored battalions advanced on the rebel camps. They were halted by a jubilantly defiant crowd—now perhaps one million strong—offering food, hugs and handshakes, ribbons, and prayers. The armored vehicle operators couldn't bring themselves to drive over the nonthreatening human obstacle, and had to turn around. Mass military defections followed. On the third day, the joyous human shield again turned back armored vehicles. Unarmed civilians, led by Catholic nuns, protecting rebel soldiers from military attack: with eloquence and irony, the moment speaks for itself. It also raises an interesting question: What if politicians and generals declare a war and only nonviolent protesters show up? In truth, the resistance was not entirely nonviolent—a helicopter unit defected to the rebels and attacked a government airbase—but the nonviolent crowds had neutralized the regime's military advantage and dramatized popular dissatisfaction. With the now infamous Marcos running out of loyal soldiers, the US government withdrew its support, and, the next day, Aquino became president; Marcos went into exile in Hawaii.[14]

Solidarity

Meanwhile, in Poland, a different type of people power movement was on the verge of an unexpected breakthrough. In the late 1970s, an alliance of Polish intellectuals, Catholic Church leaders, and labor organizers had pressed the Polish Communist Party dictatorship (PZPR) on a variety of issues. The threat of Soviet military intervention discouraged demands for political reform, but communist rhetoric—claiming to represent workers' interests—provided an opening for a labor movement. Also, the 1979 visit of Pope John Paul II, symbol of religious hope in stark contrast to communist despair, became a remarkably unifying and empowering event for millions of Poles. One year later, in 1980, economic hard times and the firing of labor organizers motivated industrial workers to halt production. Their most significant demand was the right to form trade unions independent from PZPR control. In the past, Polish resisters had gone into the street, battled with police, and burned PZPR offices, and some died from police bullets. Their use of violent tactics had played into the hands of the repressive state. This time, though, protestors occupied shipyards and other factories, and avoided physical confrontations. With hundreds of workplaces shut down, and worried that soldiers and policemen might not obey orders to attack nonviolent strikers, party officials agreed to a compromise: workers could unionize if they did not challenge the PZPR's political monopoly. Within a few months, a free trade union called Solidarity had ten million members.

A delicate balance prevailed through most of 1981. Like with Gandhi's salt satyagraha, the coordination and nonviolent discipline of the Polish strikers revealed the effectiveness of widespread noncooperation against repressive rule. Fitting with Gandhi's notion of self-rule, Poles were developing a civil society and free press outside of party control, organized instead around labor unions and the Catholic Church. In fact, religious and nationalist identity allowed for a degree of popular unity unknown in Gandhi's India. However, some Solidarity leaders, including Lech Walesa, believed a Soviet invasion could be avoided only if the façade of PZPR rule remained, so they tried to restrain the demands of the very masses they had worked to empower. Where Gandhi may have courted a violent response from his opponents, Walesa seemed to fear one. PZPR leaders had a similar balancing act, caught between a rebellious population expecting more reforms and imperial Soviet officials demanding a crackdown. The balance ended, in December, when party leader Gen. Wojciech Jaruzelski declared martial law, outlawed free unions, and unleashed carefully trained and indoctrinated troops to break up strikes and arrest thousands of union leaders and other opposition members.

Later, Walesa recalled that when he was arrested and beaten, he finally understood that the resistance had won. Jaruzelski was trying to turn back the clock, but the Polish people had discovered their power, and the resort to violence only proved the party had nothing left to offer the population—no persuasive ideas, no integrative appeal, just threat power. Faced with martial law, the resistance turned to clandestine operations. With many labor organizers imprisoned, a general strike was difficult to arrange, so resistance leaders instead focused on further development of a civil society detached from government institutions. Workers refused to join party-controlled unions and ignored party-controlled media while supporting secret factory committees and underground newspapers. The secret committees and the Catholic Church raised funds to aid the families of those fired and imprisoned. Over the next few years, Jaruzelski tried to regain some legitimacy for his regime by gradually freeing Solidarity leaders. Also, he was feeling pressure from the economic sanctions imposed by Western governments hostile to the Soviet bloc. Previously, the PZPR had raised prices on food and other consumer goods by fiat, but, in 1987, needing to make new economic adjustments, Jaruzelski knew the population was no longer complacent and obedient. He began negotiating with the familiar Solidarity leaders, offering political reforms in exchange for acceptance of austerity measures, to avoid a labor uprising led by younger activists. With new Soviet premiere Mikhail Gorbachev showing no interest in intervening, Jaruzelski was able to outmaneuver PZPR hard-liners who rejected reform measures. In 1989, talks between Solidarity and the PZPR produced agreements on free trade unions and open elections. Opting against "rivers of blood," the communists were, in effect, negotiating away their power. In June, Solidarity candidates trounced the PZPR in national elections. It had taken a decade, but people power had triumphed by delegitimizing PZPR rule and constructing alternative institutions until a government in crisis chose to abandon repression and request popular support.

This time, in 1989, after events in the Philippines and Poland, a wave of people power did follow, most strongly in east central Europe, where nonviolent uprisings evicted communist dictatorships.[15] When communist party reformers, following Gorbachev's lead, tried to direct change from above, popular movements in Poland and Hungary said, in effect, "enough is enough," and used protest and noncooperation to bring about free elections. Seeing their days numbered, communist leaders in Bulgaria moved quickly to embrace electoral politics before popular pressure forced them to it. In East Germany, Czechoslovakia, and Romania, though, hard-line communist party chiefs were more resistant to democratic demands. They fell like dominoes. In preceding years, Lutheran pastors in the East German city of Leipzig had provided safe haven for human rights groups, allowed prayer services for peace to become grievance sessions, and eventually organized the Initiative Group for Life (IGL) to teach nonviolent methods. In 1989, IGL stepped beyond the relative safety of church sanctuary and began leading public demonstrations. As protest marches in Leipzig and Berlin grew larger and larger, party officials first tried police repression, then, with policemen and militiamen on the verge of mass mutiny, opened the formerly locked-down country and agreed to popular elections.[16] In early November, the dismantling of the Berlin Wall, the hated symbol of East German and Soviet bloc totalitarianism, inspired mass rallies in Czechoslovakia. A police attack on fifteen thousand protesters in Prague brought the jujitsu effect of even greater resistance; three days later, the crowd demanding change was over one hundred thousand strong. Two weeks after that, the communist government resigned. The last to fall in 1989 was the Romanian dictator, Nicolae Ceaușescu, who had transformed party rule into a cult of his personality at the cost of a ruined country. After police fired on demonstrators, killing dozens, protests grew, but a popular front did not have time to develop fully before the army turned against Ceaușescu. Communist operatives then orchestrated an internal coup, seizing power and forestalling a stronger shift toward representative government.

To outside observers, the collapse of communist governments in Europe seemed to come from nowhere. Indeed, US officials, so accustomed to exaggerating the threat of their Cold War rivals to justify their own militarism, were caught totally unprepared. Blinded by their nationalist narcissism, US pundits insisted that President Reagan's military buildup was the primary cause of Soviet bloc demise—surely US threat power was the greatest force on the planet, so how else to explain such a dramatic political change?[17] In reality, the party dictatorships in Europe had lost popular support and relied, instead, on popular acquiescence. The threat of Soviet troops had propped up communist regimes for four decades, even when those governments could not assuage their populations with economic security, but resistance groups had survived underground after the crackdowns in Hungary, Czechoslovakia, and Poland. Gorbachev, who became Soviet chief in 1985, understood that the Soviet Union was missing out on the West's computer revolution, and he could see how nonviolent Polish workers disrupted production to express dissatisfaction. A system based on embittered laborers and centralized planning was being left behind, and either greater freedoms or greater repression would be necessary— Solidarity had made that clear. When Gorbachev announced a commitment to openness, resistance groups in the Soviet bloc took to the streets. For years they had been waiting for such a moment, and they knew what to do. Like earlier in El Salvador and Guatemala, recalcitrant regimes in East Germany and Czechoslovakia fell quickly when faced with mass nonviolent uprisings. The more a national government relies on violent repression, the more precarious its rule; when the fear is gone, the tyranny goes too. But success is not guaranteed. In demoralized and gutted Romania under Ceaușescu, resisters had little room to organize and opposition leaders had not clearly emerged, so when the populace, responding to events in neighboring countries, finally took to the streets, a violent internal coup beat them to the punch. In the end, Ceaușescu was a victim of his own repression.

He may have been wishing for greater nonviolent resistance when Romanian coup plotters summarily executed him and his wife.[18]

This brief summary of a few cases hardly does justice to the emergence of people power in all its variations. Despite failed attempts to end dictatorships in China, Burma, Kenya, and Panama, by century's end the ability of mass nonviolent protest and noncooperation to remove unpopular regimes or block military coups was well-documented and starting to be understood. In the first eleven years of the twenty-first century, variously successful civilian resistance movements—Serbia, Georgia, Ukraine, Kyrgyzstan, Lebanon, Tunisia, Egypt—were seemingly commonplace. Perhaps the "bloodiest century," with its worldwide slaughters and high-tech violence, will be followed by the century of human solidarity. Perhaps.

Sharp Thinking

Political theorist Gene Sharp has been one of the key contributors to popular understanding of civilian resistance; organizers around the world have used his handbooks, which teach nonviolent methods. Sharp concluded that Gandhian nonviolence, meaning personal commitment to ahimsa (non-harming), may be too exclusionary.[19] Not everyone, he asserted, is willing or able to be a satyagrahi, nor do they have to be—nonviolent methods can be used effectively by anyone, not just "pacifists or saints." Sharp replaced the phrase "moral jujitsu" with "political jujitsu," and even took issue with the term *nonviolence*, which he thought implied ethical values or religious beliefs and, thus, might deter potential advocates.[20] For him, "nonviolent action" and "nonviolent struggle" were more useful phrases because he was most interested in nonviolence as technique, a method of "wielding power," a "pragmatic" choice.[21] As explained earlier (see Ch. 3), so-called pragmatic nonviolence is not always pragmatic—it depends on the desired outcome—so Sharp's subject is better understood by its other name, *strategic nonviolence*, with the understanding that it may not always be the best strategy.

Of Johan Galtung's three categories of violence—direct, structural, cultural—Sharp's scholarship is primarily, though not solely, concerned with structural violence, and political structures in particular. In Sharp's theory of political power, rulers—which could be individual dictators or dominant groups—depend on a population's consent, as shaped by varying degrees of enthusiasm and agreement, ranging from passive acquiescence (obedience or submission) to active support (cooperation or loyalty). The reasons people grant consent to rulers, according to Sharp, are many and complex. In general, though, ruling power is based on *authority*, meaning acceptance of the ruler's legitimacy as decision-maker, and on *sanctions*, meaning punishment or threat of punishment to force obedience to rules. The more the population cedes authority to the ruler, the less the ruler needs to apply coercion. A beloved ruler benefits from integrative power; a hated ruler relies more on threat power—a weaker dynamic. Recall Gandhi's maxim: You cannot be ruled without your consent. Sharp's work is to understand how political rule, especially in the more extreme types of authoritarian government, is structured on that consent, and how consent can be withdrawn.[22]

Dictatorial state power is not simply one person presiding, like an overseer with a whip, over a subdued, disorganized body of individuals. People in complex societies form and participate in a variety of organizations and institutions—churches, labor unions, schools, bureaucracies, local governments, residential communities, infrastructure and service agencies— and the ruler or ruling group relies on their cooperation, obedience, knowledge, and expertise to carry out orders and maintain political and economic function. In fact, it is the cooperation and obedience of these "pillars of support," Sharp observed, that arrange and maintain the cooperation and obedience of the population in general. Try to imagine modern state power without at least a loyal police force and civilian bureaucracy. As earlier stated, Indian cooperation, which included civil and military service, *was* British colonial rule.

To weaken a ruler, to exert control *over* a ruler, a resistance movement must (1) undermine the perceived legitimacy of the ruler or ruling group, (2) withdraw popular cooperation and obedience, and (3) separate the ruler from the "pillars of support." From his study of historical examples, Sharp catalogued dozens of nonviolent techniques that, in bringing about these three changes, can force otherwise recalcitrant rulers to concede demands.[23] For example, opposition leaders can organize a variety of public demonstrations to denounce a dictator, who, if insecure enough, might order a repressive response, which further undermines his legitimacy—the jujitsu effect—enabling the opposition to recruit mass participation in a general strike, removing most "pillars of support," until the ruler and any remaining forces of repression are isolated. With popular loyalty gone, continued rule is only possible with violent sanctions to coerce obedience. Thus, the regime's moment of decision: bloodbath or negotiation. If the troops won't fire, or the ruler won't give the order, concessions follow. In this fashion, a nonviolent movement can reduce a dictator to what he always has been: a scared and tiny man, the Wizard of Oz exposed. Simple enough in theory, difficult in practice—loyalty and obedience being deeply ingrained, rulers being skilled at exploiting it—but as recent history shows us, it happens all the time.

Civilian Resistance or Armed Rebellion?

If, using the Sharp approach, nonviolent action is valued primarily as a strategy to exert popular control over an uncooperative regime, why choose nonviolent rather than violent techniques? Why civilian resistance instead of guerrilla warfare, urban terrorism, or some other armed rebellion? After successful nonviolent campaigns in Europe evicted communist regimes, social science research on nonviolent resistance blossomed in the West, providing data that address this question.[24] In general, a campaign of nonviolent resistance offers a greater chance of success than violent resistance. A study of non-state rebellions against state power, from 1900 to 2006, found "that major nonviolent campaigns have achieved success 53 percent of the time, compared with 26 percent for violent resistance campaigns."[25] There are several reasons for this significant gap. Nonviolent campaigns are more likely to win sympathy and support from the local population, members of the military and civil bureaucracy, and outside interests. Violent tactics are more likely to isolate a resistance movement and are more easily denounced. Too, a violent crackdown on unarmed resisters is more likely to produce the jujitsu effect, while, by comparison, assault on armed rebels usually generates less popular outrage, as demonstrated in the 1905 Russian uprising. These points arise from the basic tendency of humans, across cultures, to question the legitimacy of violent actions, especially when directed against noncombatants.

Furthermore, as previously observed, states usually function with some degree of threat force while claiming a monopoly on violence in the name of national defense and internal order—euphemistically called "security."[26] States invest heavily in the preparation and use of direct violence, so at the outset of a violent resistance campaign, non-state rebels are usually an inferior force, having chosen to fight against a state's strength. States depend also on integrative power—hence the symbols and propaganda of nationalism and leadership cults—but the fine words of government officials are often contradicted by divisive policies, making necessary the resort to threat power. By comparison, a nonviolent campaign usually appears more sincere in its commitment to integrative power, appealing to human interconnection and thus human skepticism of violence, which can turn the state's strength against itself.

Getting down to specifics, the decisive factor in the success or failure of a movement to oust a repressive regime is usually the ability to separate the forces of repression from the ruler's command, and historical evidence shows nonviolent methods are more likely than violent resistance to bring troop defections. One significant factor in making troops disposed to defection is popular unity. When opposition is limited or divided, soldiers and policemen may not be sure *to whom* they are defecting, and may not be convinced that any competing group has greater claim to legitimacy than the current regime. However, when the opposition is widespread and united, when a clear line is drawn between the rulers and "the people," the men with the guns are more likely to face a crisis of competing loyalties. Nonviolent methods, being more accessible to the average person, less alienating, and less destructive, are more likely than violent ones to foster such unity. Yes, a violent uprising can win sympathy, generate united popular support, and win military defections—the 1979 Nicaraguan revolution might fit this model—but history suggests the odds are against it.[27]

If greater chance of success alone is not sufficiently compelling, the nonviolent approach offers at least three other advantages. First, the likelihood of fewer casualties. While unarmed resisters appear dangerously vulnerable to armed forces and easily slaughtered, violent resistance usually brings far more casualties—among active participants and casual bystanders. Compare the devastation of almost any civil war (i.e., internal slaughter) to damage resulting from almost any nonviolent uprising. The war-level killing (in the thousands) of participants in a civilian resistance movement is rare, and when it has occurred—Burma (1988) and China (1989), perhaps Iran (1978-79)—protestor violence was a contributing factor, thus demonstrating the importance of absolute nonviolent discipline for protestor security.[28] Most nonviolent resistance campaigns suffer casualties, often in the hundreds, but not on the scale of violent campaigns. With violent resistance, two sides (or more) are killing each other, and the violent rebellion legitimizes the violent repression—there is some agreement on the rules of engagement (e.g., killing combatants is fair play). With nonviolent resistance, only one side is prepared to kill, and the nonviolent methods delegitimize the state's violence.

Simply put, soldiers and policemen are more likely to shoot at armed attackers ("self-defense") than at unarmed protestors ("murder"). There is power in vulnerability—integrative power.

A second advantage is that nonviolent methods have greater potential for empowering the general population. Violent techniques require special training and skills (handling guns, setting explosives), physical strength, and willingness to injure, and are typically seen as the province of young men. Training is also important for the more confrontational nonviolent methods, mostly for maintaining nonviolent discipline, but physical strength is not as critical, and most nonviolent actions (protests, noncooperation) are nonexclusive. Old and young, male and female—almost anyone can join a public demonstration, hold up a sign, stay home from work. (Seriously, which would *you* be more willing to do, take an unpaid day off or kill a cop?) General participation brings general empowerment, transforms passive servants into active participants, and increases popular investment in political outcomes. These should be desirable developments for opposition leaders interested in real democracy, less so for those obsessed with personal status or ideological dominance.

This points to a third advantage intrinsic to nonviolent resistance. Those who gain political power through violent means (assassination, coup, civil war) typically rule through violent means or fall back on them when feeling threatened. The threat power of direct violence is what they know and trust. Violent ascendance breeds cynicism—among the new rulers and the old, and among the general population—as violent takeover creates bitter enemies, fosters a legacy of resentment and hatred, and creates an environment of fear and distrust. Violence is decidedly undemocratic. Furthermore, a violent takeover is easily denounced by foreign states and international bodies, which may use it, hypocrisy notwithstanding, as excuse for violent intervention. In contrast, those who come to power through nonviolent means tend to be less cynical, less reliant on violent repression, more comfortable with an empowered citizenry, and harder for outsiders to demonize.

The choice, then, between civilian resistance and armed rebellion is not unlike Guy B choosing between a violent or nonviolent response to Guy A in the bar fight scenario. (See Ch. 3.)

	Loyalist casualties	resister casualties	self-esteem civilian	best likely outcome	worst likely outcome	lesson on violence
Violent Resistance	yes	yes	cynicism, resentment	?	prolonged civil war, massive casualties	military power is political power (killing = ruling)
Nonviolent Resistance	no	likely	Empowerment	few casualties, greater political participation	civilian casualties, increased repression	violence delegitimized, people power legitimized

The analogy is flawed. The bar scenario is a small, contained event, so the question regards short-term tactics—Guy B gets one "shot." Resistance movements are broader events, participants can learn from mistakes and change tactics, so the question is about overall approach or strategy, which makes for a broader, easier choice. And the bar scenario is hypothetical, the outcome can only be imagined. Resistance movements are historical and have been studied with attention to the choice between violent and nonviolent strategy. If the goal is to claim power and impose an exclusive ideology on an acquiescent population, violent rebellion has much to recommend it, though the odds may be long. Violent rebellion may also appeal to those desiring to inflict punishment or vengeance or to assert some macho notion of honor or pride. It will come with a tremendous human cost. But if the goal is to replace a repressive regime with a regime more responsive to popular participation, and to make future political violence less likely, nonviolent civilian resistance is the better strategy.

For many readers, these stories of people power will come as a surprise. The traditional lesson taught in US schools is that only great violence can bring freedom from entrenched tyranny. War brought US independence from British monarchy, war ended slavery, and war defeated Nazi Germany. From these simplistic propositions, it follows that a strong, aggressive war-machine is necessary for continued political liberty. According to official pronouncements, this is the raison d'etre of the US military: defending "our" freedom. Nonviolent accomplishments are less often included in the national narrative and in what is called "world history." The emphasis on positive change through warfare is a form of cultural violence, in that it predisposes people to initiate, support, and participate in wars. One task of teaching peace, then, is to recover and present the remarkable history of civilian resistance, to show what mass, sustained, nonviolent action can accomplish. When faced with the problem of dictatorship, mass killing is not the only possible solution. This knowledge is particularly important in the United States, where war-makers cloak their overseas interventions in claims of "liberating" foreign populations from repressive rulers. If liberation is truly the goal, wouldn't it make sense to encourage and support nonviolent resisters rather than bomb the cities where they live? When we understand that there are better ways to challenge tyranny, when we have historical evidence for the power of nonviolent resistance, we are less likely to fall for pro-war propaganda. And if our refusal to cooperate brings harsh reprisals, we'll know what to do.

NOTES TO CHAPTER 5

[1] For a discussion of the terminology, see Adam Roberts, "Introduction," in Adam Roberts and Timothy Ash, eds., *Civil Resistance and Power Politics: The Experience of Non-violent Action from Gandhi to the Present* (Oxford University Press, 2011), 2-4. Civil means "having a civic quality, relating to the interests and hopes of a society as a whole."

[2] Sections from this chapter and the following one were condensed to create Timothy Braatz, "The Limitations of Strategic Nonviolence," *Peace Review* 26:1 (2014): 4-11.

[3] Peter Ackerman and Jack Duvall, *A Force More Powerful: A Century of Nonviolent Conflict* (Palgrave, 2000); Gene Sharp, *Waging Nonviolent Struggle: 20th Century Practice and 21st Century Potential* (Porter Sargent, 2005).

[4] John Crossan and Jonathan Reed, *Excavating Jesus: Beneath the Stones, Behind the Texts* (Harper San Francisco, 2001), 143-146; Gene Sharp, *The Politics of Nonviolent Struggle* (Porter Sargent, 1973), 75-77.

[5] Richard Gregg, *The Power of Non-Violence* (Navajivan Publishing, 1938), 40-51.

[6] Quoted in Ackerman and Duvall, *A Force More Powerful*, 42.

[7] Quoted in Ackerman and Duvall, *A Force More Powerful*, 54.

[8] Gene Sharp, *Gandhi as a Political Strategist* (Porter Sargent, 1979), 26-38. Quote on 38.

[9] A quick historical glance around the world—the 1920 Jallianwala Bagh massacre in Amritsar; British slaughter of nonviolent Khudai Khidmatgar members in the Hindu Kush region around the same time; British operations in Kenya in the 1950s; recent British policy regarding the island of Diego Garcia—will dispel romantic notions of British "fair play."

[10] Judith Brown, *Gandhi: Prisoner of Hope* (Yale University Press, 1989), 234-251.

[11] Patricia Parkman, *Nonviolent Insurrection in El Salvador: The Fall of Maximiliano Hernández Martínez* (University of Arizona Press, 1988), 2-3, calls this a "civic strike," meaning political noncooperation with the state by participants from a variety of social categories, distinguishing it from a specifically working-class "general strike" over labor issues.

[12] Parkman, *Nonviolent Insurrection in El Salvador*; Tommie Sue Montgomery, *Revolution in El Salvador: From Civil Strife to Civil Peace* (Westview Press,

1995), 39-42; Sharp, *Waging Nonviolent Struggle*, 149-155.

[13] Ervand Abrahamian, "Mass Protests in the Iranian Revolution, 1977-79," in Roberts and Ash, *Civil Resistance and Power Politics*, 162-178.

[14] Sandra Burton, *Impossible Dream: The Marcoses, the Aquinos, and the Unfinished Revolution* (Warner, 1989); Sharon Nepstad, *Nonviolent Revolutions: Civil Resistance in the Late 20th Century* (Oxford University Press, 2011), 110-123; Ackerman and Duvall, *A Force More Powerful*, 369-395.

[15] Timothy Ash, *The Magic Lantern: The Revolution of '89 Witnessed in Warsaw, Budapest, Berlin and Prague* (Vintage, 1990); Gail Stokes, *The Walls Came Tumbling Down: The Collapse of Communism in Eastern Europe* (Oxford University Press, 1993), 131-167; Vladimir Tismaneanu, *Reinventing Politics: Eastern Europe from Stalin to Havel* (Free Press, 1992), 175-239.

[16] Nepstad, *Nonviolent Revolutions*, 38-55.

[17] The "Reagan Triumphant" myth claims that a Soviet attempt to match 1980s US military spending bankrupted the Soviet Union and forced Gorbachev to surrender to Western values. In fact, Soviet military spending generally remained flat, and Reagan's aggressive militarism strengthened the Soviet hard-liners, who were impeding Gorbachev's reforms. Will Bunch, *Tear Down this Myth: How the Reagan Legacy has Distorted Our Politics and Haunts Our Future* (Free Press, 2009), 82-83; Frances Fitzgerald, *Way Out There in the Blue: Reagan, Star Wars and the End of the Cold War* (Simon & Schuster), 2001, 330-331, 474-475. Notice how US propagandists want it both ways: they despaired of Soviet military supremacy—the "missile gap"—to justify US military buildup right up to the Soviet disintegration, which they then attributed to US military supremacy. Gorbachev himself said it was the computer revolution that inspired his reforms, which does make an interesting case for US military spending. After World War II, the US government used massive military budgets to support high-tech research and development. This is both military Keynesianism (federal spending to stabilize the national economy) and corporate welfare (taxpayers fund the research, then hand over the technology to private interests). Military spending led to the technological breakthroughs that left the Soviets behind. But US opinion-makers cannot make this argument because that would be admitting successful centralized planning rather than the usual celebration of (imaginary) "laissez-faire" markets and entrepreneurial enterprise.

[18] Stokes, *The Walls Came Tumbling Down*, 158-167.

[19] Sharp, *Gandhi as Political Strategist*, 292.

[20] Sharp, *Waging Nonviolent Struggle*, 20-21; Gregg, *The Power of Non-violence*,

40-51. Gregg called it "moral jujitsu"; Sharp popularized the concept as "political jujitsu." The difference is emphasis: cause versus effect. Following Gandhi, Gregg identified the moral power of nonviolence—the integrative power of suffering—which derives from human aversion to violent acts and empathy for victims. Gandhi called it Truth. Sharp found the issue of morality a potential distraction from the task of making nonviolent methods widely accessible. His formulation emphasizes how violent repression of nonviolent actors can shift the balance of power in a political struggle. "Moral jujitsu" emphasizes *why* suffering wins support; "political jujitsu" underscores *what* it can accomplish.

[21] Sharp, *Waging Nonviolent Struggle*, 27, 19.

[22] Sharp, *The Politics of Nonviolent Action*, 7-48.

[23] Sharp, *Waging Nonviolent Struggle*, 49-65.

[24] The 1989 Soviet bloc uprisings legitimized people power in the minds of Western scholars for at least four reasons. One, they happened in Europe, the non-US part of the world that matters most to Western elites, so they didn't go unnoticed. Two, the movements opposed communist states. Mainstream academics and journalists in the United States are very thorough at investigating the crimes and failures of "official" enemies such as communist regimes, so there is much enthusiasm for the study of the nonviolent campaigns in the old Warsaw Pact countries and also China. Far less attention goes to nonviolent movements against US client states in Latin America and the uprising that ousted the pro-Western Shah of Iran. The Philippines event may seem an exception, but once the US government withdrew its support for Marcos, the US media felt free to demonize first lady Imelda Marcos and the 1986 uprising became an acceptable topic of study, more than, for example, the nonviolent East Timorese independence movement against the US-supported Indonesian government in the 1990s. Still, without the 1989 European events, Philippines people power may have already been forgotten in the West. Third, the European uprisings seem to affirm the superiority of Western-style democracy and capitalism. Fourth, they seem to follow a neat and tidy narrative of good overcoming evil—so long as the story goes no further than the dictator's departure and ensuing elections. For purposes of comparison, consider how the nonviolent Shiite protests in Baghdad, in 2003-2005, which blocked the US attempt to impose direct colonial rule over Iraq, are almost completely ignored. Norman Solomon, "US out of Iraq Now," *The Progressive* 69:6 (June 2005), www.progressive.org. See also Naomi Klein, *The Shock Doctrine: The Rise of Disaster Capitalism* (Metropolitan Books), 2007, 361-365; Bob Woodward, *State of Denial* (Simon & Schuster, 2006), 206, 211, 228-229.

[25] Maria Stephan and Erica Chenowith, "Why Civil Resistance Works: The Strategic Logic of Nonviolent Conflict," *International Security* 33:1 (Summer

2008): 7-44. Quote on 8.

[26] "National security" often makes the general population less secure by increasing direct, structural, and cultural violence. Military spending detracts from social spending and also makes war more likely; the primary function of most "security forces" is repression of political opposition; and state violence contributes to the normalization of violence that contributes to individual direct violence. "National security" usually means securing the continued power of a political regime or ruling class, and the population is encouraged to believe this equates with popular well-being. Scholars who identify agents of repression as "security forces" without noting the contradiction unwittingly contribute to the cultural violence of double-speak.

[27] For the Nicaraguan revolution, see John Booth, *The End and the Beginning: The Nicaraguan Revolution* (Westview Press, 1985); Misagh Parsa, *States, Ideologies, and Social Revolutions: A Comparative Analysis of Iran, Nicaragua, and the Philippines* (Cambridge University Press, 2000).

[28] Nepstad, *Nonviolent Revolutions*, 30-37; Sharp, *Waging Nonviolent Struggle,* 245-251; Abrahamian, "Mass Protests in the Iranian Revolution, 1977-79," 175-176.

6

NOW THAT HE'S GONE

6

NOW THAT HE'S GONE

Failures

People power is not magic. It is a sensible strategy for forcing concessions from uncooperative rulers. But despite its international notice, which expanded significantly in the late 1980s, people power still sometimes fails to end political repression. One notable failure came in Burma in 1988, just two years after the dramatic success in the Philippines. At first, a Burmese popular uprising, sparked by a police massacre of student protestors, seemed close to ending several decades of military dominance. Despite occasional violent clashes, a series of general strikes and demonstrations across the country brought government resignations, a few military defections, and agreements on multi-party elections. However, as opposition leaders bickered over who would represent the pro-democracy majority, military leaders seized the moment, declared martial law, and killed hundreds more protestors. Many students fled to isolated border regions and tried to build a violent resistance movement. When the promised elections were finally held, in 1990, the National League for Democracy (NLD) claimed a landslide victory, but the military rulers refused to cede power, and, instead, killed or imprisoned many NLD members and brazenly placed party leader Aung San Suu Kyi under house arrest.[1]

In the spring of 1989, even as communist dictatorships were starting to succumb to civilian resistance movements in Europe, Communist Party rulers in China crushed a civilian uprising centered around a student-led occupation of Tiananmen Square, in Beijing. At first, students forestalled a military crackdown by cultivating sympathy and understanding among the police and army ranks. But disagreements over tactics and leadership split the movement, some protestors turned to violent methods of defense, and party officials brought in troops from distant regions who may not have understood the nature of the occupation (or even the dialect spoken in Beijing). The result: After a three-week standoff, troops finally opened fire, killing thousands of protestors. The students abandoned the square, and the resistance movement disintegrated.[2]

In the 1990s, civilian resistance in Kenya was unable to topple President Daniel arap Moi, who had survived a military coup in 1982, and then had gradually assumed dictatorial powers based on violent repression of dissent. As assassinations of opposition leaders and violent attacks on popular demonstrations received increased international scrutiny, foreign aid to Kenya slowed, contributing to economic difficulties in this impoverished country. To mute criticism, Moi agreed to multi-party elections, then carefully rigged them to assure international acceptance of his prearranged victory. He also exploited Kenya's ethnic divisions, particularly in recruiting soldiers and policemen from ethnic minorities who might feel threatened by a popular resistance movement. In this fashion—with international aid flowing and reliable troops enforcing his dictates—Moi bucked the people power trend and remained in office until voluntarily retiring in 2002.[3]

As these examples confirm, the use of nonviolence is no guarantee of success in removing unwanted rulers. But such failures are not final. If the goal is to end repressive, corrupt, unrepresentative government, the struggle may take years. A violent crackdown usually means the rulers have lost popular legitimacy, so even if a nonviolent resistance movement is beaten back, the spirit of resistance might survive as individuals know they are not alone in their rejection of the ruling regime. The example of nonviolent strategy may persist in popular memory, and the next generation of organizers can learn from earlier efforts. Repressive leaders, too, can be resourceful and persistent, so resistance leaders must be prepared to seize historical openings and to endure when such opportunities are delayed. In the 1970s, Polish workers learned they were safer and more effective taking over factories rather than taking to the streets, and they won major concessions. Then came the crackdown, and, in 1982, the Solidarity campaign for free trade unions appeared a failure, with resistance leaders in prison or hiding and free unions outlawed. Nine years later, Solidarity leader Lech Walesa was elected president of Poland, and the Solidarity movement was viewed as a glorious success of world-historic importance.

A key point here is that the success of a nonviolent resistance movement depends on the participants' efforts *and* the historical moment. While individuals and movements can shape history, history also shapes them. Solidarity leaders were courageous, creative, resourceful, and persistent, yet still needed events beyond their control—national economic decline and Gorbachev's *perestroika* reforms—to create the conditions for their political triumph in 1989. Likewise in Iran, US pressure on the Shah regarding human rights—a product of President Jimmy Carter's election in 1976—created the political opening for the street demonstrations that finally ended the Shah's 25-year reign. The world doesn't stand still, change comes in unexpected ways, and nonviolent campaigners should realize that their efforts and sacrifices are not just for a better tomorrow for themselves, but for future generations. From this perspective, then, the civilian resistance of 1968 in Czechoslovakia, known as "Prague Spring," which failed to rescue "reform socialism" from a hard-line Soviet crackdown, was not in vain; it laid the groundwork for the 1989 "Velvet Revolution," even if its only contribution was to provide a belief in the potential for nonviolent resistance, even if twenty dark years is a long time to wait.[4] And this long view may provide a ray of hope to the people of Burma, for example, where, after yet another military crackdown on nonviolent resistance, in 2007, international pressures appeared to contribute to modest electoral reforms.[5] That struggle continues.

Limits of People Power

While a nonviolent resistance movement may require years to force political reforms, there is another caveat: a successful movement, one that removes an unpopular, repressive regime, is no guarantee of long-term democratic stability, justice, equality of opportunity, and human rights protections. If failures are not final, neither are successes cemented in place. Scholarly surveys of nonviolent campaigns, in their concern with understanding and promoting the dynamics of strategic nonviolence, often end national case studies at the triumphant moment—the dictator stepped down!—and omit what came next.[6] The implication is that once a repressive regime is removed, the difficult work is finished, and society will inevitably be transformed for the better. Where power was highly centralized and coordinated, dramatic changes have, indeed, followed—for example, the opening of society in east central Europe after the removal of the communist party dictatorships. At a glance, this can give the impression that massive, spontaneous, nonviolent protests—"Whose streets? Our streets!"—are a societal panacea. But the end of European totalitarianism left many people, despite their newly won enfranchisement, less secure in their livelihoods than under party rule. Elsewhere, where traditions of popular elections already existed at local, regional, and national levels, people power movements have often proved to be little more than an extension of electoral politics—a change in leadership at the top, but minimal structural reform. For some analysts, this may be satisfactory, following the understanding of Western liberalism that often equates open elections with a healthy and just society: if the leading vote-getter takes office, all must be well. However, more careful analysis reveals that in a complex and diffuse political and economic system, a few days or weeks of mass rallies and noncooperation to ensure a moment of electoral decency are unlikely to transform society.

Johan Galtung's diagram of the causal relationship between the three types of violence can shed light on the shortcomings of successful people power movements.

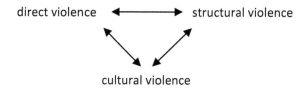

How well does strategic nonviolence address the different forms of violence, defined collectively as "avoidable insult to basic human needs"? As already explained (see Ch. 5), sustained nonviolent action can, through moral jujitsu, effectively counter an unwanted regime's direct violence; the state's use of violent repression becomes a liability, undermining its legitimacy. The visibility and drama of direct state violence—insulting the basic human need for survival and freedom—make it relatively easy to identify as a problem and target for change.[7] Structural violence is less obvious. Gene Sharp, a political theorist, has outlined the political structures that support a violent regime, and has shown how those structures can be undermined. But what he advocates is the separation of the *current* head of state from the "pillars of support," not an entire restructuring of the state system. Furthermore, even if collective refusal to cooperate with government leads to top-level resignations, economic structures are likely to remain unchanged, particularly if most property is privately owned. The dictator and his guards are gone, the violence built into the political and economic systems—marginalization, exploitation, alienation—persists. If reduction of violence, in all its forms, is the goal, the nonviolent removal of a dictatorship will not be sufficient.

The Philippines example bears this out. Marcos held a fraudulent election, the masses went into the streets, voted with their bodies, and Corazon Aquino became president. What followed was an improvement over the Marcos dictatorship, and yet, in many ways, despite the remarkable nonviolent uprising, was Filipino business as usual. The new president came from a wealthy, well-connected family. The military continued to intervene in civilian politics and commit human rights abuses. Electoral fraud returned, poverty remained widespread, the volatile question of Muslim separatism went unresolved. The US government, which had supported Marcos until the very end, maintained its military bases in the country and pushed for violent campaigns against communist rebels. For a few heady days in 1986, the people of Manila experienced real democratic participation, but, in the long term, did not institutionalize people power, and the average citizen saw little change in political and economic opportunity. The very structures that had allowed for the emergence of a dictator—powerful chief executive office, meddling military officer corps, elite-managed electoral processes—were left in place. What changed were the loyalties within those structures.[8]

In fact, this model—remove the corrupt head of state, but leave social, political, and economic structures generally intact—is typical of people power movements. The resignation of dictators in El Salvador and Guatemala, in 1944, did not end the widespread poverty and narrow concentration of wealth and political influence in those countries, did not reduce neocolonial meddling by the US government, and a long era of civil wars and brutal regimes followed. In a related scenario, the unseating of a dictatorship by a civilian resistance movement may open the door to a different type of repressive government, as happened in Iran. As an alternative to the Shah's pro-Western regime, many Iranians celebrated the return from exile of Ayatollah Khomeini, who was able to consolidate power and establish the Islamic Republic rather than a return to the 1906 Constitution. The ousted regime, originally brought to power by a CIA coup, was seen as serving US interests, while the new one seemed to stand against foreign intrusion, and, instead, brought greater social services to the country, especially to rural areas. However, the Islamic government was also a theocracy, imposing a restrictive world view on the population, and willing to use its Revolutionary Guard to repress brutally any internal political opposition.[9]

A typical strategic nonviolence campaign is *reformist*—seeking to reform the state, make government less corrupt, less repressive, and more responsive to the needs of the people. Thus, it affirms the legitimacy and efficacy of a powerful state, and, in that sense, is not *revolutionary*. The powerful state remains, with all its potential for corruption and abuse. This can be seen in the post-communist states of the old Soviet sphere. After decades of Cold War propaganda, many people believed only two options were available—US capitalism and Soviet communism—and, while focusing on the very real differences between the two models, underestimated the significance of their commonality: enormous state bureaucracy with centralized decision-making in the hands of an elite political class.[10] Under both systems, the general population concedes the authority of a relative few bureaucrats or apparatchiks to start wars, make laws, and direct government spending. Despite constant rhetoric about the interests of workers or "the people," the ruling elite in such systems will almost inevitably place their personal and class interests over the interests of the masses, and use state power to protect and extend their interests. The concentration of political and economic power makes direct violence likely. In the decades that followed the removal of Soviet-style dictatorships, the conditions which had allowed a small group to wield repressive power over an entire country were still largely present. As nonviolence scholar Robert Burrowes has pointed out, regarding Iran, the Philippines, and the nonviolent European uprisings, the structures "underwent some changes...[but] remained largely inaccessible to ordinary people and quite inappropriate for implementing the profound changes that are necessary if human needs are to be met."[11] In the former Soviet sphere, the structural violence of gangster capitalism replaced the structural violence of totalitarianism, sometimes with the same people in charge—communist elites became capitalist elites, seemingly overnight—and many citizens longed for the old regimes when at least they had secure jobs, affordable housing, and other state guarantees.[12] Nonviolent strategies shaped electoral outcomes in the former Soviet republics of Georgia (2003), Ukraine (2004-05), and Kyrgyzstan (2005), but these so-called "color revolutions" generally lacked structural change, and political corruption and direct violence promptly resumed.[13]

Poland, too, was subject to the deficiencies of a civilian resistance movement. The Polish example is unique due to the sophistication of

Solidarity organizing, the development of alternative institutions outside communist officialdom, and the length of the struggle—this was no flash-in-the-pan street takeover. The Polish people showed to the world the viability of a peaceful transition from communist totalitarianism to an open society with democratic elections and a free press. And yet, this did not ensure economic and social justice. Once they controlled the reins of state power, Solidarity leaders turned to Western bankers and capitalist ideologues for financial support and guidance, and soon submitted to "shock therapy"— privatization of state-owned industries, elimination of price controls and subsidies—a clear betrayal of the promised "third way" of worker ownership in a market economy. The predictable result of their "austerity" program was a depressed economy with chronically high unemployment and expanding poverty. Poland had fallen into the grip of international finance capitalism just as that system was accelerating the concentration of wealth and widening the poverty gap—not exactly what Polish strikers had risked their lives for in the 1980s.[14]

In the early twenty-first century, the Polish government sent troops to participate in the US invasions of Afghanistan and Iraq. After a nightmarish twentieth century—German and Soviet invasions and slaughters, communist dictatorship—and after all the Solidarity movement had revealed about the power of nonviolence, how could the people of Poland end up participating in the US imperialist wars? In fact, one might ask why Poland even maintains an army. What purpose could armed soldiers possibly serve, squeezed as the country is between the enormous Russian army on one side and the US and its allies on the other? Keep in mind, Solidarity's goal was reform—free trade unions, free press, open elections—not a transformation of Polish society. The Solidarity movement did not reject violence as unethical, just impractical. Solidarity did not reject centralized state power; it claimed it for itself. And Solidarity did not put a dent in cultural violence—that deep layer of ideologies, cosmologies, arts and sciences, and other beliefs and symbols that encourage and enable structural and direct violence.[15] While direct, structural, and cultural violence are mutually reinforcing, Galtung has identified "the major causal direction":

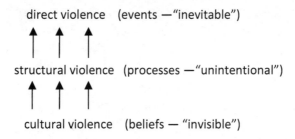

direct violence   (events — "inevitable")

structural violence   (processes — "unintentional")

cultural violence   (beliefs — "invisible")

A successful campaign of strategic nonviolence can counter cultural violence through example, teaching the power of nonviolent action and the virtue of negotiation and compromise. But cultural violence is usually multifaceted, and, for lasting change, must be addressed systematically, something strategic nonviolence does not do.

For example, belief in the legitimacy of a powerful state—so deep in the culture it is accepted as normal, natural, inevitable—is affirmed, not challenged, by a nonviolent movement that seeks to take over the reins of power. In fact, for all its efforts to be transparent and democratic, Solidarity was still led by a man who, once elected, could make unilateral decisions. But it goes deeper than that. The Solidarity movement, in its embrace of the patriarchal Catholic Church as an ally against communist rule, was affirming Catholic doctrine: authority of a male pope who supposedly spoke on behalf of a male deity, denial of the priesthood for women, rejection of many aspects of human sexuality. Catholicism also presents a story of redemption through violence (crucifixion, crusades) and a theory of "just war," which find strong parallels in the martial words of the Polish national anthem, fully endorsed by the new government. In other words, Solidarity was perpetuating, more than it was challenging, the acceptance of patriarchy and hierarchical society, and was ambivalent about violence. We can go deeper yet. Christianity includes a "chosen" people with a special relationship to an all-powerful God and the promise of individual salvation. By definition, a chosen people cannot exist without the presence of unchosen people, whose lives and identities are not as important. The promise of individual salvation in the next world teaches the superiority of certain "saved" individuals, justifies the misery of others, and makes a sustainable ecology unnecessary. This "vertical" cosmology easily accommodates Polish nationalism, with strong notions regarding the Other (Polish anti-Semitism has deep roots), and with the state assuming God-like powers. It also undergirds the ideology of capitalism, which celebrates individualism, dominance over less-fortunate others, and destruction of the natural world.[16]

Solidarity leaders and their successors were liberated from communist party rule, but not from the blinders of cosmology. Once in office, they concluded that economic security and national defense meant submitting to the dictates of the US government and its allies—an embrace of hierarchical state authority and a submission to threat power and exchange power on the macro level—and duly adopted an economic system that valued property rights over human needs and encouraged individualism and competition rather than cooperation and community. The Polish masses were not included in this decision-making. Polish politicians approached their constituency as voters to be swayed, not co-equal partners to be heard. Western leaders viewed Poles as cheap, exploitable labor. Polish troops, defenders of national honor, were sent off to fight the Other, now defined as "Islamic terrorists." The CIA constructed a secret base on Polish soil for extralegal detainment and torture.[17] The US empire had a new client state, conquered not by generals but by bankers; in other words, more verticality. Poland had traded one imperial master for another. The Polish masses could have mounted a nonviolent campaign to challenge the new political class and its submission to foreign dictates—in fact, it should have been easier in the more open post-communist society. But they had been tamed by an ideology that identified democratic participation only as voting for office-seekers and that blamed economic marginalization on personal failures—a more sophisticated form of political control than communist brutality. Simply put, Polish culture had not been transformed into a life-enhancing peace system.[18] Like people power campaigns worldwide, the strategic nonviolence of the Solidarity movement had forced out an unwanted regime weakened by historical forces, but had not confronted, and at times reinforced, many of the violent aspects of the national culture.[19]

Principled Nonviolence

We are all prisoners of cosmology or deep culture. Our deeply embedded and unexamined beliefs about the structure and function of the universe shape our ideological predispositions, including our understanding of conflict or social disharmony. Consider the concept of time. In Western thought, time is bounded; there is a beginning and an end. This comes, in part, from the Christian belief in an original creation and a cathartic or transformative conclusion. Eastern, or Buddhist, thought imagines time as an ever-flowing river, no beginning nor end. In the Western approach, then, a conflict will be bounded in time—very useful for case studies of people power, which often begin with a fraudulent election, end with electoral democracy restored, and everyone goes home: case closed. An Eastern view will see conflict as never ending, just changing shape, thus conflict resolution must be a constant, open-ended process.

Cosmology also shapes one's understanding of the restoration of social harmony. Western thought holds that the violator/sinner must be judged, punished, and then (possibly) forgiven by a higher power—God, monarch, or state. The individual transgressor must "pay a debt to society." Eastern thought is more concerned with the collective whole than with individual blame. Where there is disharmony, all involved are responsible for repairing the bad relations because the ultimate problem is bad *karma*—on all sides— not individual sinfulness. The Western tradition says adjudicate and punish the dictator and his henchman, like Nazis put on trial at Nuremberg, and the conflict is over. The Eastern tradition says start a dialogue to understand how the society tolerated and enabled such bad governance for so long—where did we *all* go wrong? Both cosmologies can learn from each other, and, in this instance, the middle ground may be a truth and reconciliation process, like in South Africa after apartheid, where individuals take responsibility for their past violent actions, but the emphasis is on decreasing hostility in society rather than on punishment, with apologies and forgiveness encouraged.[20]

The larger point is that if you want to decrease direct violence, then you must address structural and cultural violence. A cosmology that emphasizes an angry deity who punishes sinners makes likely a judicial system focused more on punishment than rehabilitation, which will likely promote the direct violence of prisons and their alumni. As previously suggested, label a teenager a "bad guy," lock him up for a few years, and see if he walks out less prone to acts of direct violence. Punishing "evil-doers" may seem righteous, may bring a sense of cosmological satisfaction, but will not decrease violence. Similarly, people power movements are only short-term fixes because, typically, they do not alter the structural violence in political and economic systems, and do not systematically address the cultural violence roots. Sorry, weekend activists, but if you are serious about reducing violence in a world of so much violence, you're going to have to re-evaluate *everything*, even the hymns you sing and the words you speak. This can also be posited in positive terms: if the goal is to cultivate direct peace (the opposite of direct violence), then work on structural and cultural peace.[21]

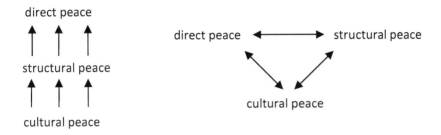

Which takes us, as usual, back to Gandhi. Sharp's strategic nonviolence is a way to remove bad government—that's the goal—and does not go much further. This is certainly a worthy enterprise, but it's easy to know what you are against, harder to identify what you are for; it's harder to build than destroy. Gandhi's principled nonviolence suggests a way to create a nonviolent society. Rather than start by destroying the old order, you begin with the nonviolent transformation of individuals—indeed, you begin with yourself—and these nonviolent actors (satyagrahis) work on the restructuring of society, the creation of alternative, nonviolent institutions to counter violence—an ongoing, never-ending process. For Gandhi, the nonviolent campaigns against British rule, against bad government, were just an initial step, teaching nonviolence, instilling fearlessness, and restoring self-esteem to a colonized, demoralized population: direct peace to counter direct violence. He spent more time on his Constructive Programme, trying to develop a decentralized network of self-reliant, self-governing communal villages—a rejection of the competition and exploitation of market capitalism, the centralized ownership and authority of communism, and powerful state systems in general. The emphasis on all individuals working to satisfy their own basic needs—making their own cloth, for example—was intended to liberate both the exploited and the exploiter from an exploitative system. Self-reliance for everybody. Structural peace to counter structural violence. Gandhi believed in the unity of life, and he preached that society must enhance all life, not just human life, and not just the lives of some privileged humans.[22] No one should use the life of another as simply the means to an end. Behavior and institutions that deny the satisfaction of basic human needs are unacceptable. Thus, he advocated interfaith cooperation, the liberation of women from patriarchy, the abolition of Untouchability, the practice of vegetarianism. He reinterpreted the Bhagavad Gita—Hindu scripture—as an allegory of selfless devotion, not a heroic battle against human enemies.[23] Cultural peace to counter cultural violence. Building from the bottom up, not the top down.

Key to all of this is *the unity of means and ends*. This is the very essence of principled nonviolence and its approach to conflict resolution—peace through peaceful means. Or, if you prefer, peace begets peace. With strategic nonviolence, the end justifies the means: sabotage, cooperation, deception, vulnerability, authoritarian leadership, even acts of direct violence—whatever it takes to remove the dictator. Principled nonviolence holds that the methods used to change society will shape the new society—the means become the end. To reduce violence, a society requires institutions of nonviolent conflict resolution, and the way to produce those institutions is through nonviolent conflict resolution. Indeed, since conflict is inevitable in human society, *the practice of creative, nonviolent conflict resolution* is a good definition of peace. Peace as an activity, an on-going process, not peace as an unreachable state of perfection.[24] Again, Muste's formulation: "There is no way to peace—peace is the way."

To understand conflict, Galtung posits another triangle. Regarding conflict between two individuals or parties, a fully formed conflict is comprised of (A) negative attitudes and/or hostile emotions, (B) predisposition or capacity for aggressive behavior, and (C) incompatible or competing goals.

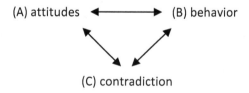

(A) attitudes ⟷ (B) behavior

(C) contradiction

For example, two individuals want to sit in a chair built for one—that's a contradiction, they have incompatible goals, they both cannot sit in the chair. If the two are friends and neither prone to violent behavior, this contradiction quickly dissolves. But if some negative attitudes or aggressive tendencies are present, the simple contradiction might develop into a conflict, perhaps escalating into a fistfight. The winner of the fight takes the chair, and the conflict may appear over—violent conflict resolution—except the negative attitudes (A) have intensified, the value of aggressive behavior (B) has been affirmed, and the next contradiction (C) that occurs will mean more conflict. The river keeps flowing: the seeds of the next conflict are planted in the resolution of the current one. Nonviolent conflict resolution addresses all three points on the conflict triangle by viewing the contradiction (C) as an *opportunity* to improve the relationship (A) between the parties, meaning a chance to make their attitudes toward and assumptions about each other more positive, by inviting cooperation (B) in finding the solution. There is more than one goal: resolving the current conflict, but also increasing fearlessness, self-reliance, and self-esteem for all parties involved, and building better social relations and structures. In this fashion, not only is the current contradiction resolved, but the potential for future conflict is decreased.[25]

Two people arguing over a chair is a very simple conflict. Most conflicts, especially at the level of politics, are far more complex, involving multiple parties, goals, and contradictions. But strategic nonviolence tries to keep things simple—two parties (rulers and ruled) and one contradiction (disagreement over distribution of decision-making power, i.e., who gets to be chairman)—and does not carefully address all three points. Rather than recognize the importance of the ruling group's basic need for self-esteem and participation—they, too, need a dignified place in the reformed society—a typical people power movement demonizes the opponent, targeting bad actors not bad structures. ("He's finished" was the rallying cry in Serbia in 1999.[26]) Negative attitudes (A) are reinforced, and the value of victory *over* the opponent, defeating the "bad guys," is affirmed. Conflict resolution is viewed as win-lose, not win-win, not victory *with*, and this mindset, and all its potential for violence, shapes the reformed society.

In contrast, Gandhi did not try to demonize the British residents of India, and did not seek to evict them. He wanted to replace "British civilization" with a nonviolent society, and he invited the Brits to be partners in the endeavor. Punishing deposed rulers—isolation, expulsion, execution— may bring righteous satisfaction to some, but will alienate others, affirm the new ruling party's authority over life, and perpetuate a climate of fear. Furthermore, a dictator and his henchmen will likely be more determined to use violence to defend themselves if they fear punishment. They may eventually be defeated by sustained nonviolent noncooperation, but how will society be changed?[27] Strategic violence may remove a dictator, but

Gandhian nonviolence has a much greater goal: the rehumanization of a dehumanized society.

To summarize, the violence triad (direct, structural, cultural) is mutually reinforcing. To reduce and prevent violence in society, all three points of the triangle must be addressed, with cultural violence possibly the most crucial. In positive terms, the peace triad (direct, structural, cultural) is mutually reinforcing. To increase and cultivate peace in society, all three points must be addressed, with cultural peace possibly the most crucial. The conflict triad (attitudes, behavior, contradiction) is also mutually reinforcing, and long-term conflict resolution requires attention to all three concerns. A typical people power movement, for all its virtue, does not meet these requirements. Sharp's nonviolence may be strategic, but if the goal is nonviolent transformation of society, including prevention of future dictatorships, it is not pragmatic. If, like in the Philippines and Polish examples, a nonviolent resistance campaign does not seek to build nonviolent structures, does not systematically address the violent aspects of deep culture, does not work to bring opponents closer together, making them partners in conflict resolution, it simply is not peaceful enough.

NOTES TO CHAPTER 6

[1] Gene Sharp, *Waging Nonviolent Struggle: 20th Century Practice and 21st Century Potential* (Porter Sargent, 2005), 245-251; Maria Stephan and Erica Chenoweth, "Why Civil Resistance Works: The Strategic Logic of Nonviolent Conflict," *International Security* 33:1 (Summer 2008): 37-40.

[2] Sharon Nepstad, *Nonviolent Revolutions: Civil Resistance in the Late 20th Century* (Oxford University Press, 2011), 21-37; Sharp, *Waging Nonviolent Struggle*, 253-269.

[3] Nepstad, *Nonviolent Revolutions*, 95-109.

[4] Kieran Williams, "Civil Resistance in Czechoslovakia: From Soviet Invasion to 'Velvet Revolution,' 1968-89," in Adam Roberts and Timothy Ash, eds., *Civil Resistance and Power Politics: The Experience of Non-violent Action from Gandhi to the Present* (Oxford University Press, 2011), 126.

[5] Christina Fink, "The Moment of the Monks: Burma, 2007," in Roberts and Ash, *Civil Resistance and Power Politics*, 354-370.

[6] Examples can be found in Sharp, *Waging Nonviolent Struggle*; and Peter Ackerman and Jack Duvall, *A Force More Powerful: A Century of Nonviolent Conflict* (Palgrave, 2000).

[7] Direct state violence, in fact, may violate the need for survival (through killing), well-being (misery), identity (forced socialization), freedom (repression), and more. Johan Galtung, *Peace by Peaceful Means: Peace and Conflict, Development and Civilization* (Sage Publications, 1996), 197.

[8] Amado Mendoza Jr., "'People Power' in the Philippines, 1983-1986," in Roberts and Ash, *Civil Resistance and Power Politics*, 179-196. With no major structural changes underway, no danger of downward wealth redistribution, US officials were willing to abandon Marcos once he lost military support. Continued unrest, they feared, might create an opening for more radical leaders than Aquino.

[9] Abrahamian, "Mass Protests in the Iranian Revolution, 1977-79," in Roberts and Ash, *Civil Resistance and Power Politics*, 174-178.

[10] It is easy to understand why insightful dissidents in closed communist states—like Vaclav Havel in Czechoslovakia—believed that the US government, which supported their resistance to communist dictatorship, stood for democracy, freedom, and self-determination, despite all the evidence that US foreign policy supported death squads and dictators wherever it served the real goal: access to markets and resources.

[11] Robert Burrowes, *The Strategy of Nonviolent Defense: A Gandhian Approach* (State University of New York Press, 1996),166.

[12] Rossen Vassilev, "The Tragic Failure of 'Post Communism' in Eastern Europe," *Global Research*, Mar. 8, 2011, http://www.globalresearch.ca/the-tragic-failure-of-post-communism-in-eastern-europe/23616. Vassilev wrote, "Nearly all of these twenty-eight Eurasian countries have experienced a long-term economic decline of catastrophic proportions (only Poland has thus far surpassed its Communist-era GDP). Grave economic setbacks, deep-rooted corruption, and widespread popular frustration with the hardships and deprivations of the seemingly endless post-Communist transition are undermining the prestige of the new authorities and even the population's belief in Western-style democracy and market-based capitalism. A new breed of rapacious and ruthless plutocrats with insatiable appetites for wealth and power has pillaged—through an unjust and corrupt process of privatization—the assets of the formerly state-owned economy and has re-created at home the worst excesses of 19th-century Dickensian capitalism, as if the social progress of the 20th century had never existed. In the midst of widespread joblessness, penury, malnutrition and even hunger, multimillion-dollar private mansions have sprung up in all major cities as palace-like symbols of ill-gotten gains and of unattainable wealth for ordinary people who are struggling just to find jobs, pay daily bills, and find affordable housing."

[13] Andrew Wilson, "Ukraine's 'Orange Revolution' of 2004: The Paradoxes of Negotiation," in Roberts and Ash, *Civil Resistance and Power Politics*, 353, describes a "very non-revolutionary revolution." Stephen Jones, "Georgia's 'Rose Revolution' of 2003: Enforcing Peaceful Change," in Roberts and Ash, 318, sees an ideologically "colourless" phenomenon that "made no demands for major economic, social, or systemic change."

[14] Naomi Klein, *The Shock Doctrine: The Rise of Disaster Capitalism* (Metropolitan Books, 2007), 171-181, 191-193.

[15] For cultural violence, see Galtung, *Peace by Peaceful Means*, 196-210.

[16] Galtung, *Peace by Peaceful Means*, 201-204.

[17] Jane Meyer, "The Black Sites," *The New Yorker*, Aug. 13, 2007, http://www.newyorker.com/reporting/2007/08/13/070813fa_fact_mayer?currentPage=all; "Secret Prisons in Poland and Romania?" *DW*, Nov. 4, 2005, http://www.dw.de/secret-prisons-in-poland-and-romania/a-1765288-1.

[18] For examples of peace systems, see Douglas Fry, *Beyond War: The Human Potential for Peace* (Oxford University Press), 21-32, 113-130.

[19] This is not intended as a general condemnation of Polish culture or the Polish

population. Polish culture, like Western industrial society in general, is filled with contradictions, including enough peaceful aspects to make life tolerable and enough violent aspects to make one shudder.

[20] Galtung, *Peace by Peaceful Means*, 82-85.

[21] Galtung, *Peace by Peaceful Means*, esp. 32-34.

[22] Galtung, *Peace by Peaceful Means*, 207-208.

[23] Mohandas Gandhi, *The Bhagavad Gita According to Gandhi* (Wilder, 2012).

[24] Regarding the end of apartheid in South Africa, in 1994, Nadine Gordimer has explained that "Democracy is not an on-off affair, it has to be learned, day by day." Gordimer, *Telling Times: Writing and Living, 1954-2008* (Norton, 2010), 501. The same should be said about nonviolent conflict resolution. In fact, nonviolent conflict resolution may be the purest form of democracy: non-coercive, full-participation problem-solving.

[25] Galtung, *Peace by Peaceful Means*, 70-80.

[26] Ivan Vejvoda, "Civil Society versus Slobodan Milošević: Serbia, 1991-2000," in Roberts and Ash, *Civil Resistance and Power Politics*, 295-316. Strategic nonviolence did remove the Serbian dictator, with limited structural and cultural change, and Serbian society was far from transformed. Serbian resistance organizers then provided guidance to nonviolent resisters in Ukraine, Georgia, and elsewhere, with similar results.

[27] Burrowes, *The Strategy of Nonviolence Defense*, esp. 67-68, 156-161, 106-112.

7

NONVIOLENCE AND WORLD WAR II

NONVIOLENCE AND WORLD WAR II

What about Hitler?

Yes, what about Hitler? That's the question that usually follows the Crazed Gunman trap (see Ch. 3), again trying to force one to admit that sometimes nonviolence is inadequate and a violent response is appropriate and beneficial. This time, though, the scenario is historical, not hypothetical: How could a mass, sustained, nonviolent movement succeed against a genocidal regime like Nazi Germany, which gassed, shot, starved, and worked to death millions upon millions of noncombatants? How could moral jujitsu be applied against a regime without conscience that didn't care about popular opinion and wouldn't hesitate to kill anyone standing in its way? How can anyone believe war is always wrong when only the Soviet and US armies, fighting their way to Berlin, could shut down the gas chambers, liberate the concentration camps, and end the Holocaust? This is the Crazed Gunman writ large—the head of state as psychopath, government as serial murderer— also known as the problem of the "ruthless opponent."[1]

One might point out that Germans never actually employed mass, sustained nonviolence against the Nazi regime, so we don't know if it would have worked or not, but perhaps it wasn't tried because it simply wasn't possible. If a German police battalion—not the highly trained sadists in the Gestapo and SS, but "ordinary men"—willingly shot thousands of unarmed, nonresistant Jews, one by one, in the forests of Poland, how could anyone hope to organize, for example, a nonviolent protest march to fill the streets, to shut down a major German city?[2] The Nazis didn't tolerate opposition voices; participation would be suicide. No, nonviolence would not have worked against Adolf Hitler.

Except it did.

There is a tendency, at least in US popular discourse, to view the policies and actions of Nazi leadership as so monstrous as to defy human understanding—perhaps because evaluating Nazi behavior as anything other than inexplicable "evil" is to admit that ordinary human beings, meaning any of us, are capable of the vilest acts.[3] Furthermore, many erroneously imagine that Hitler's government faced no internal opposition, believing that Nazi propaganda had thoroughly won over the German people or that Nazi terror had cowed all Germans of goodwill into silent submission and obedience.[4] But Nazis were not automatons. They were human beings, with human needs, desires, and emotions, and, like all politicians, Nazi leaders were concerned about popular opinion. Adolf Hitler was just one man, no matter how charismatic, cunning, or ruthless, and his reign depended on, if not popular support, at least the tacit consent of the German population. Nazis needed the cooperation of the citizenry to run their bureaucracies, maintain economic production, and fill the ranks of the armed forces, especially during wartime. They needed, in Gene Sharp's words, "pillars of support." Thus, even the monstrous Hitler was vulnerable to pressure from nonviolent protest if it weakened his pillars.

The Nazis came to power in 1933 and institutionalized a propaganda campaign that demonized the Jewish minority as racially inferior and an obstacle to the rebirth of the German nation. Discriminatory laws and violent intimidation forced Jews out of the economic mainstream and into relocation, from rural areas to cities and from cities to foreign countries. In response to Nazi bullying, many Jews were choosing avoidance rather than passivity or active resistance, and understandably so. The hate campaign intensified in 1938, and, by October, a quarter of the Jewish population had departed Germany. Then, on November 9-10, Propaganda Minister Joseph Goebbels unleashed the *Reichskristallnacht* pogrom, or "Crystal Night." Nazi thugs destroyed Jewish homes, shops, and synagogues, and detained thousands of Jews. While a small percentage of Germans approved of the anti-Jewish violence, a far more common response was disgust, outrage, and shame, even among Nazi officials. Goebbels received a letter from a Nazi sympathizer who wrote, regarding the destructive acts and arrests, "Nobody dares to say a word against them, though 85 percent of the population is angry as never before." For some Germans, the pogrom was materially wasteful, illegal, and distasteful. Others had humanitarian concerns, and a few staged public protests against the racist barbarity. German attitudes were far from uniform on the so-called "Jewish Question," and Nazi leaders were not indifferent to the mood of the citizenry. Indeed, the negative responses seem to have convinced Goebbels not to repeat the tactics of Crystal Night, even though the event dramatically accelerated Jewish emigration.[5]

Hitler was particularly concerned about potential opposition from Catholic and Protestant church leaders, who were highly respected and influential in German society. In 1939, he initiated a secret program, known as T4, that euthanized, through carbon monoxide asphyxiation, tens of thousands of mentally ill Germans, as a step toward "purifying the race." When word got out, Germans generally were appalled but hesitant to protest. A few churchmen spoke publicly, if somewhat belatedly, against the euthanizing, and military men objected to the inclusion of wounded veterans in the murderous program. It only took a few respected individuals giving public voice to popular concern to trouble the German leadership. With war begun against the Soviet Union, in 1941, Hitler decided it best to discontinue T4, at least temporarily, rather than risk unrest at home (but soon approved the gassing of Jews in Poland).[6]

Two years later, another public protest interrupted, however slightly, the Nazi death machine. When SS troops began the "final roundup" of Jews in Berlin, a group of women spontaneously gathered outside a Jewish community center on a central Berlin street called Rosenstrasse. These were the non-Jewish wives of Jewish men, and their husbands were being held in the community center by SS guards in preparation for deportation to Auschwitz. The women went to Rosenstrasse seeking information about their missing husbands, but as their numbers grew into the hundreds, they began shouting for the release of the prisoners. Despite Gestapo threats, SS warning shots, and Nazi laws against public gatherings, the women returned the following day, and the next, and eventually numbered one thousand protestors, including women not in mixed marriages and also some men. Nazi leaders argued over the appropriate response to the agitated women, and ruled out a violent crackdown—Nazi ideology, after all, claimed to defend "German motherhood." After a week of the noisy demonstrations, Goebbels ordered the release, with Hitler's approval, of close to two thousand intermarried Berlin Jews and their "half-Jewish" children. Intermarried Jews who had already been sent to concentration camps were also released.

Nonviolence had succeeded against an indisputably ruthless opponent. A group of German housewives saved their husbands and children because they dared to protest against SS actions and because the Nazi leadership feared public displays of opposition, especially in Berlin, and understood that an assault on the women might increase disloyalty in the capital city.[7] Nazi threat power had become a potential liability. Far from omnipotent, Nazi leaders needed German cooperation and were aware of the possibility of moral jujitsu. As one of Goebbels's deputies put it after the war, "The police could have arrested them and sent them to a concentration camp, but that wasn't handled that way because the people openly made public that they weren't in agreement with what was happening."[8]

If an unplanned convergence of several hundred housewives could give the Nazi leaders pause, how would Hitler and Goebbels have responded to tens of thousands of Berliners, in opposition to anti-Jewish laws, occupying the Kurfürstendamm—the city's renowned boulevard—perhaps followed by a general strike in major cities across the country? How would SS troops have responded to orders to shoot into unarmed crowds of German citizens, fellow members of the *Herrenvolk*, the supposed master race? The answers are unknowable, but the T4 and Rosenstrasse protests suggest that the German people might have been able to stop Hitler's persecution of German Jews—the potential was there. Certainly, the "German character," sometimes described as orderly, loyal, and legalistic, was not an obstacle. In 1920, a general strike of German workers, including civil servants and military leaders, reversed a rightwing coup after four days; a German noncooperation campaign, in 1923, stymied French military occupation and economic exploitation of the Ruhr industrial region; and, in 1989, Germans nonviolently forced out a ruthless communist dictator.[9]

One question *can* be answered: Why didn't the masses act to protect the Jewish minority? Again, attitudes were mixed. A small percentage of Germans were blatantly anti-Jewish, and this group increased in size as children grew up under the pernicious influence of Nazi propaganda. Another minority group, consisting mostly of Catholics, urban bourgeoisie, socialists, and communists, felt sympathy and humanitarian concern for their Jewish neighbors. The majority of the population held latent anti-Jewish attitudes. They weren't actively involved in Jew-baiting, but easily accepted the enforcement of discriminatory and exclusionary laws that had little effect on their own daily lives. As Jews became more and more isolated, most Germans simply gave little thought to their plight—out of sight, out of mind—two exceptions being the women of Rosenstrasse, who were defending their families, and the widespread disapproval of the highly visible Crystal Night onslaught. Simply put, the majority of Germans were not virulently anti-Jewish, despite the Nazi propaganda efforts, but they were overwhelmingly, tragically indifferent. The cruel cynicism of Nazi rule, coupled with the outbreak of war, caused Germans to shrink inward, harden their attitudes, and focus on their own well-being, even as reports filtered in about German atrocities against Jews in Poland.[10]

Resistance to Occupation

A German nonviolent resistance movement might have looked similar to the Danish and Norwegian resistance to German occupation. Germans had accepted the legitimacy of Nazi rule; the Nazis were fellow Germans, they had come to power through ostensibly legal means, and Hitler's policies seemed to serve the economic interests of the German middle class. By comparison, the vast majority of Danes and Norwegians rejected the legitimacy of Nazi rule, imposed from outside by German military invasion in 1940.[11] In Denmark, at first, the German occupation appeared relatively benign. The Germans wanted the products of Danish farms and factories, and they wanted to maintain Denmark, with happy, well-treated citizens, as a "model protectorate" on international display—Nazis were concerned about *world* opinion too. Thinking resistance hopeless and cooperation the only way to protect Danish lives, the Danish king and his ministers grudgingly acceded to German demands. The Danish people, though, did not want to be ruled by Germans, and a resistance movement gradually took shape. Young Danes led the way, with protests, acts of sabotage, and creation of an underground press. When German officials pressured the Danish government to crack down on saboteurs, Danes took to work slowdowns and general strikes. In response, Hitler ordered the Danish government to cooperate in the establishment of martial law. Caught between a toughened German presence and a widening Danish resistance, the Danish government finally resigned, ending the fiction of inoffensive German administration. For the remainder of the war, the German occupiers struggled to rule Denmark, as increased German brutality, including the killing of nonviolent resisters, only brought more noncooperation.[12]

In Norway, two months of military resistance failed to prevent a German takeover, but did make clear that German forces were the enemy, as did the sharp economic decline that came with German occupation. The invaders had little gripe against the Norwegians—the Germans were mostly concerned with access to north Atlantic ports and mines in neighboring Sweden—but the Norwegian population overwhelmingly rejected German and local Nazi rule and participated in or supported noncooperation efforts. The king and his government fled to England rather than collaborate. The Supreme Court tried to maintain the Norwegian constitution against the demands of German commissioners, then resigned when this was no longer possible. Churches, labor unions, and athletic associations refused to cooperate with efforts by the Norwegian Nazi party, backed by German officials, to organize the country along corporatist lines. Bishops in the state church renounced their state responsibilities. Over eighty percent of teachers signed letters of protest and held out against participation in a fascist union, despite school closures and the imprisonment under harsh conditions of one thousand male teachers.[13] The teachers' public stand was particularly inspiring and unifying, as confirmed, in 1942, by Vidkun Quisling, the infamous Norwegian who was appointed "minister-president" by the German occupiers to win Norwegian allegiance to fascist policies. Quisling complained, "The teachers are responsible for the fact that we have not yet made peace with Germany. You teachers have destroyed everything for me."[14]

To be sure, the emphasis in Norway and Denmark was on strategic, not principled, nonviolence, on what Mohandas Gandhi called "nonviolence of the weak." Widespread noncooperation sprung up only after military resistance and sabotage proved ineffective or counterproductive. The goal of strategic noncooperation was to resist unacceptable German demands, not to take a principled stand against violence of all types, not to transform society. One particular event in Denmark is instructive. After the Germans outlawed strikes and imposed an 8 P.M. curfew, factory workers in Copenhagen walked out at 1 P.M., saying they weren't on strike, they just had to tend their gardens before the curfew hour. A clever ruse, but trying to get off on a technicality is not patient suffering. Many of the workers barricaded the streets and threw stones at German soldiers, who responded with bullets, killing twenty-three and wounding over two hundred. The Germans also shut off gas, electricity, and water in the city. After negotiations, the Germans suspended the curfew, restored utilities, and stopped the shooting. The Danes went back to work—grudgingly, sluggishly, inefficiently, but still serving the German war effort.

Norwegian and Danish resistance did not force out the foreign occupiers, but, in both countries, people were discovering the power of noncooperation— even against Nazi Germany. Indeed, a British military theorist who interviewed German generals after the war concluded that nonviolent resistance confused them. "They were experts in violence, and had been trained to deal with opponents who used that method. But other forms of resistance baffled them....It was a relief to them when resistance became violent, and when non-violent forms were mixed with guerrilla action, thus making it easier to combine drastic suppressive action against both at the same time."[15] This point is worth emphasizing: A repressive government may feel more threatened by nonviolent rather than violent resistance, since violence is what agents of repression understand and where they have the advantage.

Noncooperation with the Holocaust

The most critical act of Danish resistance was refusal to assist in the roundup of Jews. During the first three and a half years of occupation, the Germans didn't target Danish Jews, believing anti-Jewish violence would only increase Danish unrest—again, the concern with popular opinion. German officials tried pressuring the Danish government to pass anti-Jewish legislation, but the Danes refused. A German commissioner reported, "Denmark considers the Jewish question a constitutional issue. Equality of all citizens before the law is a basic pillar of the constitution." The Danish king, who had become a rallying symbol of defiant nationalism, publicly expressed sympathy for Danish Jews. The Danish Church issued an official statement of support for "our Jewish brothers and sisters." In autumn 1943, though, after the Danish government had resigned, the German leadership decided it was time to sweep the country of Jews. Given advance warning by a sympathetic German official and Danish resisters, most Jews were able to find safe hiding places, usually with the assistance of non-Jews. The Germans ordered the hidden ones handed over, but, instead, Danes arranged for small fishing boats to smuggle seven thousand Jews to safety in Sweden. The rescue effort was a national affair, with contributions made by churches, professional organizations, and police.[16] Unlike in Germany, where the majority population was indifferent to Jewish suffering and most Jews who had failed to emigrate early did not survive the war, over ninety percent of

Danish Jews evaded the Holocaust apparatus. In Norway, where Quisling's fascist government collaborated with German demands and local policemen participated in the Jewish roundup, resistance efforts saved only fifty percent of a population of two thousand.[17]

Across Europe, Jewish survival following German invasion largely depended on their fellow countrymen. Two factors were key: the level of German control and the extent of anti-Jewish attitudes. Countries placed under direct German administration, including Poland, Holland, Greece, and Slovakia, had the highest Jewish death tolls as a percentage of the prewar Jewish population. Where the German overlords depended on previously existing national governments, they were hesitant to employ harsh methods for fear of alienating domestic administrators who the general population accepted as legitimate. Thus, national officials, if so inclined, could use their intermediary position as a shield against Nazi demands for Jewish roundups and could use their domestic influence to encourage pro-Jewish sympathies. But national leaders were limited in their capacity to save Jews if anti-Jewish attitudes were deeply entrenched and the general population viewed the expansion of Nazism as opportunity to persecute their Jewish neighbors rather than a call to protect them. In Denmark, Finland, Bulgaria, and Italy, where local administration endured and anti-Jewish attitudes were insignificant, the death tolls were relatively low.

Perhaps most remarkable was Bulgaria, where the national government enacted anti-Jewish laws and entered the war on Germany's side. Many Bulgarians, led by Orthodox Church officials, opposed the anti-Jewish measures, Jews openly protested against the yellow star requirement, and the administration backed down. Political opposition and protests against Jewish deportations, including by a bishop who threatened to lie down on the train tracks, convinced the Bulgarian king to stop cooperating with German demands. The Bulgarian government did participate in the transport of thirteen thousand Jews from Macedonia and Thrace to the Treblinka extermination camp, and many Bulgarian Jews suffered expulsion from the capital city and endured difficult conditions in work camps, but almost the entire prewar population of fifty thousand Bulgarian Jews survived the war. In sum, where non-Jews protected Jews, survival rates were highest, and where non-Jews, including government officials and policemen, assisted Nazis in identifying and capturing Jews, the Jewish population was doomed.[18] In this sense, the Holocaust was not only a Nazi or German undertaking, it was a European enterprise, and European cooperation or noncooperation was not only a very real choice but of utmost importance.

A Jewish Satyagraha?

Returning to Germany and hypothetical scenarios, what if German Jews, without the support of the indifferent non-Jewish population, had responded to persecution with a strategy of nonviolent resistance rather than avoidance or passivity? Recall the bar fight scenario (see Ch. 3) and the list of potential strategies and outcomes: nonviolent resistance holds the most promise if the goal is transformation of participants and onlookers. What if, rather than fleeing the country, hiding behind closed doors, or going quietly to the trucks and trains, German Jews had held mass marches and sit-ins in major urban centers? What if they had communicated a message of ahimsa: You can kill us but we will not hurt you because we care about you. Big what-if's, and a complicated thought experiment to carry out, in part because Nazi propaganda played on latent anti-Jewish attitudes, characterizing Jews as subhuman and making them scapegoats for all sorts of societal ills. Public acts of large-scale resistance, even if nonviolent, would have been easy to construe as further "evidence" of a Jewish "problem."

There is an important point here: Historically, the nonviolent removal of an autocratic head of state has been accomplished by an awakened majority opposition with a shared identity based on common ethnicity, religion, and/or nationality, and usually with the dictator and his enforcers included in that identity group. Unable to divide the opposition and unwilling to expand the violent repression against his "own people," the ruler steps aside.[19] In that regard, German Jews tormented by Hitler faced a greater challenge than did the Salvadorans who drove out Hernández Martínez, for example, or the Filipinos who stopped Marcos's tanks. How could a relatively inconsequential minority, increasingly cast as racially different outsiders, at times portrayed as religious or political enemies and specifically targeted for abuse, turn the masses against a charismatic, nationalistic leader? Most likely, Hitler would have approved Nazi requests for a bloody crackdown on the Jewish "agitators."

But here's the unknown: If German forces had openly massacred thousands of unarmed Jewish protesters, how would the German population have responded? Could they have maintained their willful ignorance, self-absorption, and passivity with mass murder occurring in downtown Berlin and Munich, in front of reporters and foreign diplomats? In other words, German Jews might have said, "If they're going to slaughter us, let's bring it out into the light of day"—like Crystal Night, only far worse. It would have taken a lot of corpses, a mass action of self-sacrifice, but visible, courageous suffering in the face of extreme anti-Jewish brutality might have awakened the collective moral conscience of the non-Jewish population, including members of the armed forces, compelling them into active rejection of Nazism and withdrawal of the cooperation and obedience that enabled Nazi rule.

Or perhaps not. SS troops might have obeyed orders and gone right on machine-gunning the lines of Jewish marchers; the German masses might have remained silent, shocked into paralysis rather than action; the German military leadership might have remained loyal to Hitler; the hypothetical Jewish satyagraha might have failed miserably. But with the benefit of hindsight, we can say that a Jewish nonviolent resistance campaign would have been worth the concomitant risks because either way, success or failure, transformation of society or non-redemptive bloodbath, the overall outcome for Germany's Jews couldn't have been much worse than what actually happened.

This is not offered as a criticism of Jewish behavior in the face of Nazi persecution. We can no more condemn German Jews for not using patient suffering and Gandhian nonviolence than condemn them for not defending themselves with AK-47s and "suitcase" nuclear bombs.[20] We cannot hold people responsible for failing to use tools they don't possess. Most nonviolent resistance in Europe in the early twentieth century, like with the women at Rosenstrasse, was spontaneous. Participants lacked training, deliberate strategizing, and a nuanced understanding of the dynamics of nonviolence. The long history of nonviolent resistance to state power, dating back at least to Jewish resistance against Roman rulers in Palestine in the first century A.D., was largely unknown at the time, and the dynamics of nonviolence were only beginning to be investigated.[21] Perhaps the only places in the world offering extensive training in direct nonviolence were on the Indian subcontinent—at Gandhi's ashrams and at the Khudai Khidmatgar camps in the Hindu Kush. German Jews were in no way prepared to mount an adequate nonviolent defense against Hitler's genocidal intentions as perpetrated by a thoroughly dehumanized Nazi regime that operated with extensive training, shrewd strategizing, and a cultivated understanding and embrace of the dynamics of violence. In fact, many Jews refused to believe reports of gas vans and extermination camps, refused to imagine the situation could get any worse, refused to comprehend that they were being sent to their deaths. Not having the tools to combat such extreme persecution, it was, for some, easiest to pretend it wasn't happening. But just because his victims weren't adequately equipped for satyagraha, and just because the German masses didn't stand with their Jewish neighbors, doesn't mean Hitler and Nazism were immune to the power of nonviolent resistance.

Start Early

Conflicts are not static—unresolved, they almost always intensify, as the triangle of attitudes, behavior, and contradiction suggests. (See Ch. 6.) As a conflict intensifies, a greater degree of dehumanization develops, meaning loss of compassion. Participants focus more and more on their own victimization, less on the harm they might be causing. Peace scholar Michael Nagler, in his cogent discussion of the efficacy of nonviolent resistance to Nazism, offers an "escalation of violence" chart to illustrate how, over time, an unchecked conflict will increase in intensity.[22] Moving left to right (forward in time), the intensity ramps upward, gradually at first, then rising sharply.

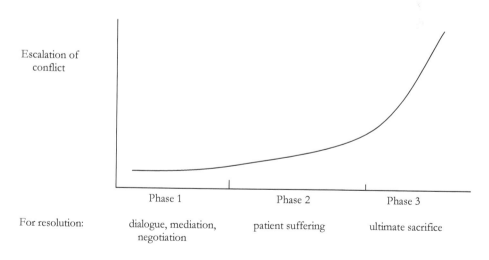

Following Gandhi, Nagler points out that as a conflict intensifies, as hearts harden and dehumanization increases, the amount of compassion ("to

171

suffer with") necessary to defuse or resolve the conflict must be proportional to the level of inhumanity being expressed; the direct nonviolence must match or exceed the direct violence. In Phase 1, where most conflicts remain, resolution can come through dialogue and negotiation. If a conflict reaches Phase 2, resolution requires an act of sacrifice, someone willing to suffer, to take on the pain of another. In the extreme intensity of Phase 3, the dehumanization is such that only the willingness to die can ease the conflict.

Imagine two neighboring landowners, in a poorly policed region, arguing over the boundary line between their adjoined properties. Early on in the conflict, the actors may be able to "talk it out." But if the conflict is not quickly resolved, meanness may emerge and resentments build—particularly if the initial attitudes were not friendship and empathy. Perhaps the neighbors stop talking, avoid eye contact, tell their children not to play with the other's children. Name-calling and small acts of vandalism follow, perhaps even fistfights and threats of arson. In time, the families may even forget the original disagreement, and only remember that they hate each other. (Consider how this same dynamic works on a larger scale: replace "neighbors" and "families" with "governments" and "countries," and you have a recipe for war.) When, in Phase 2, the relationship has turned hostile and dangerous, when at least one party has lost sight of mutual humanity, resolution may only come with self-sacrifice, some act that reaches the opponents' hearts (since ears are closed and vision clouded), something that restores the humanity of both parties. For example, a third neighbor sits on the disputed property line and announces she will fast until they agree to negotiate a resolution (i.e., return to Phase 1). She would rather go hungry, she tells them, than see them consumed by hatred. The alienated neighbors must now choose: negotiate with each other or watch a sympathetic person suffer day after day.[23] If the conflict has intensified to Phase 3, to the point of extreme dehumanization, when the neighbors are engaged in direct and deadly violence—perhaps firing bullets at each other in a blood feud between families—rehumanization may require the ultimate sacrifice, the third neighbor may have to suffer more than hunger pains. She may have to fast to death to touch the landowners' calloused hearts—like Mary Dyer shocking theocratic Massachusetts, and like old John Brown going happily to the gallows, suffering on behalf of "His despised poor," in a deeply dehumanized society of slaves and slave owners.

Nagler tells the story of Father Maximilian Mary Kolbe, a Polish Catholic priest who was murdered by Germans at Auschwitz in 1941. Father

Kolbe volunteered to die in place of a Jewish prisoner randomly selected for execution. A solitary act of patient suffering was hardly enough to rehumanize millions of Germans and Poles in the midst of the Holocaust, but, as a prisoner who was present later testified, Kolbe's sacrifice restored many prisoners' faith in humanity: "Thousands of prisoners were convinced the true world continued to exist and that our torturers would not be able to destroy it....To say that Father Kolbe died for one of us or that person's family is too great a simplification. His death was the salvation of thousands."[24] According to one Auschwitz survivor, in the camps it was obvious when a fellow prisoner had lost hope and given up the fight for survival. These walking dead were called *klepsydra*, the Polish word for hourglass, either referring to the gaunt shape of their faces or because their time was running out.[25] By giving hope to Auschwitz inmates, by giving them something to live for, Father Kolbe may have, indeed, saved thousands. Again, nonviolence *did* work against German oppressors, even some in Nazi uniform. As with John Brown in his final days, it wasn't Father Kolbe's biological death that changed things, it was his *willingness* to sacrifice his life for another, his response to deepest hate with deepest love. But Kolbe's act had even more integrative power than Brown's. The willingness to die for others *while refusing to kill* is the greatest affirmation of mutual humanity, and is the antidote for the willingness to torture and kill, which is the negation of mutual humanity. Most people are not yet prepared to make the ultimate sacrifice, even if it offers hope of rehumanizing a society, but the "steep curve" of Nagler's graph provides a reassuring insight: if we nonviolently resolve conflicts before they escalate into hatred and violence, risking death to restore humanity may become unnecessary.

The lesson is *start early*. In the question "What about Hitler?," the word *Hitler* represents the German war machine that spread across Europe in the early 1940s and also the systematic murder of millions of Jews, Roma, Jehovah's Witnesses, homosexuals, war prisoners, and anyone else condemned by Adolf Hitler. At that most intense level of conflict and dehumanization, only a proportional nonviolent response—hundreds of thousands of Father Kolbes—could dissolve the hatred, savagery, callousness, resentment, and fear consuming Europe. But why answer the Hitler question only in terms of Phase 3 conflict intensity? Consider, instead, a nonviolent response to Nazism beginning in 1933, before the newly elected *führer* had initiated mass murder, or even earlier, in the 1920s, when Hitler first began spewing his venom. Imagine if Germans of goodwill had protested against the Nazi message of hate, fear, and German victimhood; if they had responded to the order to boycott Jewish-owned businesses with a boycott of Nazi-owned businesses instead; if millions had rallied to proclaim their rejection of militarism and racism rather than their loyalty to the red-and-black swastika. Imagine if, in the early 1930s, German clergy, particularly at the higher levels of church bureaucracy, had spoken against the persecution of Jews, the way a few individual churchmen would openly oppose T4, the way the Orthodox Church in Bulgaria and the Danish Church denounced anti-Jewish enactments. The power of church authority, turned against Nazism rather than providing tacit approval, might have legitimized public dissent and given rise to a protest movement, perhaps with German wives and mothers at the forefront, stopping the Holocaust *before it began*.[26] But that did not happen; nonviolent resistance did not start early. Germans of goodwill, including those in influential positions, kept their heads and voices down—more out of indifference than fear—and Hitler's anti-Jewish measures escalated toward the "final solution." The oft-quoted confession attributed to Pastor Martin Niemoller is a cry of regret, but also an affirmation of what might have been:

> When the Nazis stopped the Communists, I said nothing, because I was not a Communist. When they locked up the Socialists, I said nothing, because I was not a Socialist. When they came to get the Jews, I did not protest, because I was not a Jew. When they came to get me, there was no one left who could protest.

Le Chambon

The life of André Trocmé demonstrates the importance of starting early. Trocmé was born in 1901, grew up in northern France, and saw firsthand the ravages and futility of World War I. He was disgusted by the way German soldiers abused Russian prisoners, but found inspiration in a German soldier who served as a telegrapher but refused to carry a weapon into battle. After the war, Trocmé studied theology in Paris and joined the Fellowship of Reconciliation, a nonviolent organization. He later attended Union Theological Seminary, in New York City, known for its Social Gospel emphasis on helping the less fortunate. Because Pastor Trocmé was a free-thinker who taught nonviolence—a character type always threatening to institutional authority—the French Reformed (Protestant) Church sent him off, in 1938, to a congregation in Le Chambon-sur-Lignon, a rural town of five thousand on the Vivarais-Lignon Plateau of southern France. Two years later, the German army invaded France, occupied Paris and the northern region, and allowed the collaborationist Vichy government to administer the south.

When the Germans and their French allies began enforcing Nazi policies, the people of Le Chambon and nearby villages were more prepared than most to respond with nonviolence. First, as Huguenot (Calvinist) Protestants, the Chambonnais had suffered persecution at the hands of Catholics, in the sixteenth through eighteenth centuries, and, later, provided shelter to Protestant refugees, sometimes guiding them through the mountains to safety in Switzerland, almost two hundred miles away. This history created a deep skepticism of outside political authority and a compassion for persecuted people. In the 1930s, led by Trocmé's predecessor, Pastor Charles Guillon, the Chambonnais welcomed refugees from the Spanish Civil War and Jews fleeing Nazi persecution in Germany and Austria.

Second, Pastor Trocmé had cultivated a philosophy of nonviolence in the town through his sermons, personal example, and in a boarding school he founded with his wife Magda and Pastor Édouard Theis. The day after the French government surrendered to the Germans, Trocmé told his congregation, "The responsibility of Christians is to resist the violence that will be brought to bear on their consciences." While other French resisters turned to violent tactics to challenge fascist rule, the Chambonnais employed what Trocmé called "weapons of the spirit." The people of the plateau refused to take an oath swearing allegiance to the Vichy government. They supported a boarding school for Jewish refugee children, established by the American Friends (Quakers) Service Committee and directed by Daniel Trocmé, Andre's nephew. When forced deportation began, in 1942, hundreds of French Jews fled to the plateau region, and found refuge in homes and farms, churches, schools, and hotels. Some remained in hiding for the duration of the war, while others made the dangerous trek to Switzerland.

Although the rescue enterprise was secretive by nature, and the townsfolk had to take extra precautions to hide Jews during raids by the Vichy police or German SS, Trocmé did not deny his participation. When Vichy officials demanded Jews be turned over, Trocmé replied, "A shepherd does not forsake his flock....I do not know what a Jew is. I know only human beings." In 1942, Vichy police arrested Trocmé, Theis, and a school director, held them in an internment camp, and pressured them to sign the Vichy loyalty oath. The three refused, and were released five weeks later. Trocmé and Theis reluctantly went into hiding, but the people of the Le Chambon region, including Magda Trocmé, continued their rescue work. It is estimated they sheltered five thousand people during the war, most of them Jews, but also Spanish Republicans, German oppositionists, and young Frenchmen dodging deportation to German labor camps.[27]

At first glance, the story of Le Chambon's open resistance appears miraculous. The Germans knew the town was a "nest of Jews," yet never destroyed it, never attacked it with the brutality they used against armed resisters.[28] The town's two spiritual leaders were released from incarceration rather than killed. Vichy officials sometimes warned the community before police raids. More often, Vichy policemen would eat lunch at a hotel restaurant in Le Chambon and loudly discuss which houses they were about to search, giving time for word to spread and those houses to be evacuated. Plain good luck does not explain why the people of the plateau, for the most part, went unpunished. Vichy officials were careful because they knew the region was united in its efforts; a crackdown on Le Chambon or the murder of an influential priest would only bring greater resistance. In other words, they feared moral jujitsu.

Furthermore, Pastor Trocmé and others, rather than denying their subversive activities, made clear their willingness to suffer on behalf of others. A Vichy cabinet official visited Le Chambon and was handed a letter from students advising him, "We feel obliged to tell you that there are among us a certain number of Jews," and adding that any Jews would be welcomed and protected. The official protested that this was not his concern; Jewish deportation was the responsibility of Robert Bach, the local prefect, who was standing right beside him. Bach saw the courage and honesty of the students, and it was Bach who made sure Le Chambon had advance warning of raids, Bach who requested the release of Trocmé and Theis, arguing that the number of Jews around Le Chambon and the illegal activity of the pastors had been greatly exaggerated.[29] When Daniel Trocmé heard that the Gestapo had searched his school and arrested eighteen students including five Jews, he hurried to Le Chambon and joined the arrested students rather than flee. Accused of aiding Jews, he responded that he was obeying the Christian imperative to help the oppressed. For this, he was transported to his death in a Polish concentration camp.

Roger Le Forestier, the town doctor, made a similar sacrifice. He gave a ride to members of the Maquis, the armed resistance, and when the car was stopped by police, he was accused of possessing a banned weapon. An SS colonel wanted Dr. Le Forestier executed, but the regional German military commander, Major Schmehling, arranged instead for the physician to help bombing victims in Germany. In the end, the SS colonel got his wish: the Gestapo killed Le Forestier before he could leave France. His death, though, was not in vain. Le Forestier had not denied his rescue work, and the honesty and humility of his testimony reached Schmehling's heart, as the major explained when Pastor Trocmé interviewed him after the war. Trocmé said to Schmehling,

> You knew that Le Chambon was a nest of resistance; you knew we had Jews there, and the Maquis nearby. It is true that your German police did us harm, but why did you not send a punitive expedition to destroy the village in those last few months? Surely you were doing this elsewhere in France, and in places near Le Chambon.

Schmehling replied,

> Well, Colonel Metzger was a hard one, and he kept insisting that we move on Le Chambon. But I kept telling him to wait. At his trial I had heard the words of Le Forestier, who was a Christian and who had explained to me very clearly why you were all disobeying our orders in Le Chambon. I believed that your doctor was sincere. I am a good Catholic, you understand, and I can grasp these things....I told Metzger that this kind of resistance had nothing to do with violence, nothing to do with anything we could destroy with violence. With all my personal and military power I opposed sending his legion into Le Chambon.[30]

This is a clear example of the integrative power of principled nonviolence—not magic, but a comprehensible, traceable dynamic (and quite different from when Danish strikers announced they were going home to tend their gardens). Honesty, sincerity, courage, and compassion, the refusal to prevaricate or hide, the willingness to suffer on behalf of others—this powerful combination touched the hearts of a German major and a French prefect, rehumanized them to some degree, and they worked to constrain the more dehumanized SS men. Such power may arise spontaneously, like at Rosenstrasse, but years of compassionate service, practicing tolerance and selfless love, embracing honesty and transparency in one's motives, cultivating the human capacity to do good rather than the human capacity to do harm, can prepare one for moments of crisis and can give an individual, like Father Kolbe, more integrative power than a spontaneous group of hundreds. Because of their history and preparation, because they had refined their humanity, the Chambonnais considered their actions during the war unremarkable. One resident later recalled, "We didn't protect the Jews because we were moral or heroic people. We helped them because it was the human thing to do." These simple words—not from a university philosopher or evolutionary biologist, but a rural villager—take us back to the first peace lesson: the human tendency toward goodness is built into our DNA. With cultivation and encouragement, that basic urge can be strengthened so that in times of great stress—for example, when confronted with hateful propaganda and threats of violence—it does not waver.

Many years after the war, Pastor Theis explained why Soviet forces could not use nonviolence against German forces:

> They had to use violence then. It was too late for nonviolence. Both the Germans and the Russians were *embarques* [embarked on a journey], committed to mass murder—that is, to warfare— and they had to play out their terrible roles upon each other. Besides, nonviolence involves preparation and organization, methods patiently and unswervingly employed—the Russians knew nothing of all this. Nonviolence must have deep roots and strong branches before it can bear the fruit it bore in Le Chambon. Nonviolence for them would have been suicide; it was too late.[31]

Start Now

If the lesson is start early, the time to start is *now*, and the place to begin is *everywhere*. Why wait until the next *führer* grimly takes office, his dark mind buzzing with sinister designs? Why delay until goose-stepping neo-Nazis are fouling the streets? American folksinger Woody Guthrie's guitar famously bore the slogan "THIS MACHINE KILLS FASCISTS." Guthrie, who wrote "This Land is Your Land," in 1940, argued that singing antifascist songs was the most valuable contribution he could make to the US war effort. (The US government insisted he serve in the military instead.) Guthrie's slogan may not have been a call for nonviolent resolution to World War II, but his point about using music to combat fascism is a good one. *Fascism* means authoritarian ultranationalism, worshiping the state—in particular, an exalted head of state—as protector of a chosen people, and promoting a perceived national purity, rejuvenation, and power through aggressive militarism: an almost perfect blueprint—xenophobic hatred whipped with highly centralized authoritarian government—for racist persecution and war. Indeed, a self-perpetuating triangle:

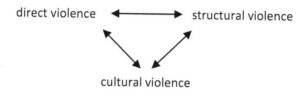

Racism, nationalism, and demonization of others (cultural violence) facilitates war against "inferior" peoples, legitimizes repression, and delegitimizes voices of tolerance. Authoritarian government (structural violence) demonizes out-groups to build popular support, and pursues war for personal aggrandizement, economic gain, and to justify repressive rule. War (direct violence) intensifies hatred of perceived enemies, necessitates more centralized administration, and sharpens the tools of repression.

In contrast, songs that teach tolerance of others (rather than hatred of differences) and celebrate critical thinking (rather than unquestioning obedience) are cultivating cultural peace and, thereby, undermining structural and direct violence.[32] "My country right or wrong" is a foothold for fascism. "I should like to be able to love my country and still love justice" is profoundly antifascist.[33] The best strategy for defeating a ruthless opponent is for parents, teachers, ministers, writers, coaches, artists, entertainers, and public figures of all sorts to use their influence to promote tolerance, compassion, and nonviolent conflict resolution, and, following Gandhi, to encourage fearlessness, self-reliance, and self-confidence to minimize vulnerability to threat power, exchange power, and persuasive power. That way, ministers of hate won't gain followings, schoolyard bullies won't win elections, the ruthless opponent will never command an army. Teach your children Phase 1 nonviolent conflict resolution, and your grandchildren may be spared the need to employ Phase 2 and Phase 3 nonviolence.

Nonviolent Army

Since the masses did not start early, were not prepared to use nonviolence to counter proportionally German militarism and genocide, and did not nonviolently expel the German occupiers and unseat Hitler, it is, instead, the 1945 military conquest of Germany by US and Soviet armed forces that has been memorialized as the salvation of Europe. However, as previously discussed (see Ch. 1), war is not a contest to be won but a tragedy for most all concerned, and World War II was no human triumph. War is a disease, and the planet Earth is infected. World War I led to World War II, which led to wars in Korea, Vietnam, and Afghanistan, which led to war in Iraq, and so forth, *ad nauseam*. Trying to cure war with war is insanity. As Nagler asked, "Is there no other way?"[34]

One possible "other way" to respond to armed invasion is *nonviolent interposition*. Consider this scenario: In summer 2002, the US government began a propaganda campaign to build public and institutional support for an intensification of its war on the people of Iraq. They called their planned offensive "Shock and Awe"—the most powerful military in the history of the world preparing for full-scale invasion of a country with no standing army of any substance.[35] Public protests by millions of people, in the United States and around the world, did not dissuade the Bush-Cheney administration, and, in March 2003, the invasion began, with disastrous consequences for all involved (except, as usual, the profiteers). The antiwar world had not started early enough. Imagine, though, if an international nonviolent army had existed—tens of thousands of trained volunteers committed to principled nonviolence. Imagine if, as soon as the US government began hinting at invasion, those satyagrahis had rushed en masse to Baghdad, and, with their computers, smart phones, and cameras, publicized to the world their nonviolent intentions, actions, and goals. Imagine if, rather than building airbases and high-walled "green zones," they had undertaken service projects, including nonviolent training, and taken up residence in neighborhoods and around targeted buildings. Nonviolent interposition means unarmed third parties inserting themselves into conflict zones, living with individuals and groups who face violent attack, serving as mediators, witnesses, and human shields, offering to absorb suffering if necessary (like the hypothetical third neighbor fasting on a disputed property line). Peace Brigades International, Witness for Peace, Nonviolent Peaceforce, and other organizations have been doing such work for several decades, sending small teams and individual peacekeepers to Guatemala, the Philippines, Sri Lanka, and elsewhere.[36] But stopping a major military offensive would probably require masses of unarmed peacekeepers—and there's precedent for that too.

In 1929, Pashtuns (Pathans) in the Hindu Kush region of India formed the Khudai Khidmatgar (Servants of God) as a nonviolent army to work for independence from British rule. They wore red uniforms, organized into ranks, maintained military-like discipline, and exercised and performed drills, but carried no weapons. The foremost leader in the region's independence movement was Khan Abdul Ghaffar Khan, a physically towering man known as the "frontier Gandhi." Like his friend Gandhi, Ghaffar Khan preached the importance of reforming society from within as a way to resist domination from without. In that spirit, volunteers who attended Khudai Khidmatgar training camps learned cleanliness and hygiene, spun cotton for cloth, and ground seeds into flour. They opened schools, held community meetings, performed skits, and worked to raise political awareness. They organized tax strikes, boycotts of foreign goods, and other forms of noncooperation with British rule. By 1938, despite violent persecution by the British, over one hundred thousand Pashtuns had joined the "Red Shirts."[37]

Gandhi, too, had envisioned a *shanti sena* (peace army) in India, and, at the time of his assassination, in 1948, had begun planning for nonviolent platoons to quell deadly rioting between Hindus and Muslims. In 1957, Gandhi disciple Vinoba Bhave revived the idea in response to communal riots. Led by Jayaprakash Narayan and Narayan Desai, the Shanti Sena grew to some six thousand *shanti sainiks* (peace soldiers) in the mid-1960s, and often intervened to stop riots. One dramatic success came in 1965, in the city of Baroda, Gujarat. After communal riots broke out, and police violence exasperated the situation, a platoon of thirty-two shanti sainiks met with police officers and political opposition groups and convinced them to abandon violent tactics. The sainiks also quashed inflammatory rumors, organized peace-building actions, patrolled the streets as a pacifying influence, and interposed themselves between rioters and police. Once-skeptical city leaders were impressed enough to request the sainiks remain in Baroda as peacekeepers, even after the rioting ended. The Shanti Sena broke apart, in the 1970s, due to internal politics, but Sarvodaya Movement founder A.T.

Ariyaratne organized a nonviolent army for Sri Lankan youths, in 1978, as ethnic conflict was intensifying between Sinhalese and Tamils. Called Sarvodaya Shanthi Sena Sansadaya, the Sarvodaya peace brigades emphasized peace-building, community development, and relief work. In the early twenty-first century, membership exceeded eighty thousand men and women, ages fifteen to thirty, organized into eight thousand units across Sri Lanka.[38]

An international shanti sena does not exist, yet, but one successful, high-profile peace army intervention would change the way people around the world think about nonviolence and about war.[39] The US government could proceed with the destruction of Baghdad and occupation of Iraq because US propaganda had convinced enough US citizens and foreign leaders, despite all evidence to the contrary, that Iraqi despot Saddam Hussein was somehow responsible for the World Trade Center attacks, that he remained a threat to Western "security," and that "preventive" war was the only reasonable defense.[40] More hypotheticals to ponder: If one hundred thousand nonviolent international volunteers had been living and serving in Baghdad by December 2002, would the US population have rejected the cynical fear-mongering? Would their congressional representatives have opposed a violent invasion that jeopardized the lives of all those compassionate international volunteers? Would the volunteers' willingness to risk suffering to protect Iraqis have moved enough hearts? Would the peace army have convinced enough people that nonviolent interposition is a better response to security threats than bombing a city? No? What if *five hundred thousand* nonviolent volunteers had arrived in Baghdad, or *one million*, supported by millions of protestors in major cities? Certainly, that many courageous, compassionate humans could be found. What if they included Nobel Prize laureates, church leaders, former heads of state, and international celebrities? (Would George W. Bush have given the go-ahead to air assault on a city hosting Desmond Tutu, Nelson Mandela, Jimmy Carter, Mikhail Gorbachev, Pope John Paul II, A.T. Ariyaratne, Vandana Shiva, Rigoberta Menchú Tum, Arundhati Roy, Jody Williams, Harry Belafonte, John Lewis, Yoko Ono, Howard Zinn, Tom Hayden, Joan Baez, Thich Nhat Hanh, and the Dalai Lama, with music by Shakira, Ani DiFranco, Sweet Honey in the Rock, and Ladysmith Black Mambazo, and special guest appearances by Angelina Jolie and Brad Pitt? Killing thousands of "faceless" Iraqis is one thing, killing "The Sexiest Man Alive" quite another.) What if the shanti sainiks, half a million strong and led by Ariyaratne, refused to leave until representatives of all parties in the conflict endorsed a mediated nonviolent conflict resolution?

And what if, while in Baghdad, they gave support and protection to Iraqis nonviolently resisting the repressive Hussein regime? Hypothetical but imaginable, and the potential short-term and long-term results are worth considering. A new way of thinking might follow: In a crisis—any crisis—send in the peace army. Success is never guaranteed, but mass nonviolent interposition is more likely than armed resistance to resolve conflicts, reduce violence, and make future armed conflicts less likely.

War is not inevitable, stopping war is not impossible. It's a question of nonviolent organizing and training, and human imagination and will. Start early, start now, build a peace army, change the culture.

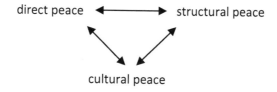

NOTES TO CHAPTER 7

---

[1] The "ruthless opponent" question is historically settled. The examples from Latin America and Europe have shown that nonviolence *can* oust a ruthless dictator. For discussion of the minimization of casualties against a ruthless opponent "in a tactical situation," see Robert Burrowes, *The Strategy of Nonviolent Defense: A Gandhian Approach* (State University of New York Press, 1996), 238-245. Still, the question of nonviolence versus Hitler is worth discussing, as "Hitler," in Western discourse, represents the personification of evil, the worst of the worst (though Germany's World War II foes—the British and US governments that directed the destruction of German and Japanese cities, and the Soviet forces that terrorized eastern Europe—also fit the model of "ruthless opponent").

[2] Christopher Browning, *Ordinary Men: Reserve Police Battalion 101 and the Final Solution in Poland* (HarperCollins, 1993).

[3] Ian Kershaw, *Hitler, the Germans, and the Final Solution* (Yale University Press, 2008), 237-238. There are other reasons. The reduction of Hitler and company to inexplicable "evil" can be used to argue that US participation in World War II— fighting against "evil"—was indisputably "good." It can also be used to characterize European Jews as unique and special among populations targeted for genocide, deserving greater memorialization than, say, Native Americans or East Timorese. The uniqueness of Jewish suffering in World War II is also used, by some, to excuse Israeli war crimes.

[4] Kershaw, *Hitler, the Germans, and the Final Solution*, 139-140.

[5] Kershaw, *Hitler, the Germans, and the Final Solution*, 173-182. Letter quoted on 179.

[6] Jacques Semelin, *Unarmed Against Hitler: Civilian Resistance in Europe, 1939-1943* (Praeger, 1993), 97-104.

[7] Peter Ackerman and Jack Duval, *A Force More Powerful: A Century of Nonviolent Conflict* (Palgrave, 2000), 236-238.

[8] Gene Sharp, *Waging Nonviolent Struggle: 20th Century Practice and 21st Century Potential* (Porter Sargent, 2005), 143-147. Quotes on 147.

[9] Sharp, *Waging Nonviolent Struggle*, 91-99; Ackerman and Duval, *A Force More Powerful*, 177-206.

[10] Kershaw, *Hitler, the Germans, and the Final Solution*, 151-196, esp. 183-185.

[11] Nationalistic thinking makes it easier to rise against bad government imposed from without (e.g., invasion) than to rise against bad government arriving internally through avenues perceived as legitimate (e.g., election). National politicians, to increase support, typically present themselves as heroic defenders against foreign threats.

[12] Ackerman and Duvall, *A Force More Powerful*, 207-231.

[13] Semelin, *Unarmed Against Hitler*, 50-54, 66-70; Sharp, *Waging Nonviolent Struggle*, 135-140.

[14] Quoted in Semelin, *Unarmed Against Hitler*, 69.

[15] B.H. Liddell Hart, "Lessons from Resistance Movements—Guerilla and Non-violent," in Adam Roberts, ed., *Civilian Resistance as a National Defense: Nonviolent Action against Aggression* (Stackpole Books, 1968), 195-211.

[16] Leo Goldberger, ed., *The Rescue of the Danish Jews: Moral Courage Under Stress* (New York University Press, 1987), 6-9; Emmy Werner, *A Conspiracy of Decency: The Rescue of the Danish Jews during World War II* (Westview Press, 2002); Bo Lidegaard, *Countrymen: The Untold Story of How Denmark's Jews Escaped the Nazis* (Alfred Knopf, 2013); Sofie Bak, *Nothing to Speak of: Wartime Experiences of the Danish Jews 1943-1945* (Museum Tusculanum Press, 2013).

[17] Semelin, *Unarmed Against Hitler*, 137-139, 151-154. In 1933, over 520,000 Jews, by religious definition, lived in Germany. Slightly over 300,000 emigrated to escape Nazi persecution, leaving approximately 214,000 within German borders on the eve of World War II. Of these, an estimated 160,000 to 180,000 were killed in the Holocaust. "German Jews During the Holocaust, 1939-1945," United States Holocaust Memorial Museum website, http://www.ushmm.org/wlc/en/article.php?ModuleId=10005469.

[18] Tzvetan Todorov, *The Fragility of Goodness: Why Bulgarian Jews Survived the Holocaust* (Princeton University Press, 2001), 3-13; Semelin, *Unarmed Against Hitler*, 129-160.

[19] Among Western opinion-makers, killing one's "own people" is typically considered a greater crime than the violent invasion of foreign lands, at least for the propaganda purposes of demonizing a foreign leader as a psychopath. Foreign invasion, for which Western leaders claim a monopoly, can be understood as well-intended, if misguided, "national defense."

[20] The AK-47 assault rifle went into production at the end of World War II. Portable nuclear weapons were first developed in the 1950s (but probably no longer exist).

[21] John Crossan and Jonathan Reed, *Excavating Jesus: Beneath the Stones, Behind the Texts* (Harper San Francisco, 2001), 143-146.

[22] Michael Nagler, *The Search for a Nonviolent Future: A Promise of Peace for Ourselves, Our Families, Our World* (Inner Ocean Publishing, 2004), 100-111, reprinted with permission of New World Library, www.newworldlibrary.com.

[23] Notice how this voluntary self-sacrifice creates a dynamic different from King Solomon's solution to a dispute between two claimant mothers, as described in the Biblical passage 1 Kings 3:16-28. When Solomon ordered the disputed baby sliced in half, the real mother relinquished her maternal claim in order to save the child. The wise king then concluded that she was, indeed, the mother, and ordered the child returned to her. A clever solution (and a tidy story), but if the real mother hadn't made the right move—hadn't resorted to dishonesty—would the king have proceeded with this terrible act of violence against a child? His death threat was not an act of compassion, but a test of nerves for the two women—who would blink first? Perhaps the king should have offered his own life instead.

[24] Patricia Treece, *A Man for Others: Maximilian Kolbe, Saint of Auschwitz, in the Words of Those Who Knew Him* (Harper and Row, 1982), 178, quoted in Nagler, *The Search for a Nonviolent Future*, 105.

[25] Anatol Chari and Timothy Braatz, *From Ghetto to Death Camp: A Memoir of Privilege and Luck* (Disproportionate Press, 2011), 48-49

[26] The German clergy generally resisted Nazi anti-Church measures, but only a few German ministers courageously spoke against anti-Jewish activity. Kershaw, *Hitler, the Germans, and the Final Solution*, 165-173.

[27] Philip Hallie, *Lest Innocent Blood Be Shed: The Story of the Village of Le Chambon and How Goodness Happened There* (Harper Perennial, 1994); Richard Unsworth, *A Portrait of Pacifists: Le Chambon, the Holocaust, and the Lives of André and Magda Trocmé* (Syracuse University Press, 2012).

[28] For example, German SS troops torched the southern French village of Oradour-sur-Glane, and shot and burned 642 villagers, almost the entire population, in 1944, supposedly in retaliation for armed resistance activity. Sarah Bennett Farmer, *Martyred Village: Commemorating the 1944 Massacre at Oradour-sur-Glane* (University of California Press, 1999), 18-28.

[29] Tim Carroll, "A Haven from Hitler," *Sunday Times Magazine* (London), June 4, 2006, accessed at http://www.chambon.org/chambon_sunday_times_mag_06-06-04.htm.

[30] Philip Hallie, *Lest Innocent Blood Be Shed*, 240-246. Quotes on 245.

[31] Hallie, *Lest Innocent Blood Be Shed*, 34-35.

[32] One verse of Guthrie's "This Land is Your Land" reads, "In the squares of the city, in the shadow of a steeple;/By the relief office I seen my people,/As they stood there hungry, I stood there asking,/Is this land made for you and me?" Guthrie, the son of a Ku Klux Kan member, married a Jewish woman and collaborated on songs with his Jewish mother-in-law. His famous refrain—"This land was made for you and me"—leaves *you* unspecified. Sung in public, to and with strangers, this is a very welcoming, tolerant, sharing, and antifascist line—though it does have an unfortunate Manifest Destiny ring to it.

[33] Albert Camus, *Resistance, Rebellion, and Death* (Modern Library, 1960), 5.

[34] Nagler, *The Search for a Nonviolent Future*, was originally entitled, *Is There No Other Way?* (Berkeley Hills Books, 2001).

[35] The US war on Iraq began in 1991, five months after the Iraqi army invaded Kuwait. The US military entered the fray from bases in Saudi Arabia, slaughtered fleeing Iraqi forces, and established military control over Iraqi airspace. Over the next decade, the US government enforced devastating economic sanctions on the Iraqi population and regularly bombed Iraqi military installations. The 2003 invasion was intended to complete the US takeover of the oil-rich country.

[36] For examples, see Liam Mahony, *Unarmed Bodyguards: International Accompaniment for the Protection of Human Rights* (Kumarian Press, 1997); Daniel Hunter and George Lakey, *Opening Space for Democracy: Third-Party Nonviolent Intervention Curriculum and Trainer's Manual* (CreateSpace Publishing, 2013); Burt Berlowe, *The Compassionate Rebel Revolution: Ordinary People Changing the World* (Mill City Press, 2011).

[37] Eknath Easwaran, *Nonviolent Soldier of Islam: Badshah Khan, A Man to Match His Mountains* (Nilgiri Press, 1999); Mukulika Banerjee, *The Pathan Unarmed: Opposition and Memory in the North West Frontier* (School of American Research Press, 2000).

[38] Thomas Weber, *Gandhi's Peace Army: The Shanti Sena and Unarmed Peacekeeping* (Syracuse University Press, 1996); "Shanti Sena (Indian Peace Brigade) Intervenes in Baroda Language Riots, 1965," *Global Nonviolent Action Database*, http://nvdatabase.swarthmore.edu/content/shanti-sena-indian-peace-brigade-intervenes-baroda-language-riots-1965. For the Shanthi Sena in Sri Lanka, see www.shantisena.org.

[39] The blue-helmeted UN soldiers, who often carry guns (thus reducing their

integrative power) yet aren't allowed to use them (thus reducing their threat power), should not be confused with a peace army of volunteers fully committed to nonviolence.

[40] Underlying and facilitating the acceptance of US pro-war propaganda was a deep layer of cultural violence: the veneration of military service, the desire for punishment of "sin" and defeat of "evil," and the devaluation of lives not perceived as white, Christian, and Western. From a US perspective, Hussein was an intolerable evil deserving a painful death; Iraqis were less "civilized" than Westerners, required salvation, and, if killed, were "faceless" collateral damage; and US soldiers were heroic, always well-meaning, and beyond criticism.

8

STUDENTS OF NONVIOLENCE

STUDENTS OF NONVIOLENCE

Starting Locally

To identify a starting point for the Civil Rights Movement in the United States is to court controversy. Was the beginning in 1942, in Chicago, when James Farmer and other members of the Fellowship of Reconciliation (FOR) organized the Congress of Racial Equality (CORE) to employ Gandhian principles and nonviolent action against racial segregation? CORE initiated the use of sit-ins to desegregate public accommodations, and, in 1947, sent black and white activists by bus on a two-week "Journey of Reconciliation" through the upper South, testing a Supreme Court ruling against segregation on interstate transportation. Was it in 1941, when A. Philip Randolph, head of the Brotherhood of Sleeping Car Porters, began planning a mass convergence on Washington, DC, to protest segregation in the armed forces and discriminatory hiring in war-related industries? With war on the near horizon, President Franklin Roosevelt wanted to avoid unrest in the nation's capital, so, to obviate the demonstration, signed an executive order banning the racist hiring practices—an act of concession, albeit partial and poorly enforced, that confirmed the political power of black citizens united in nonviolent protest.[1] Perhaps the start came in 1909, in New York City, when W.E.B. Du Bois, Ida Wells-Barnett, and other black activists joined white liberals in forming the NAACP to challenge segregation laws and lobby for federal anti-lynching legislation. Or perhaps we should look to an earlier century, to when Harriet Tubman, Frederick Douglass, and John Brown planted the seeds of black empowerment by recruiting black soldiers and promoting violent resistance to slavocracy.

In fact, the Civil Rights Movement had many starting points—that's what made it a movement. The founders of the NAACP, CORE, and the March on Washington Movement envisioned nationwide changes, but less ambitious beginnings, often spontaneous or accidental, were just as critical to the destruction of Jim Crow segregation. ("Jim Crow" is shorthand for, collectively, the racial discrimination laws and customs enforced by whites after the Civil War.) One of the more remarkable starting points occurred at R.R. Moton High School, in Farmville, Virginia, in 1951. A 16-year-old junior named Barbara Johns took the lead in organizing a student walkout to protest classroom conditions: poorly built, poorly heated, and overcrowded. NAACP lawyers tried to convince the students to end their strike—it was dangerous for blacks to challenge the status quo (status Crow) in Virginia, and illegal to boycott school. The jails can't hold all of us, argued the students. The lawyers believed the proper way to address institutionalized racial injustice was in court, and explained that the only legal recourse was to challenge the Supreme Court's doctrine of "separate but equal"—in other words, sue for complete integration, all the way to the top. Fine, said the Moton students, get us a lawsuit. They hadn't anticipated initiating a movement, they were simply demanding the new school long promised by white officials—if not for their own benefit, then for the students who came after them. But their lawsuit against Prince Edward County, bundled with four similar cases, eventually reached the Supreme Court as *Brown v. Board of Education of Topeka* (1954), which resulted in the high court repudiating "separate but equal" in education and ordering the desegregation of public schools—which led to another starting point.[2]

In Little Rock, Arkansas, in 1957, nine black students decided they would enroll at all-white Central High School. They knew they might face harassment, but someone had to go first. When eight of the nine tried to enter the school, in early September, not even a police escort could get them past a dangerous white mob and the Arkansas National Guard. The ninth student—15-year-old Elizabeth Eckford—was not informed of the plan that day. As she approached the school without escort, guardsmen with bayonets blocked her path. She sought a different entrance, then, finally comprehending the situation, retreated to a bus stop, trailed by whites shouting slurs and death threats. A photograph of the dramatic scene—a calm Eckford wearing a crisply pressed white dress, the features of her agitated tormentors animated by hate—appeared on the front page of the *New York Times*. Eckford, in her naïveté, had put human faces on the battle over school desegregation, and kept the Eisenhower administration from sidestepping the brewing constitutional crisis of state and local officials defying a Supreme Court order. On their second attempt, three weeks later, the nine students snuck in a side door while the infuriated mob out front battered four journalists. President Dwight Eisenhower, who had wanted to avoid the issue, now felt compelled to send US troops to occupy Central High. Under armed federal protection, the Little Rock Nine desegregated the school.

The best-known starting point, of course, is Rosa Parks refusing to give up her bus seat, in Montgomery, Alabama, in 1955. Parks was better prepared than Eckford for her moment—she was the local NAACP secretary and had recently participated in nonviolence training at the Highlander Folk School in Tennessee—but her noncooperation on the bus was spontaneous. The arrest of Parks put into motion a black boycott of Montgomery buses, and provided the NAACP, buoyed by their victory in *Brown*, with a court case to challenge busing segregation. The boycott financially damaged the bus company, but it was a Supreme Court decision that forced the Montgomery city council to repeal its law requiring segregation on local buses. Like the Moton students and Little Rock Nine, the Montgomery boycott organizers were not trying to start a nationwide movement, they were addressing a local problem. However, a young Montgomery minister named Martin Luther King Jr. was developing a broader vision, which he proclaimed the night before the boycott began.

> Right here in Montgomery, when the history books are written in the future, somebody will have to say, "There lived a race of people, a black people, 'fleecy locks and black complexion,' a people who had the moral courage to stand up for their rights. And thereby they injected a new meaning into the veins of history and of civilization." And we're going to do that. God grant that we will do it before it is too late.[3]

The boycott elevated King's powerful message of Christian righteousness and civil disobedience, and transformed him from a fledgling minister into a nationally prominent civil rights leader. (King's emergence in Montgomery is one reason Parks's arrest is considered so significant.) With other black ministers, he formed the Southern Christian Leadership Conference (SCLC) to advance the struggle for desegregation, which was facing a racist backlash. In the late 1950s, sit-ins desegregated a few stores and food establishments in Oklahoma, Missouri, and even Florida, but, across the South, whites continued to resist school desegregation, and blacks remained too intimidated to register to vote.

Then, on February 1, 1960, came another memorable starting point. In Greensboro, North Carolina, four college freshmen, former members of the NAACP Youth Council, talked each other into doing something about their frustration with whites-only facilities.[4] A Sunday night bull session became a Monday morning action: the four students seated themselves at a Woolworth's lunch counter in downtown Greensboro, and remained until closing time, waiting to be served. That night, they met with other students, agreed to remain strictly nonviolent, and planned a larger occupation of the downtown lunch counters. With the number of participants growing quickly—from twenty-seven on Tuesday to over three hundred on Friday— city officials tried negotiating and stalling, then began arresting students, which only garnered sympathy for the sit-ins. In support of the students, Greensboro blacks began boycotting downtown department stores, and, after a few months of declining profits, the store managers and city officials agreed to desegregate the lunch counters.

More sit-ins quickly followed—across North Carolina, and then around the South. CORE's occupation of the Jack Spratt diner, in Chicago in 1943, may have pioneered the use of sit-ins to desegregate public accommodations, but Greensboro proved a highly visible starting point because the situation had changed, conditions were right—and not simply by accident. The Little Rock drama had captured the attention of the national media, and reporters were now paying more attention to civil rights confrontations. News broadcasts and newspaper headlines spread the Greensboro story across the South, where a generation of college students was primed for activism. These students had been in elementary school when the Farmville kids walked out of Moton High, had become teenagers around the time of the *Brown* decision, and had expected their high schools to desegregate. Instead, they saw white officials resist federal law, often by shuttering public schools rather than integrating them. As college students, they watched as African nations gained independence from western European colonizers seemingly overnight, while US desegregation crept along, as King put it, "at horse and buggy pace."[5] Expectations raised then frustrated: a precondition for revolt. The courage of the Little Rock Nine inspired this generation of students, King's words instructed them, and a network of civil rights workers organized them. In the years since *Brown*, the NAACP, CORE, and SCLC had been recruiting southern blacks, training volunteers, and raising community awareness. When they heard about Greensboro, these activists contacted their connections in local organizations, church congregations, and black colleges, and encouraged them to seize the moment. In 1960, over seventy thousand people—mostly college students—participated in sit-ins, and by the end of 1961, businesses in nearly one hundred southern towns had desegregated their public facilities.[6]

From Farmville to Montgomery and Little Rock and Greensboro: there is a lesson here about beginnings. Trying to correct injustices in an entrenched political and economic system can be demoralizing. Problems seem so vast, one doesn't know where to start. High school and college students, especially, as their energy and optimism mix with growing social and political awareness, ask, "What can I do?" Most well-intended people who want to "make a difference" are not yet prepared to make big sacrifices, are unwilling or unable to adopt a lifestyle that actively rejects all forms of violence, are not ready for satyagraha. For many, the question is really, "What can I do *for a few hours on Saturday afternoon*?" Those people are important too—indeed, there are far more weekend warriors than fully committed activists—and the stories of Barbara Johns and Elizabeth Eckford and the Greensboro Four offer an instructive answer: find like-minded people, identify a *local* problem, and together, using nonviolent means, try to fix it. You might fail. You might succeed and be satisfied. You might succeed and inspire yourself and others to continue the work. In a rare instance, you might start a movement.[7]

Freedom Behind Bars

If Greensboro is remembered as the first, the sit-in campaign in Nashville, Tennessee, was probably the most important—in part because the Nashville Student Movement, of all the major direct action campaigns in the Civil Rights Movement, was the truest to Gandhian principles. The guiding figure in Nashville was a 32-year-old minister named James Lawson, who had learned from A.J. Muste (FOR) and James Farmer (CORE), and whose principled rejection of violence had already earned him fourteen months in federal prison. Lawson had refused to register with a military draft board, declined even to apply for conscientious objector status, student deferment, or ministerial exemption, choosing to suffer the penalty for civil disobedience rather than escape on a technicality. His time in prison didn't for a second stymie US war-making in Korea, perhaps had no immediately discernible social effect whatsoever, but it was a form of nonviolence training—developing fearlessness, strengthening personal integrity (Mohandas Gandhi called it "purifying")—and it helped prepare Lawson for work that eventually did contribute to historic changes. Following prison and college graduation, Lawson spent three years (1953-56) in India as a missionary and teacher, but also studying the Gandhian method.[8] Back in the United States, after King told him the movement desperately needed a Gandhian organizer in the South, Lawson moved to Nashville to enter the divinity program at Vanderbilt University and to serve as an FOR field secretary. In 1959, he began a workshop for college students, teaching nonviolent philosophy and strategy, and leading role-playing exercises, as the students carefully researched and planned for a campaign to desegregate downtown Nashville.

As a teacher, Lawson was more concerned with empowering students than promoting his own authority, and he encouraged other workshop participants to lead the Nashville Student Movement. After the Greensboro organizers requested actions of support, the Nashville student leaders agreed to speed up their schedule. Late on a Friday night, Lawson gave a crash course in nonviolent tactics to hundreds of new volunteers, and the next day over one hundred disciplined students—neatly dressed, polite, committed to nonviolence—sat silently in Woolworth's and other department stores, studying their schoolbooks, even after befuddled store employees closed down the lunch counters. Two weeks later, on the fourth sit-in day, white thugs attacked the sitting students, who were then promptly arrested—the students, not their attackers. But as police escorted the noncombative arrestees out the door, another squad of students quietly took their vacated seats, with more squads waiting in the wings. The students had been warned to expect trouble that day, but rather than stay home, they had dubbed it "Big Saturday" and faced it head on.[9]

Critics often accuse nonviolent activists like the Nashville students of intentionally and hypocritically provoking violence. Such critics insist that inherent contradictions (e.g., nonviolence needs violence) discredit the philosophy of nonviolence—a conclusion that conveniently justifies their own continued endorsement of violent conflict resolution. But this is something of a misunderstanding. Nonviolent action does not *cause* violence, it *exposes* violence. In most cases, the violence is already present, like the culture of racism, system of segregation, and environment of intimidation that persisted in Nashville. The demonstrators were *dramatizing* the violence, inviting it to show itself in a more recognizable form; cultural and structural violence might run deeper, but direct violence is more readily understood as violence. Put another way, the students were interrupting the smooth functioning of a violent system. Refusing to vacate a lunch counter or restaurant booth was direct nonviolent intervention, and a far more confrontational tactic than holding protest signs or withholding consumer dollars. The Moton students had walked *out*; the Montgomery boycotters had stayed *away* from the buses; the lunch counter activists were sitting *in*, putting their unwelcome bodies on the line, announcing they would not longer cooperate in their own oppression. No surprise, then, that the defenders of the status quo chose a violent response. The sit-in shattered the shiny façade of amiable segregation, and direct violence bubbled to the surface. The surprise—for the police officers, anyway—was that their crackdown didn't deter the students, it only increased support for the campaign. Lawson's insistence on nonviolent discipline and role rehearsals had prepared the students to effect moral jujitsu. Their respectable attire and polite demeanor made them difficult to characterize as criminal; their refusal to strike back delegitimized their assailant's choice of fists and paddy wagons; the sitters-in held the moral high ground. Had the students been rowdy and fought back with violence of their own, not only would they have perpetuated the cycle of violence they were trying to stop, but the newspapers, safe to say, would have reported that black youths were "rioting," and the students would have found little sympathy.

As the student leaders understood, there were other important participants in the conflict. Nashville blacks generally wanted to avoid trouble, had accommodated themselves to Jim Crow laws and customs, were partners in their own marginalization. They had chosen passivity and appeasement over active resistance. The students' profound humanity—willing to suffer to reduce suffering for others, unwilling to cause suffering, holding firmly to Truth—stirred moral consciences, reawakened local blacks to the repression they had internalized, and black shoppers began boycotting downtown stores. Some of the storeowners were prepared to serve black diners, but feared alienating white customers. Likewise, the mayor was trying to balance his sympathy for the students with his fear of a segregationist backlash. When the arrested students refused bail, even after it was lowered to five dollars, he ordered them freed anyway. When they refused to pay court-ordered fines and were sentenced to the county workhouse, he again had them released. The mayor was trying to defuse the situation while arranging for a compromise solution that would create lunch counters with a whites-only section and an all-comers section—a reasonable approach, perhaps, but the Nashville Student Movement rejected half-measures. Like Lawson facing the draft board a few years earlier, the students were practicing noncooperation with a violent system, and were not letting anyone off easily, not moderate whites and not themselves.[10]

Over seventy Nashville students were arrested on "Big Saturday," and they found that being placed behind bars didn't frighten or discourage them. Quite the opposite—they knew why they were there and what purpose it was serving. Incarceration has long been used by governments to intimidate or punish opposition voices, and fear of the isolation and brutality of imprisonment has certainly silenced many, but some individuals have found enlightenment and empowerment behind bars. Part of it is facing one's fear, part of it is realizing that one's mind can remain free, and part of it, at least for nonviolent resisters, is the emancipation one feels when no longer cooperating with a violent system. In 1943, antiwar activist Dave Dellinger discovered this paradox for himself. Locked up for World War II draft resistance, and thrown into isolation in "the Hole" for principled noncooperation with prison rules, Dellinger experienced a moment of euphoria, realizing that his jailers had taken everything from him and still they couldn't touch him. When he had nothing left to lose, they had nothing left to take, thus no threat power over him. "For the first time in my life," he later explained, "I had nothing, and for the first time in my life I had everything."[11] *Imprisonment brought freedom.* They could kill him, but they couldn't rule him. Dellinger's epiphany echoes Henry David Thoreau's account of spending a night in jail for refusing to pay poll taxes that financed both the US invasion of Mexico and the enforcement of slavery. Thoreau wrote that he "did not for a moment feel confined," and he "pitied" the state for being unaware of its inability to stop the one thing that was "dangerous"—his "meditations." He concluded, "The State never intentionally confronts a man's sense, intellectual or moral, but only his body, his senses. It is not armed with superior wit or honesty, but with superior physical strength. I was not born to be forced. I will breathe after my own fashion. Let us see who is the strongest."[12] Ralph Waldo Emerson supposedly visited Thoreau in jail and asked, "Henry, what are you doing in there?" Thoreau relied, "Waldo, the question is what are you doing out there?" Apocryphal but instructive: In a violent system, quiet acquiescence equates to tacit approval, while imprisonment for principled noncooperation is near to purity. As Dellinger put it, "I was in the right place at the right time with the right people."[13]

The experiences of the Nashville students behind bars were probably closer to Dellinger's joy than Thoreau's quiet contemplation, but neither of those two white, male New Englanders had squirmed under the boot of white supremacy. The students had found a way to stand up, face their fears, and challenge racist oppression without becoming violent, without becoming oppressors themselves. Also, they had strength in numbers, supported by their cellmates inside and the student organization on the outside. On the ride to jail, John Lewis, who had admonished his fellow students to "Remember the teachings of Jesus Christ, Mahatma Gandhi, and Martin Luther King," discovered his fear giving way to unprecedented exhilaration. Bernard Lafayette later recalled that the "kind of power we felt was more forceful than all of their police force…and all of their dogs or billy clubs or jails."[14] The students were activating what Gandhi called "soul force." Arresting the students not only empowered them, it did their work for them by expanding the nonviolent occupation to the jailhouse. Sitting behind bars, they were in no way cooperating with the unjust system, and actually were encumbering it by placing an added burden on jail and court personnel. Indeed, the police eventually asked the store managers to shut down the lunch counters on "Big Saturday" so they wouldn't have to arrest any more students.

Two months into the Nashville campaign, a bomb destroyed the house of the black lawyer who regularly defended the arrested students in court. If the bombing shook the city, two of Lawson's precepts also resonated: (1) a sharp, violent reprisal usually means nonviolence is having an effect and (2) never let violence stop the movement. In that spirit, the student leaders immediately organized a protest march. The bomb exploded at 5:30 A.M.; by noon, two thousand demonstrators had gathered. They walked in silence to the city courthouse, three and four abreast, led by Lafayette, Diane Nash, and C.T. Vivian, their numbers growing to three or four thousand—the largest civil rights demonstration the South had seen. A remarkable moment ensued. On the courthouse steps, in front of the crowd, and captured on newsreel, the eloquent and intellectual Vivian confronted the mayor and accused him of tolerating racist violence and arresting the wrong people. Vivian may have been correct, but his approach only made the congenial mayor defensive and argumentative, and a heated public debate did not serve the campaign's goal.

Then the 21-year-old Nash interrupted, eloquent in her own way, sweet-voiced and plainspoken, persistent but not aggressive. "Do you, Mr. Mayor, feel that it's wrong to discriminate against a person solely on the basis of his race or color?" The mayor agreed that it was wrong, and said he hoped for an end to segregation and bigotry. "Then, Mayor, do you recommend that the lunch counters be desegregated?" The mayor hesitated. He saw cameras and microphones pointed toward him, his political instincts said be careful. When Nash repeated the question, it seems her gentle and charming demeanor reached the mayor's heart, her forthright words appealed to his awakened moral conscience, and they overcame his calculating mind. "Yes," he replied, and, as the crowd cheered, he hugged the students around him.[15] The happiest politician is one who finally finds a reason to do the morally right thing, and Nash, by employing integrative power, had shown him the way out of cynicism. (Perhaps the city should be named for her.)

With the mayor having taken the first step, the downtown storeowners were now willing to abolish their discriminatory policies. The student leaders understood that this was a victory *with*, not *over*, the mayor and the merchants, and, their immediate goal accomplished, worked out a plan that quietly, gradually integrated the lunch counters with the hope of minimizing segregationist reprisals against the stores. A seemingly minor victory—a few lunch counters in one city—but a model for a growing movement: in near-perfect Gandhian fashion, the Nashville Student Movement's nonviolence had converted black bystanders into activists, won the cooperation of hesitant white moderates, and turned violent tactics into a liability when employed by their more recalcitrant opponents. It took more years of picketing and sit-ins, beatings and arrests, to desegregate Nashville theaters, restaurants, and hotels, one by one, but the tide was turning, the course was clear.[16]

Of course, the individuals most changed by nonviolent action are the active participants, and Nashville was the proving ground for Nash, Lafayette, Lewis, James Bevel, Marion Barry, and others who would spend many years in the Civil Rights Movement. That April, in Raleigh, North Carolina, college students from around the South met with representatives from CORE and SCLC. When the students formed their own organization—the Student Nonviolent Coordinating Committee (SNCC)—the leadership came largely from Nashville, ensuring a continued embrace of principled nonviolence. Their "Statement of Purpose" began, "We affirm the philosophical or religious ideal of nonviolence as the foundation of our purpose, the presupposition of our faith, the manner of our action."[17]

Interstate Satyagraha

As the movement spread farther south, the SNCC satyagrahis found many more opportunities to put their bodies on the line, to test their resolve, to bring nighttime terrorism into the light of day. The sit-in successes had been mostly in the Upper South, in places like Tennessee, Virginia, and North Carolina. The Deep South—primarily Georgia, Alabama, Mississippi— presented an even greater challenge: a thoroughly cowed black population, fewer white moderates willing to accept desegregation, and public policymaking and police forces dominated by callous bigots. Many whites in the region didn't have much by way of education and material wealth—in fact, may have inherited transgenerational trauma reaching back to violent conquest by Union forces in the Civil War—but at least they were superior to blacks, or so they told themselves, and they found the slightest notion of black equality profoundly threatening.[18] With such fragile self-esteem, and often living in close proximity to large populations of blacks, these "rednecks" were quick to employ terror to make sure blacks, too, shaped their psyches around an ideology of white supremacy. Simply put, southern bigots could be ruthless opponents to blacks who dared challenge Jim Crow segregation.

In spring 1961, CORE director James Farmer called for nonviolent intervention to expose southern resistance to desegregation of interstate transportation and to test the federal government's commitment to enforcing Supreme Court decisions on the matter.[19] CORE organizers prepared in Gandhian fashion—carefully selecting volunteers, holding training sessions, and announcing their intentions to the US government and to the Trailways and Greyhound bus companies. Just as Gandhi had led eighty satyagrahis on the Salt March to the sea to commit civil disobedience, CORE sent two small, interracial groups southbound by chartered bus, headed for New Orleans. In the first ten days of the Freedom Ride, local police arrested three of the thirteen participants for sitting in whites-only sections of bus terminals, and thugs in South Carolina beat up Nashville student John Lewis for entering the wrong waiting room. Then came Alabama. In Anniston, on May 14, a vicious mob led by Ku Klux Klan members chased down one bus, tossed in a firebomb, and pummeled the smoke-stricken passengers as they stumbled out. White goons boarded a second bus and beat one rider nearly to death.[20]

In Birmingham, after suffering more beatings, and unable to find a cooperative bus driver, the freedom riders ended their satyagraha and flew to New Orleans. A tragic trip, but not without accomplishment: the nonviolence of the riders had revealed to the newspaper-reading world the intensity of the conflict in the Deep South, the severity of the racist oppression, and had brought southern noncompliance to the attention of the otherwise indifferent US Justice Department.[21]

Meanwhile, in Nashville, Nash decided the Freedom Ride wasn't over: never let violence stop the movement. She quickly recruited sit-in veterans, got them to Birmingham despite police resistance, and, three days after the original riders flew out, twenty-one satyagrahis purchased bus tickets and resumed the trek.[22] As Nagler's "escalation of violence" graph predicts, the Deep South environment of deep dehumanization would require an equivalent degree of nonviolent sacrifice and patient suffering to de-escalate the conflict—it's too late to start early when the conflict (white oppression of blacks) goes back hundreds of years—and the Nashville reinforcements had a pretty clear idea of what they might encounter; they even wrote letters to be sent home if they didn't survive the trip. When the freedom riders arrived in Montgomery, an escort of police cars vanished, and another Klan-led mob attacked with bats, pipes, and bricks. Among the most brutally beaten were Lewis and a white student named James Zwerg.[23] As he faced his attackers, Zwerg felt a great sense of peace because, he later recalled, "I knew I was doing what I should be doing." It was, for him, "a wonderful religious experience," and, while he never considered himself a perfectly nonviolent person, "the strength of those people with me gave me strength beyond my own abilities."[24] Like when the Nashville students went to jail together, a triangle of mutual reinforcement was at work:

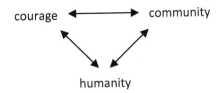

Seeing Zwerg pinned down and taking blows to the head, a local black man stepped in, inviting the rioters to beat him instead. Both Zwerg and the heroic, anonymous passerby were hospitalized. Zwerg sustained a broken back and other serious injuries, but told a television reporter, "We're willing to accept death, but we are going to keep coming until we can ride anywhere in the South."[25] The following night, several thousand armed and agitated whites surrounded a church where King and an estimated twelve hundred people were rallying in support of the riders. Directed by the Kennedy White House, federal marshals repulsed the attackers with tear gas and billy clubs until local policemen and Alabama National guardsmen with bayonets belatedly cleared the streets. Inside, King and other ministers urged the frightened congregants to remain nonviolent; outside it looked reminiscent of the Civil War.[26]

Still, the Freedom Ride wasn't over. More volunteers had arrived, including Nash and Lawson, and, four days after the bloody reception in Montgomery, twenty-seven freedom riders on two buses traveled the next leg. With them went almost as many reporters and a federal and state entourage—FBI, Border Patrol, National Guard, highway patrol—to maintain order, despite Lawson's insistence that riders didn't want armed protection. "We will accept the violence and hate," he told reporters, "absorb it without returning it." Arriving in Jackson, Mississippi, where police had kept a mob from gathering, the riders immediately violated whites-only rules in the bus terminal and were arrested. Like in Nashville, they refused bail and made it clear they wouldn't pay fines. They weren't going quietly, and more riders—over one thousand in the next three months, it turned out—were coming to join them. But the Hinds County prison farm and Parchman Penitentiary, where the first arrestees served their time, were a long way from the Nashville jail. Imprisoned freedom riders suffered oppressive conditions, psychological abuse, and physical torture. Some bailed out early, but most endured and came out steeled for nonviolent revolution. Behind bars, they buoyed themselves with sermons, movement songs like "Oh, Freedom" and "We Shall Overcome," and knowledge of what they were accomplishing.

Like the Little Rock Nine, the freedom riders had given the US president a choice he would have preferred to avoid: do his job as chief executive and enforce Supreme Court desegregation decisions or watch white mobs attack nonviolent black students. At King's suggestion, the Kennedy administration pressed the Interstate Commerce Commission (ICC) into action. Beginning on November 1, exactly six months after the first freedom riders had begun nonviolent training in Washington DC, the ICC required interstate carriers and terminals to post anti-segregation signs, and banned interstate buses from stopping at segregated facilities. Across the South, the buses and terminals and the airports and train stations began inching toward racial integration. The direct nonviolence of the movement was slowly undermining the direct violence of Jim Crow segregation. But, as Lawson understood, the structural and cultural violence were largely intact. "The sit-ins won concessions, not structural changes; the Freedom Rides won great concessions, but not real change," he wrote in 1961. Not enough freedom riders had gone to prison to make it a "jail-in" that seriously inconvenienced the state. Thousands of volunteers were needed, Lawson continued, "to establish work camps for training, study, reading, meditation, and constructive work in voting, repairing neighborhood slums, community centers…people who will be willing to go at a given moment and stay in jail indefinitely"—a call that echoed Gandhi's Constructive Programme and Ghaffar Khan's Khudai Khidmatgar troops. "Remember that the way to get this revolution off the ground is to forge the moral, spiritual and political pressure which the president, the nation, and the world cannot ignore….The only way is through a nonviolent army."[27]

Constructive Program

At the start of 1962, civil rights activists did not constitute a disciplined army. In bringing activists from Nashville, Atlanta, and northern cities to Birmingham, Montgomery, and Jackson, the Freedom Ride had produced a greater sense of a single, unified project, but the movement was still a collection of spirited organizers and disparate organizations that cooperated in campaigns, competed for volunteers and donations, and argued passionately about strategy and philosophy. If the importance of media presence made King the recognizable face and inspirational voice of the movement, the Gandhians of SNCC and CORE were the beating heart, yet even they had internal schisms. In particular, a debate developed over whether to follow up the Freedom Ride with additional direct action campaigns to expose Jim Crow violence and to season nonviolent activists, or with a voter registration drive to build black political power.

In fact, efforts to register black voters in the Deep South had already begun, with the notable contribution of two remarkable individuals. Septima Clark was born in South Carolina in 1898, her father had been a slave, but she eventually earned a degree from Columbia University and became a teacher. At the Highlander Folk School in the 1950s, Clark created a "citizenship school" that included intensive, week-long workshops that taught practical reading skills, explained basic civil rights, and encouraged resistance to Jim Crow.[28] Clark also recruited promising teachers, particularly women, to duplicate her program in their hometowns. In 1961, Clark and her niece, Bernice Robinson, relocated to Dorchester, Georgia, where, under the auspices of the SCLC's Citizen Education Program, they soon trained hundreds of women who started their own citizenship schools across the Deep South.[29]

Robert Moses, a Harvard graduate student, was, like Leo Tolstoy, influenced by Quaker pacifism and Eastern thought. He had little interest in movement politics or theatrics, but had a satyagrahi's fearlessness. In 1961, he traveled alone across the Deep South, recruiting volunteers for SNCC. The following summer, while imprisoned freedom riders were debating the next step, Moses was quietly leading night classes in McComb, Mississippi, preparing blacks for the daunting task of registering to vote in a region where whites, as a minority population, were particularly nervous about black enfranchisement. After Moses suffered a beating and dared to bring charges against his white assailant, more SNCC field secretaries arrived, expanded the classes, and canvassed door to door to recruit participants. Mississippi segregationists responded with tenant evictions, job dismissals, and other economic reprisals against local recruits, as well as arrests, beatings, torture, bombings, and murder. The terror wore down the organizers and intimidated the local population. The few blacks willing to risk life and livelihood to visit the courthouse registrar typically encountered bureaucratic obstruction, and, from 1961 through 1964, black voter enrollment increased only slightly in Mississippi. But, despite the almost constant harassment, a constructive program was underway. It didn't make big headlines, wasn't dominated by self-important clergymen. It was merely the dangerous, uncelebrated, grassroots work of empowering poor black citizens, raising their political awareness and expectations, teaching them to read and to stand up for their rights. Moses and Clark and the people they worked with, including Fannie Lou Hamer and Dorothy Cotton, were the movement's very soul.[30]

The citizenship teachers and field secretaries encouraged other nonviolent actions across the Deep South—for example, in McComb, where SNCC workers organized local sit-ins—but the Albany, Georgia, campaign, begun in late 1961 by SNCC organizers Charles Sherrod and Cordell Reagon, stands out for two reasons. First, in a pioneering attempt at a citywide mobilization, it combined many key elements of earlier campaigns, including student recruitment and nonviolent training, voter registration workshops, a local bus boycott, downtown sit-ins and kneel-ins, freedom riders arriving from out of town, jailed demonstrators refusing bail, cautious adults drawn in by the courage of students and inspired by song-filled church meetings, and high-profile visits from ministers King and Ralph Abernathy representing the SCLC. Second, the local police chief studied the Montgomery boycott and the Freedom Ride, and formulated a plan to thwart nonviolent direct action and to forestall Supreme Court desegregation rulings and federal intervention. Understanding that overt violence was counterproductive, the chief closely watched white troublemakers to prevent mob violence, and instructed his officers to refrain from brutality. After a police officer beat a prominent black woman, causing her to miscarry, a large protest march turned violent. Policemen may have instigated the fighting, but they withdrew rather than strike back when angry blacks started throwing bricks and bottles. The chief also directed that civil rights demonstrators be arrested for disrupting the peace and disobeying police orders, not for violation of potentially unconstitutional segregation ordinances. To make mass arrests an effective tool rather than an impediment, he borrowed cell space from surrounding counties. Hundreds of Albany demonstrators went to jail, and many refused to bail out, but never enough to disrupt city operations. When King and Abernathy opted for prison time rather than pay fines, the police chief secretly arranged their release to deter national media scrutiny.[31]

A nonviolent army did not materialize in Albany, and the police plan worked: no scandalous, front-page photos of bloodied protestors, no federal troops securing downtown streets, no broadening of federal integration policy. In Nashville lunch counters and Alabama bus terminals, direct nonviolence had exposed direct violence and won sympathy for the movement. In Albany, the police strategy, essentially, was to minimize direct violence and, instead, allow structural violence to wear down the desegregation campaign. Gandhian resistance to structural violence includes the development of self-reliance, but most southern blacks were financially dependent on white employers, bankers, and landlords. As long as blacks feared losing what little they possessed, whites had power over them. Challenging Jim Crow usually meant going to jail, and for blacks with families to support and mortgages to pay, jail time was a great risk—even without police brutality. They couldn't afford to pay fines, and if they stayed behind bars they might lose their jobs, see the foreclosure of their houses, their cars repossessed. Furthermore, all the policemen, judges, and jury members were whites steeped in the ideology of white supremacy; even if well intended, they couldn't help but see blacks as inferior, dangerous, and, therefore, guilty. Structural and cultural violence: the system had blacks pinned down and could outlast them, as organizers in Albany soon learned. White leaders delayed, negotiated, promised concessions, and quickly reneged as the local campaign lost momentum for lack of volunteers willing to go to jail. City officials closed rather than desegregate the public parks, and removed the chairs from the "integrated" library to prevent integrated seating. Downtown businesses and schools remained segregated. King left town after being tossed *out* of jail, and the national media departed with him.[32]

General accounts of the Civil Rights Movement tend to depict the Albany Movement as a failed effort marred by internal conflicts. Jealous NAACP leaders tried to undermine SNCC organizing, SNCC members resented the SCLC's sudden entrances and exits, and local leaders were unprepared for such a broad campaign. Movement activists were indeed divided, and the numerous acts of civil disobedience in Albany, while holding to nonviolent principles, lacked the careful strategizing that Lawson had overseen in Nashville. But to note only failure is to take the short view. In Albany, SNCC organizers gained more experience and understanding of the challenges they faced, and they continued the grassroots organizing in the region long after the SCLC and the media had turned their attention elsewhere. SNCC workers also founded the Freedom Singers, a choral group that became, like King, an inspirational voice for the movement. King, too, learned valuable lessons—about his weighty role as spokesperson, charismatic leader, and media magnet. If nothing else, he now realized the importance of balancing and coordinating the strengths of the different organizations: SNCC direct action and ground-level organizing, NAACP lawsuits, SCLC fundraising and access to federal officials.

As usual, the most important development was how nonviolent action changed the nonviolent actors. Gandhi considered the Salt Satyagraha and other nonviolent campaigns to be exercises in purification, developing fearlessness, self-reliance, and self-respect—changing Indians, not the British. The Salt Satyagraha wasn't the end of British rule, but it awakened millions of Indians into active rejection of British rule. Likewise the civil rights campaigns in the United States. Short-term failures notwithstanding, events in Albany awakened and empowered a black community otherwise resigned to life under Jim Crow. The Albany Movement president called the campaign "an overwhelming success, in that there was a change in the attitude of the people involved. They had [decided] that they would never accept that segregated society as it was anymore."[33] As the song went, "Ain't gonna let nobody gonna turn me 'round." Bernice Johnson, the original Freedom Singer, experienced that change while leading a song after her first stint in jail. She later realized, "I'd never heard that voice before. I had never been that me before. And once I became that me, I have never let that me go." Blacks had been afraid to challenge segregation, they feared jail and lynching, but freedom songs gave them courage, gave them a way to express themselves. The act of full-throated singing takes the singer's focus away from the thinking mind and into the present moment, where there is little room for fear of what will happen next. There is remarkable integrative power in uninhibited group song; the hearts of a choir literally beat as one.[34] Johnson later explained,

> Albany settled the issue of jail and I think songs helped do that....Sometimes [the police] would plead and say, "Please stop singing." And you would know that your word is being heard. There was a real sense of platformness and clearly empowerment, and it was like just saying, "Put me in jail, that's not an issue of power. My freedom has nothing to do with putting me in jail." And so there was this joy.

For Johnson, "Discussion about whether it was a failure or success...that was not central." Her experience in the Albany Movement was empowerment.

> There was a sense of confronting things that terrified you, like jail, the police, walking in the street—you know, a whole lot of black folks couldn't even walk in the street in those places in the South. So you were saying in some basic way, "I will never again stay inside these boundaries." The Civil Rights Movement gave me the power to challenge *any* line that limits me.[35]

Violence stifles self-realization; nonviolence opens individuals to their full human potential.[36]

A Marvelous Chapter

In 1963, the SCLC ministers turned their attention to Birmingham, over forty percent black and, according to King, "by far the worst big city in race relations in the United States."[37] Wyatt Walker formulated a broad strategy: sit-ins and mass meetings to raise awareness and inspire courage, a boycott of downtown businesses to pressure influential merchants, and mass marches to fill the jails and disrupt civic operations. The hope was that the inconvenience to the business community and the law enforcement system, and the threat of federal intervention, would convince city leaders to accept integration of schools, businesses, and public accommodations in general. Unlike the Nashville Student Movement, which used college students to target individual businesses, this would be a citywide mobilization against citywide segregation—like in Albany, only with better planning and greater unity. The Albany police chief advised restraint to Birmingham officials, but Walker expected the local police commissioner, Eugene "Bull" Connor, a mean and desperate man, to order a violent crackdown on demonstrators, which could bring on the jujitsu effect, provided the campaign had enough volunteers to absorb his hatred and fill his jails. There was also the likelihood of Klan violence. "If it comes," King said, "we will surface it for the world to see," but he predicted that some of the organizers "will not come back alive from this campaign."[38]

Birmingham is today remembered as the most spectacular triumph of the Civil Rights Movement, but in the first month, the campaign appeared doomed for lack of volunteers. Bail money was running out, and a court injunction made public demonstrations a serious offense, so getting arrested could mean months behind bars and all the attendant financial problems. Frustrated and unsure of himself, King took a Gandhian step—"a faith act," he called it. "I have to go," he told his demoralized colleagues, "I am going to march if I have to march by myself."[39] King may have hoped to lead by example, but only Abernathy and forty volunteers followed him to jail on April 12. The SCLC leadership—typically ministers from large urban congregations—were accustomed to being in charge. SNCC field secretaries knocked on doors, met dirt-poor sharecroppers, recruited students; SCLC ministers expected the people to come to them. King, though, was learning that true movements begin with local organizing and that a high-profile, inspirational spokesperson is not necessarily in charge.[40] In fact, he was becoming fond of quoting Gandhi: "There go my people. I must catch them, for I am their leader."[41] King had gone to India, in 1959, to study the Gandhian method, but it may have been at this moment—Good Friday in Birmingham—that King, who had declined to join the 1961 Freedom Ride, consciously decided to put his own well-being on the line.

Before going to jail, King contacted James Bevel, a young Mississippi preacher who had participated in the Nashville sit-in campaign and the Freedom Ride, had married Diane Nash, and was back in his home state as a SNCC field secretary. Bevel was a brilliant and creative sermonizer, at times outrageous and obnoxious—exactly, it turned out, what Birmingham needed. Upon arriving, he took the pulpit and lit up a mass meeting: "Some Negroes don't want to get well. If they do, they would have to compete with the white man. There are some Negroes who want segregation as much as Bull Connor." Bevel was criticizing blacks who had grown complacent in mid-life, middle-class comfort, big fish in a small, fetid pond. "The Negro has been sitting here dead for three hundred years. It's time he got up and walked." He scolded the SCLC for staging media events rather than empowering the black community. "You guys are running a scam movement," he said. "A movement is when people actually do it out of conviction."[42] Bevel was, in essence, making a distinction between Walker's plan for strategic nonviolence and the principled nonviolence of SNCC field secretaries and freedom riders. Lawson, who King later acknowledged as "the leading theorist and strategist of nonviolence in the world," had been doing his part in Birmingham, training adults to commit civil disobedience and go to jail, and had coaxed pledges from several hundred. Bevel and Nash set about organizing the school children, and enlisted thousands.[43] They encouraged high school sports stars and beauty queens to start a "whisper campaign," and asked local disc jockeys to spread the word. In after-school rallies, Bevel exhorted and educated, showed a film about the Nashville campaign, and even took students to a graveyard to tell them, "In forty years you're going to be here. Now, what are you going to do while you are alive?"[44] Some of the SCLC ministers were concerned that using children would backfire—kids would get hurt, organizers would appear irresponsible and cowardly and be charged with contributing to delinquency of minors—but Bevel was undeterred. "King told me to fill the jails," Bevel later recalled, "but *how* I filled the jails was *my* business." The adults had economic concerns and decades of submission to overcome. The children felt less restraint, and as for getting hurt, one later explained, "We were born black in Alabama—we were already hurt."[45]

The story has been told elsewhere, but not often enough. On May 2, Bevel sent children, in squads of fifty, marching out of the Sixteenth Street Baptist Church, next to Kelly Ingram Park in the black part of downtown. The youngsters were heading for city hall, but the police didn't let them get that far. Six hundred children, most younger than sixteen, went to jail for demonstrating illegally. They had ditched school and walked long miles to the church just to get arrested. On May 3 and 4, with singing children packed into jail cells and hundreds more ready to go, the angry commissioner ordered his men to limit arrests and, instead, use German shepherds and high-powered fire hoses to clear the park and surrounding streets. Undisciplined spectators fought back with bricks and bottles, but the world only saw newspaper and television images of neatly dressed children blasted by water and bitten by police dogs. As SCLC leaders had hoped, the jujitsu effect brought sympathy and moral and financial support. SNCC and CORE members arrived, as did famous entertainers and veteran activists, including Dave Dellinger.[46]

In response to the violence of black bystanders, Bevel called for a day off, on Sunday, May 5, to purify the campaign and to rest his troops. But, at a mass meeting that night, he spontaneously dispatched a column of two thousand marchers, led by a local minister named Charles Billups, toward the city jail in support of the young prisoners. This time it was Birmingham adults, shamed and inspired by the children, who faced the fire hoses. The marchers knelt on the pavement and prayed, then Billups stood up and addressed the policemen and firemen, "We haven't done anything wrong. All we want is our freedom. How do you feel doing these things?" With tears in his eyes, he began a chant, "Turn on your water! Turn loose your dogs! We will stand here till we die."[47] The police commissioner, who had rushed to the scene, twice ordered firemen to blast the marchers. The firemen refused. Ever the strategist, Walker quickly negotiated an agreement with the police: the marchers went to pray in a normally segregated park rather than proceed to the jail. It was a compromise, but also a victory. The marchers had faced their fears, stood up to the police, and saw integrative power at work—the firemen couldn't bring themselves to harm nonviolent Christians who prayed for their opponents and who were demonstrating their willingness to absorb hatred. The commissioner had ceded the park because, like a dictator whose security forces won't fire, his threat power was shrinking before his eyes.

The next day, May 6, children marched in even greater numbers, and the police reverted to making mass arrests. Student leaders had distributed flyers that read, "Fight for freedom first, then go to school," and "It's up to you to free our teachers, our parents, yourself, and our country."[48] Kids wore bathing suits for the fire hoses, and carried toothbrushes for jail. Some had already been bailed out once and were going back in. Getting arrested had been, in Walker's words, "transformed into a badge of honor."[49] At least one police officer realized the implication: "There was no way to keep a lid on this. The fear was gone." The jails were beyond full, children were being held in animal stalls at the fairgrounds—some three thousand demonstrators were incarcerated—and, that night, five to ten thousand people packed four churches. King made the rounds, reminding the congregants to stay nonviolent. "Don't worry about your children," he said, "they are doing work for all men and for all mankind."[50] The SCLC's strategy was finally working. The jails were overflowing, and hundreds more volunteers were ready to march; whites were avoiding downtown, unwittingly contributing to the boycott of segregated stores; and white city leaders were grudgingly negotiating a truce. Once frustrated with the reticence of Birmingham adults, King was now optimistic, telling them, "You will make it possible for the historians of the future to write a marvelous chapter. Never in the history of this nation have so many people been arrested for the cause of freedom and human dignity."[51] On May 7, to squeeze the merchants further, campaign organizers sent six hundred picketers and sitters-in to downtown businesses, and their protests drew three times as many black spectators. The police didn't want to make any more arrests, didn't want to use tear gas in the business district, and the fire hoses and dogs were busy battling the brick-throwers back at Kelly Ingram Park. Nonviolent black demonstrators had neutralized the police, taken over downtown, and white leaders soon agreed to gradual desegregation of schools and public accommodations.

Freeing the Oppressor

Birmingham remained, for the moment, a brutal, segregated city—white resistance resumed after the marches stopped, city officials violated their agreements, terrorists bombed blacks homes and churches. But the "Children's March" remade the movement. The initial capitulation by white leaders in Birmingham reinvigorated movement activists after frustrations in Mississippi and Albany; if black children could stand up to "Bombingham," Jim Crow would soon be finished. Images of schoolchildren facing police dogs and fire hoses awakened the country and the world to the violent nature of white rule in the South, and brought greater support for the movement. With blacks across the country standing up to Jim Crow—over 750 demonstrations and close to 15,000 arrests in 186 cities in the ensuing ten weeks alone—President John Kennedy went on national television to denounce racial discrimination and to announce that he was submitting a civil rights bill to Congress.[52] Birmingham changed the movement, and the movement changed the country. The movement's first great achievement was the awakening and empowerment of blacks, particularly in the South, including the very poor. Farmer called it "a spiritual emancipation." Walker said, "We threw off the slave mentality."[53] The second great achievement was the end of Jim Crow through nonviolent protest and intervention. Birmingham led to the transformative Civil Rights Act of 1964, which included, among other things, a ban on public segregation and discriminatory hiring practices—the first of several major federal civil rights bills passed in the decade.

The third great achievement was the radicalization and mobilization of other marginalized groups. In the late 1960s, even as the Civil Rights Movement was waning, the challenge to the political status quo was broadening. Northerners worked with SNCC and CORE in the South, then went home and helped create the women's rights movement and Students for a Democratic Society, and became leaders in the antiwar movement. The mobilization of Chicanos began as a labor action in the grape fields of central California, but Dolores Huerta, Cesar Chavez, and other organizers adopted the philosophy of nonviolence, employed boycotts and marches, and sparked a civil rights movement for Latinos. The American Indian Movement, though not nonviolent, held dramatic sit-ins and staged their own march on Washington, which they called "The Trail of Broken Treaties." A gay rights movement also emerged. In India, Gandhi had mobilized a majority population against rule by a tiny minority occupier. The Civil Rights Movement awakened minority groups in the United States, and taught them how to use nonviolent resistance against majority oppressors—a lesson for the world at a time when violent uprising, as espoused by Che Guevara and other celebrated revolutionaries, was in vogue. The Civil Rights Movement put direct nonviolent action on television screens just as television was becoming the dominant media, and, in melding Gandhian nonviolence with Judeo-Christian theology, made tolerance and inclusion the professed cultural ideal in the West. The movement was, as Lawson described it, "a moment in history when God saw fit to call America back from the depths of moral depravity and onto his path of righteousness."[54] The CIA had recently directed violent coups in Iran, Guatemala, and the Congo, and a hostile invasion of Cuba, and the US military was perpetrating mass murder across much of southeast Asia, yet the post-1950 United States was also where civil rights activists were fulfilling Gandhi's speculation that "It may be through the Negroes that the unadulterated message of nonviolence will be delivered to the world."[55] As the poet sang, "It's coming to America first, the cradle of the best and of the worst."[56] If the worst included US airborne terror inflicted on Vietnamese farm families, the best was the children of Birmingham becoming their own song, words made flesh: "I ain't scared of your jail 'cause I want my freedom now."

Jim Crow segregation was, at root, a cycle of fear. Southern blacks feared white violence—they had for centuries—and southern whites feared blacks might lose their fear. Like slave owners before them, segregationists had a deep, unexamined dread of blacks taking revenge. Whites had constructed a system of oppressors and oppressed, and could only imagine a perpetuation of status quo Crow or a role reversal, with blacks becoming the oppressors; the bigots couldn't imagine racial harmony.[57] One could argue that vengeance against southern whites would be well deserved. One could also point to the lack of retribution by former slaves after emancipation and conclude that the white fear was irrational. But if the goal is nonviolent conflict resolution—in this case, dismantling the oppressors-oppressed structure—one must lay aside the prideful desire for revenge and acknowledge and address the fears of all concerned.[58] The principled nonviolence of civil rights activists offered a way out of the cycle of fear by cultivating courage among the oppressed and by expressing Christian love for the oppressors. Nonviolent activists who welcomed arrest and sang freedom songs in jail, and who refused to use violence against their attackers, were demonstrating that they would no longer cooperate in their own oppression, yet had no desire to become oppressors. King understood this:

> Our aim must never be to defeat or humiliate the white man but to win his friendship and understanding. We must come to see that the end we seek is a society at peace with itself, a society that can live with its conscience. That will be a day not of the white man, not of the black man. That will be the day of man *as* man.[59]

In other words, a rehumanized society.

Oppressors and oppressed are caught in a bad relationship, both are dependent rather than independent, both are fearful, but, counterintuitive to traditional views of power and justice, *the oppressed have the better chance of emancipating both parties.* It may appear that the oppressed have the motivation but not the power (except through self-elimination) to end an oppressors-oppressed relationship, and the oppressors have the power but not the motivation—a seeming dilemma for those pursuing harmonious relations. Yet this is only true where the type of power under consideration is exchange and threat power. When the oppressed discover integrative power, when they learn to appeal to the shared humanity of all concerned—oppressors, oppressed, bystanders—they can combine method with motivation to change the relationship, to dismantle the exploitative relationship. (Which is more likely—the oppressed discovering their nonviolent power or the oppressors tiring of privilege? Here's a clue: The organizers of protest movements in the United States learned the power of direct nonviolence from the actions of southern black kids, not from the distinguished mouths of white professors, advertising executives, and elected officials.) King understood that southern officials were "imprisoned by their own lies. It is history's wry paradox that when Negroes win their struggle to be free, those who have held them down will themselves be freed for the first time."[60]

A wry paradox indeed: Only the oppressed masses can save us. That may be terribly unfair, a tremendous weight for the already burdened, more suffering required of the already pained, but, physical peril notwithstanding, the personal and societal rewards are unmatched. Even as they patiently dismantled Jim Crow, even as they risked death and suffered beatings and confinement to remake US society for the better—more tolerant, just, vibrant, creative, humane—even as they did a job for all humankind, John Lewis experienced joy, Jim Zwerg felt great peace, Bernice Johnson found her voice, the children of Birmingham set themselves free. Blessed are the meek.

NOTES TO CHAPTER 8

[1] Farmer was introduced to Gandhian ideas by Howard Thurman, who had traveled to India to meet Mohandas Gandhi. CORE founders embraced the nonviolent strategies described by Krishnalal Shridharani in *War Without Violence: A Study of Gandhi's Method and Its Accomplishments* (Harcourt Brace, 1939). Shridharani had been one of Gandhi's satyagrahis in the Salt March. James Farmer, *Lay Bare the Heart: An Autobiography of the Civil Rights Movement,* (Texas Christian University Press, 1998), 101-116; August Meier and Elliott Rudwick, *CORE: A Study in the Civil Rights Movement, 1942-1968* (Oxford University Press, 1973).

[2] Jill Titus, *Brown's Battleground: Students, Segregationists, and the Struggle for Justice in Prince Edward County, Virginia* (University of North Carolina Press, 2011), 1-8; Lynne Olson, *Freedom's Daughters: The Unsung Heroines of the Civil Rights Movement from 1830 to 1970* (Scribner, 2001), 79-82; Taylor Branch, *Parting the Waters: America in the King Years, 1954-63* (Simon & Schuster, 1988), 19-21.

[3] King, "Address to the first Montgomery Improvement Association mass meeting," Holt Street Baptist Church, Montgomery, Dec. 5, 1955, in Clayborne Carson, et al., eds., *The Eyes on the Prize Civil Rights Reader* (Penguin, 1991), 50-51.

[4] The Greensboro Four were Joseph McNeill, Ezell Blair Jr., Franklin McCain, and David Richmond.

[5] Martin Luther King Jr., "Letter from Birmingham City Jail," Apr. 16, 1963.

[6] Harvard Sitkoff, *The Struggle for Black Equality, 1954-1992* (Hill & Wang, 1993), 61-82; John Lewis, *Walking with the Wind: A Memoir of the Movement* (Simon & Schuster, 1998), 55-58.

[7] Margaret Mead (supposedly) said it best: "Never doubt that a small group of thoughtful, committed citizens can change the world. Indeed, it is the only thing that ever has."

[8] Lawson's time in India, and King's visit there in 1959, were part of a bigger story of international cooperation. Blacks in the United States watched with interest as Gandhi experimented with nonviolence to liberate brown-skinned people from exploitation and repression by racist white governments. Civil rights organizations sent representatives to study Gandhi's movement in India, and invited Gandhian advocates to visit North America. Sudarshan Kapur, *Raising Up a Prophet: The African-American Encounter with Gandhi* (Beacon Press, 1992).

[9] Peter Ackerman and Jack Duvall, *A Force More Powerful: A Century of*

Nonviolent Conflict (Palgrave, 2000), 306-322; Branch, *Parting the Waters*, 274, 278-283; Lewis, *Walking with the Wind*, 93-108

[10] Lewis, *Walking with the Wind*, 108-113.

[11] David Dellinger, *From Yale to Jail: The Life Story of a Moral Dissenter* (Pantheon, 1993), 82-96. Quote on 86.

[12] Henry David Thoreau, "Civil Disobedience," 1849, 2:13-14.

[13] Dellinger, *From Yale to Jail*, 65.

[14] Ackerman and Duvall, *A Force More Powerful*, 321-322; Branch, *Parting the Waters*, 279-80; Lewis, *Walking with the Wind*, 106-108.

[15] Olson, *Freedom's Daughters*, 151-160; Branch, *Parting the Waters*, 295.

[16] Ackerman and Duvall, *A Force More Powerful*, 323-38; Branch, *Parting the Waters*, 279-280; Lewis, *Walking with the Wind*, 115-117.

[17] "We affirm the philosophical or religious ideal of nonviolence as the foundation of our purpose, the presupposition of our faith, and the manner of our action. Nonviolence as it grows from the Judaeo-Christian tradition seeks a social order of justice permeated by love. Integration of human endeavor represents the crucial first step towards such a society.

Through nonviolence, courage displaces fear; love transforms hate. Acceptance dissipates prejudice; hope ends despair. Peace dominates war; faith reconciles doubt. Mutual regard cancels enmity. Justice for all overcomes injustice. The redemptive community supersedes systems of gross social immorality. Love is the central motif of nonviolence.

Love is the force by which God binds man to himself and man to man. Such love goes to the extreme; it remains loving and forgiving even in the midst of hostility. It matches the capacity of evil to inflict suffering with an even more enduring capacity to absorb evil, all the while persisting in love.

By appealing to conscience and standing on the moral nature of human existence, nonviolence nurtures the atmosphere in which reconciliation and justice become actual possibilities." Student Nonviolent Coordinating Committee, "Statement of Purpose," revised 1962, in Staughton Lynd and Alice Lynd, eds., *Nonviolence in America: A Documentary History* (Orbis Books, 1995), 222.

[18] Ending slavery through massive slaughter, rather than through nonviolent conflict resolution, guaranteed an intensification of southern white resentment, hatred, and fear. Whites mourning the loss of slavocracy may not merit pity, but if the goal is improvement of racial relations and reduction of violence, they must be understood as participants in the conflict with the legitimate need for inclusion;

their basic needs must also be addressed.

[19] In 1946, in *Morgan v. Virginia*, the US Supreme Court ruled segregation on interstate buses unconstitutional and, thus, illegal. The following year, CORE and FOR sponsored a "Journey of Reconciliation" bus ride to test this ruling. Bayard Rustin led a group of eight black and eight white riders into the Upper South. Some of the riders were arrested and imprisoned, but this very first "freedom ride" received little media attention. In *Boynton v. Virginia* (1960), the court extended the desegregation ruling to include bus station facilities—washrooms, waiting rooms, lunch counters, drinking fountains, ticket windows, and the like—inspiring the 1961 Freedom Ride.

[20] Dr. Walter Bergman, a 61-year-old professor, World War II veteran of the Normandy landing, and long-time social activist, survived cruel beatings in Anniston and Birmingham, but suffered a stroke and permanent brain damage, and lost the ability to walk. His wife, Frances, was also a freedom rider. Douglas Martin, "Walter Bergman, Champion of Civil Liberties, Dies at 100," *New York Times*, Oct. 10, 1999.

[21] Raymond Arsenault, *Freedom Riders: 1961 and the Struggle for Racial Justice* (Oxford University Press, 2007); Branch, *Parting the Waters*, 412-427; Sitkoff, *The Struggle for Black Equality*, 88-93. James Farmer had been called away from the ride for his father's funeral, and John Lewis had temporarily left to meet with the American Friends Service Committee regarding a possible grant to study the Gandhian method in India, like Lawson before him. The reinvigorated Freedom Ride inspired Lewis to stay in the United States and work with the movement.

[22] For Nash's role in Freedom Ride, see Olson, *Freedom's Daughters*, 182-194.

[23] Lewis, *Walking with the Wind*, 147-161. Lewis rejoined the ride in Birmingham with the Nashville reinforcements, which included Zwerg, a white exchange student at Fisk University.

[24] "Interview with Jim Zwerg, Civil Rights Activist, United States," http://www.pbs.org/wgbh/peoplescentury/ episodes/skindeep/zwergtranscript.html.

[25] Sitkoff, *The Struggle for Black Equality*, 94-95; Ann Bausum, "James Zwerg Recalls His Freedom Ride," *Beloit Magazine* (Winter-Spring 1989), http://www.beloit.edu/archives/documents/archival_documents/james_zwerg_free dom_ride/; John Blake, *Children of the Movement* (Lawrence Hill Books, 2004), 25-36.

[26] Branch, *Parting the Waters*, 454-468.

[27] Lawson, "Eve of Nonviolent Revolution," *Southern Patriot* (Nov. 1961), quoted

in Carson, et al., *The Eyes on the Prize Civil Rights Reader*, 131-132. Just as Gandhi had predicted that total noncooperation with British rule would bring Indian independence in year's time, Lawson asserted that "in the next twelve months if we had such an army ready…the Deep South would begin to realize that…the moment of truth was not far off."

[28] The Highlander Folk School in Monteagle, Tennessee, not far from Alabama and Georgia, was founded in 1932 by Myles Horton, who had studied Social Gospel at Union Theological Seminary, as did Dave Dellinger and André Trocmé. Highlander was similar to Trocmé's school in Le Chambon and Gandhi's ashrams in that it was building an alternative, nonviolent society in the midst of an extremely violent one.

[29] Katherine Charron, *Freedom's Teacher: The Life of Septima Clark* (University of North Carolina Press, 2009); Septima Clark, *Ready From Within: Septima Clark & The Civil Rights Movement* (Africa World Press, 1990); Branch, *Parting the Waters*, 263-263, 381-382, 575-578.

[30] Branch, *Parting the Waters*, 325-331; Sitkoff, *The Struggle for Black Equality*, 104-114; Olson, *Freedom's Daughters*, 212-224.

[31] For the Albany Movement, see Branch, *Parting the Waters*, 524-560, 601-607.

[32] Branch, *Parting the Waters*, 524-557.

[33] Quoted in Juan Williams, *Eyes on the Prize: America's Civil Rights Years, 1954-1965* (Viking Penguin, 1987), 178.

[34] Björn Vickhoff, et al., "Music Structure Determines Heart Rate Variability of Singers," *Frontiers in Neuroscience* 4:334 (July 9, 2013), http://www.frontiersin.org/Journal/10.3389/fpsyg.2013.00334/full#h4.

[35] Carson, et al., *The Eyes on the Prize Civil Rights Reader*, 144-145; Olson, *Freedom's Daughter*, 232-238.

[36] Dr. Bernice Johnson Reagon's remarkable career as a performer, composer, teacher, and scholar is irrefutable evidence of the empowering dynamic of nonviolence that allowed her to discover her voice.

[37] Quoted in Branch, *Parting the Waters*, 684.

[38] Quoted in Branch, *Parting the Waters*, 691-692.

[39] Quoted in Branch, *Parting the Waters*, 729-730.

[40] In Birmingham, despite the gallant, awe-inspiring efforts of Fred Shuttlesworth and the working-class women of the Alabama Christian Movement for Human Rights, when the SCLC leaders arrived there was not much movement for them to lead. Shuttlesworth was a nonviolent dynamo, a satyagrahi, at times a one-man desegregation campaign. He took his children to desegregate a school, took his wife to desegregate a train station, and led a local freedom ride. For his troubles, he was repeatedly arrested, beaten, and charged with conspiracy; his house was bombed; he was nearly killed by a fire hose. Through it all, he expressed Christian love, not hatred, for his persecutors. But, like Father Kolbe in Auschwitz, his personal sacrifice alone could not match the level of inhumanity around him—including black ministers who looked with contempt on poor blacks. Even with his congregation, his human rights organization, and his few courageous comrades, before 1963 Shuttlesworth couldn't get far in rehumanizing "Bombingham." Diane McWhorter, *Carry Me Home: Birmingham, Alabama, the Climactic Battle of the Civil Rights Revolution* (Simon & Schuster, 2001), esp. 87-88, 110-118, 127-129, 154.

[41] Sitkoff, *The Struggle for Black Equality*, 135.

[42] McWhorter, *Carry Me Home*, 355.

[43] "This Far by Faith: James Lawson," http://www.pbs.org/thisfarbyfaith/witnesses/james_lawson.html.

[44] McWhorter, *Carry Me Home*, 359-361.

[45] Quotes from *Mighty Times: The Children's March*, a film by Teaching Tolerance and HBO, 2009.

[46] Celebrity participation brings media attention, but also raises the stakes. The nature of celebrity is that the lives of the rich and famous are considered more valuable than others. Thus, celebrity arrests are more scandalous, and celebrity suffering considered more tragic. Like it or not, celebrities generally have greater than average integrative power—people want to know them, stand near them, be like them—which can make them particularly effective as nonviolent activists.

[47] Quoted in McWhorter, *Carry Me Home*, 387.

[48] Quoted in Sitkoff, *The Struggle for Black Equality*, 129; McWhorter, *Carry Me Home*, 390.

[49] Sitkoff, *The Struggle for Black Equality*, 134.

[50] Quotes from *Mighty Times: The Children's March*.

[51] Sitkoff, *The Struggle for Black Equality*, 118.

[52] Branch, *Parting the Waters*, 825.

[53] Sitkoff, *The Struggle for Black Equality*, 133-134.

[54] "This Far by Faith: James Lawson."

[55] Nico Slate, *Colored Cosmopolitanism: The Shared Struggle for Freedom in the United States and India* (Harvard University Press, 2012), 115.

[56] Leonard Cohen, "Democracy," *The Future*, audio CD (Columbia, 1992).

[57] This was true not only in the South. A century earlier, Abraham Lincoln, a clever politician who knew his northern white audience, spoke in favor of exporting blacks to foreign lands after emancipation.

[58] In his shameful but award-winning film, *Django Unchained*, Quentin Tarantino told a story of a heroic former slave bringing spectacularly violent vengeance against a slave owner—perhaps providing short-term emotional satisfaction to viewers, but disregarding the nobility and wisdom of real-life former slaves who never sought revenge. On the whole, former slaves in the South acted with greater humanity than former slave owners, and Tarantino seems to wish they hadn't. He created a similar violent revenge fantasy that punished Nazis. The celebrated filmmaker, who thinks direct violence is entertaining and redemptive, who sees profundity in films that imitate the cheap and gratuitous violence of earlier films, whose point of reference is cinema tradition not human history, is a high-profile contributor to cultural violence—part of the problem, not the solution.

[59] King, "Our God is Marching On!" Alabama State Capitol, Montgomery, Mar. 25, 1965, in Carson, et al., *The Eyes on the Prize Civil Rights Reader*, 227.

[60] Branch, *Parting the Waters*, 589.

9

GETTING RADICAL

9

GETTING RADICAL

Successes and Failures

The Civil Rights Movement was the greatest force for positive change in US history. Working against the weight of centuries of racist oppression, the movement ended Jim Crow segregation, empowered the least powerful, made US society more inclusive and creative, and taught nonviolent resistance to minority groups and oppressed peoples around the world. Fifty years later, though, the United States remains a country of great violence, residential segregation by race still prevails, and blacks remain politically underrepresented, disproportionately poor, and the preferred target of the police, courts, and prisons—the new Jim Crow. The work of racial justice is far from over, and an understanding of the shortcomings of the movement in the 1960s can be instructive for future campaigns. Judging the movement by conventional standards, it was the second "American Revolution," a great leap closer to the equality and liberty promised in the 1770s.[1] Judging it by Gandhian principles, it was insufficiently revolutionary, which is to say insufficiently nonviolent.

Scholars typically characterize major political change as reformist or revolutionary. Political *revolution* is understood to mean the complete overthrow of a power structure or system of government, usually through violent means. Political *reform*, by comparison, means repairing or altering the current system. As defined by NAACP, CORE, SCLC, and SNCC organizing, the Civil Rights Movement was reformist in objective. The general goal was freedom for a despised, oppressed minority—freedom to attend the schools, eat in the restaurants, pursue the careers, live in the

227

neighborhoods, and vote for the candidates of one's own choosing. Black activists were demanding first-class citizenship, meaning full participation in the existing political, social, and economic institutions.[2] In giving southern blacks significantly greater access to mainstream institutions, the reform movement was a success. Indeed, it expanded voter rolls far more than did the celebrated violent revolt against British rule in the 1770s.[3] Along the way, though, some activists concluded that the system itself was incompatible with their goals, especially as their goals changed from personal justice (full inclusion) to a truly just system. For them, revolution was required—the work of true radicals—going beyond fixing the old system to, instead, creating a new one. In 1966, SNCC chairman Stokely Carmichael wrote, "For racism to die, a totally different America must be born."[4] But as a political revolution, the movement proved largely unsuccessful; the political and economic foundations remained intact.

Liberal thinkers tend to evaluate political regimes based on who is permitted participation in decision-making (democracy versus autocracy), while Marxist thinkers are concerned more with distribution of wealth. Peace theory views both political exclusion and material deprivation as forms of violence requiring immediate attention. The complete overthrow of a system of government, even through nonviolent means, does not guarantee more democracy or less poverty. (See Ch. 6.) True nonviolent revolution—the replacement of a violent system with a peace system—requires systematically addressing all three categories of violence: direct, structural, cultural.[5] By definition, this must be done through nonviolent means. Getting to the root of things, radical nonviolence means rejection of all forms of violence. More violence means less revolution.[6]

The most obvious concern and greatest area of success for the Civil Rights Movement was direct violence—the active, intentional denial of basic human needs (survival, well-being, identity, freedom), in this case through Jim Crow segregation and exclusion, lynching, and other forms of terrorism. Direct nonviolent action exposed the direct violence, empowered blacks, attracted white sympathy and support, and led to federal action against Jim Crow, thus creating numerous new opportunities and avenues for black individuals to reach their full potential. Structural violence, though less dramatic, presented a greater challenge. A bigoted southern sheriff is easy to identify, but who is the enemy when you can't find a decent job or afford decent housing in a prosperous industrial city like Chicago or Detroit? The US political economy greatly favors those with access to material wealth.

Generally speaking, it takes money to make money, and greater wealth brings greater influence on public decision-making, which is used to secure and increase economic privilege. Nice work if you can get it. The masses are excluded from decision-making that profoundly affects their lives, and material poverty obstructs fulfillment of basic needs. "The rich stay healthy, the sick stay poor," even if no one means harm—that's structural violence.[7] Civil rights activists found that civil rights alone were not enough—not after centuries of slavery and Jim Crow had created a black underclass in a system of limited upward mobility. What good is legal access to the best schools and safest neighborhoods if you can't afford the tuition and the mortgage? The Civil Rights Act of 1964 began the process of state action to overcome structural obstacles to black upward mobility. Over the next few decades, "affirmative action" allowed for emergence of a sizeable black middle class— no small achievement—but it didn't change the structures themselves. In sum, the movement reformed the system by dramatically reducing the direct violence of Jim Crow, but did not generate a revolution to counter the structural violence of two-party oligarchy, concentration of wealth, and capitalist exploitation of labor.

Of the three points on the violence triangle, cultural violence is arguably the most complex and deeply rooted. Across the few centuries of US history, the dominant ideology insisted on patriarchy as a natural condition, the necessity of punishment for sin, the primacy of property rights over human rights, and other received truths that encourage structural and direct violence. For the movement, the most problematic belief system was racial hierarchy. Assumptions of white supremacy and black inferiority lay anchored in the subconscious of most US residents, no matter their skin color. By exposing the violence of racism; by presenting images of blacks as nonviolent, organized, eloquent, and courageous; and by increasing interracial coexistence and cooperation in schools, work places, and public accommodations, the movement contributed to a dramatic decline in personal bigotry.[8] However, centuries-old beliefs do not quickly disappear, and conscious and subconscious assumptions of black inferiority remained.

The movement also ran up against belief in the efficacy of threat power in a culture that glorified militarism and mythologized violent men. Despite the success of the movement's nonviolent campaigns, and despite the numerous nonviolent protest movements that followed, most people did not yet fully appreciate integrative power and could not understand how bloodied freedom riders were anything but passive victims. James Lawson, Diane

Nash, Septima Clark, and other movement teachers trained hundreds of satyagrahis and taught thousands more to remain nonviolent, but millions clung to their faith in conflict resolution through violent action: throw punches, hurl bricks, send in the Marines. And get yourself a gun, there's a black man in the neighborhood.

The reform/revolution paradigm says fix or change the system, and things will be better. Certainly this was true of the movement's reform efforts; US society became less violent and more democratic. The violence triangle, with six directions of causation, reminds us that one type of violence, if left unaddressed, will reinforce the other two types. Here, again, is the diagram (with change brought by the Civil Rights Movement):

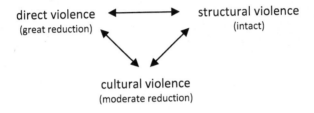

direct violence
(great reduction)

structural violence
(intact)

cultural violence
(moderate reduction)

Movement organizers focused primarily on reducing direct violence, and hoped their example would bring a decline in cultural violence—sympathy would replace bigotry, the power of nonviolence would become apparent. But they mostly left structural violence alone, and this made their achievements tenuous. The structural obstacles that kept blacks disproportionately poor reinforced assumptions of inherent black inferiority: structural → cultural. Racist fear of "dangerous" blacks, coupled with embrace of violence conflict resolution, allowed for passage of draconian laws—the "War on Drugs"—that disproportionately incarcerated and disenfranchised black males: cultural → direct. Conflict between police and inner city residents contributed to expansion of overwhelmingly white suburbia, thus extending de facto school segregation and perpetuating the old racist assumptions: direct → structural → cultural. With six directions of possible causation, reduction of violence is a never ending process—one rotten apple can spoil the barrel—and the process must be grounded in creative, nonviolent conflict resolution. From this perspective, the movement was a positive development but incomplete. Accepting that a few decades of nonviolent campaigning will not completely overcome centuries of violence, the questions remain: Where did the movement fall short of nonviolent principles? How did it fail to address all points on the violence triangle? What might it have done differently?

Missed Opportunity

On August 28, 1963, an estimated 250,000 people, from across the country, converged on Washington, DC, to demonstrate their support for the Civil Rights Movement. They filled the National Mall and listened politely to a slate of singers and speakers that peaked with Martin Luther King Jr.'s iconic "I Have a Dream" speech. Movement leaders then met with President Kennedy in the White House to discuss his proposed civil rights bill. The March on Washington for Jobs and Freedom, as this celebrated event was named, can be understood as a high point and culmination, the day a regional movement went national and mainstream. An enormous monument to King now stands near the Mall, between the Lincoln and Jefferson memorials, a testament to his significance as a truly national leader. Approximately one third of the March attendees were white—a display of racial accord perhaps unprecedented in US history—and organizers had arranged for the presence of well-known entertainment celebrities. Television networks broadcast the program live, the first time viewers could experience a King speech in its entirety. The message—of King's speech and the entire event—was of racial harmony as a national value, a "beautiful symphony of brotherhood." Less than eight years after the arrest of Rosa Parks had sparked the Montgomery bus boycott, she was standing center stage in the national capital, along with Fred Shuttlesworth, Bernice Johnson, John Lewis, and others who, in preceding years, had been brutalized for sitting or walking in the wrong places in southern cities. Then evening came, and they all went home. A quick departure was not the original plan, and there may be value in pondering what might have been.[9]

In the weeks after the Children's March, protests had pervaded the country. People were on the move in the summer of '63, and Kennedy felt he must act to prevent more "Birminghams." Images of white policemen assaulting nonviolent black children reflected poorly on the Kennedy administration, and were perfect for use by Soviet propagandists as evidence of capitalist immorality. Kennedy weighed stifling the protests versus ceding to movement demands for stronger federal action against Jim Crow; in other words, act to decrease or increase civil rights—never an easy choice for a US president. He considered enacting "a reasonable limitation of the right to demonstrate," but decided, instead, to announce support for civil rights legislation. He wasn't ceding much, though, because he expected a filibuster by southern Democrats to block passage of any bill that outlawed segregation. (Indeed, two months later, to reassure southern whites that the administration wasn't entirely in the desegregationist camp, Attorney General Robert Kennedy announced federal criminal indictments against the "Albany Nine" for picketing a white-owned grocery store.[10]) The president's real intent was to redirect the movement's energy into conventional politics. He hoped his televised announcement would bring calm and obviate more protests while the legislative process dragged along. Put another way, Kennedy was calling for reforms to preempt possible demands for revolution.[11]

Civil rights leaders, though, with a burgeoning movement behind them, were not settling for noble gestures and political delay. "We are on a breakthrough and need a mass protest," King told his advisors. "We are ready to go on a national level with our protests."[12] They discussed taking the Birmingham strategy to Washington, knowing that A. Philip Randolph's Negro American Labor Council (NALC) was already planning a similar action. They would recruit thousands of volunteers to set up an encampment, hold marches, and stage sit-ins in the halls of government, essentially taking over the city until Congress passed the law.[13] Imagine if the SCLC, NALC, SNCC, and CORE had gone forward with such an open-ended occupation, if they had organized more than enough participants to fill the district's jails, thus neutralizing the threat of mass arrests. Imagine James Lawson guiding the strategy sessions, Bayard Rustin working out the logistics, Bob Moses and Septima Clark training volunteers, King and James Bevel preaching in nightly mass meetings, Bernice Johnson leading the singing, John Lewis and Bernard Lafayette leading carefully selected satyagrahis to occupy congressional offices and absorb police violence, and Diane Nash gracefully confronting the president. Imagine a nonviolent "dream team," rather than just "I Have a Dream." Then consider two possible outcomes: First, Congress might concede the campaign's demands and pass robust civil rights legislation, confirming for observers a valuable lesson in democracy: mass, sustained, nonviolent action, more so than voting or letter-writing, is the way for those without great wealth to influence federal lawmakers. If you want real change, nonviolently overwhelm the capital. Second, echoing the 1932 attack on the Bonus Marchers, federal officials might order police and military forces to remove the protestors and clear the streets, possibly producing a display of state-sanctioned violence against nonviolent citizens that would make Birmingham's police dogs and fire hoses seem tame by comparison.[14] In this case, the nationally televised lesson would be that the federal government is part of the problem, an obstacle to civil rights, and, thus, reform might be insufficient. If you want real change, get rid of the capital.

So, either empowerment of the masses or destruction of the myth of a genuinely democratic system, possibly leading to empowerment of the masses. For the Kennedy brothers—rich, white, northeastern, and seated atop the political class—neither option was appealing. The Kennedys may not have fully understood integrative power and moral jujitsu, but they knew that a nonviolent occupation of Washington would force them to take a stand. In typical Cold War rhetoric, they claimed to represent moral decency (and seemed to believe their claims), but had struggled mightily behind the scenes with movement leaders and southern governors—negotiating, manipulating, threatening—to avoid appearing in full support of the civil rights activists in their efforts against state-sanctioned violence in the Deep South. Now, they might have to choose between a nonviolent movement that held the moral high ground and the political structure that generated their wealth and power. They couldn't have it both ways anymore, not if nonviolent intervention targeted the entire Washington ruling class rather than just the southern bigots. Forced to choose, the Kennedys most likely would have defended class interest—Clear the streets!—and the violent nature of the underlying political structures would have been revealed in the direct violence of government thuggery.

The Kennedy administration avoided that dilemma by nipping occupation plans in the bud. In late June, the president met with King, Lewis, Randolph, and other movement leaders, and presented himself as courageously committed to passing legislation: "I may lose the next election because of this. I don't care." He and his vice president insisted that traditional Capitol Hill deal-making was the only way to get the law passed, and they wanted their guests to support lobbying efforts. Again, the Kennedy strategy was to channel movement energy away from potentially revolutionary nonviolence and into conventional politics. Just as President Roosevelt, in 1941, asked Randolph to cancel the first planned March on Washington, Kennedy argued against the movement coming to town.[15] Street demonstrations, he assumed, would turn violent and be counterproductive: "We want success in the Congress, not a big show on the Capitol."[16] Employing a carrot-and-stick approach, the president promised financial support to cooperative leaders, and threatened to arrest potential occupiers before they reached the city.[17] The movement representatives, aside from NAACP chief Roy Wilkins, were committed to an event in Washington—they couldn't afford *not* to build on the Birmingham momentum—but struck a compromise. Instead of protests, they would hold a one-day rally that, by increasing national support, would serve to lobby Congress, but would not pressure or threaten anyone. There is an old saw claiming that the violent rhetoric of Malcolm X and other black nationalists forced government officials to cooperate with movement moderates like King.[18] But, in fact, just as German generals knew how to respond to violent resistance during World War II, government officials knew how to deal with violent blacks; they worked with moderates because radical *nonviolence* confounded and unsettled them even more. In convincing movement leaders not to occupy Washington, Kennedy had forestalled revolutionary action by promising support for reforms. The March on Washington wouldn't be nonviolent intervention. It would barely be a march.

In 1930, Mohandas Gandhi went to the beach and gathered sunbaked salt in violation of the British monopoly on salt production in India—by itself, a simple act of civil disobedience, but Gandhi first organized a journey by foot. He informed the British viceroy of his plans, then set out, with eighty trained satyagrahis from his ashram, on a 240-mile trek to the sea. Along the way, he stopped in villages to explain his noncooperation campaign, to denounce British colonial rule, and to call on local officials to resign their collaborationist posts. Thousands of volunteers joined the satyagrahis, national journalists reported on their progress, and the suspense grew: When would they arrive at the coast? Would they really defy the law? Would the British try to stop them?

Years earlier, in South Africa, Gandhi had led Indian marchers in violation of racist border restrictions. A nonviolent march, he understood, can be powerful. First, there is the spectacle of it, the drama, as a large number of people walk knowingly into a dangerous situation. A march draws attention to a cause, attracts an audience along the route, and displays the courage and commitment of the marchers. Second, a march can be an act of nonviolent resistance and intervention, going where you are not wanted or allowed. Marchers are, essentially, daring the opposition to stop them, to show their violence in broad daylight. Third, a march symbolizes moving forward, delivering a message, and, in a world of violent armies, is readily understood as the taking of territory. Fourth, an extended march, with participants living together, sharing the hardships of life on the road, creates community, builds commitment, and attracts more volunteers. Marchers find themselves with time to think about what they are doing and why. If they stick it out, they gain a greater sense of purpose, belonging, and investment in the cause. All of this just by going for a long walk. The Salt March started with eighty, grew into the thousands, and set off a movement of illegal salt production in India.[19]

There have been a few actual protest marches *to* Washington—notably "Coxey's Army" (1894) and "Cox's Army" (1932)—but sometime in the early twentieth century, a march *on* Washington came to mean a large political demonstration that drew participants from across the country, no matter how they made the trip.[20] As such, the 1963 March on Washington did not fully reap the benefits of extended, collective, overland travel at walking pace. Individuals and small groups undertook remarkable pilgrimages—by train and bus, even on roller skates and by bicycle—and there was a collective and somewhat chaotic procession of less than a mile—a march *in* Washington— ending at the Jefferson Memorial. On the whole, though, the March was less an exercise in community-building and nonviolent resistance, more a political rally and media event.[21] The gathering certainly had power, it influenced many people, but as a march it was more symbolic than real. The dramatic build and taking of territory had come in sit-ins, freedom rides, and illegal street processions in the Deep South. (As nonviolent intervention, the Children's March shared important characteristics with a Gandhi-led march.) The rally in the national capital was the symbolic arrival. It was a great day, but didn't convince Congress to pass President Kennedy's civil rights bill— the opposition from southern senators was too strong.

In November, though, Kennedy was assassinated, and his presidential successor, Lyndon Johnson, told Congress that the best way to honor Kennedy's memory was with "the earliest possible passage of the civil rights bill for which he fought so long." Kennedy was handsome, charming, rich, eloquent, powerful, and white—the type of personage celebrated in US culture. A great many people considered his death, like that of his former lover Marilyn Monroe, an enormous tragedy. In exaggerating Kennedy's support for the movement, Johnson was harnessing the integrative power of Kennedy's death to the proposed legislation. The following spring, with the NALC threatening a nationwide, one-day labor strike to protest congressional inaction, northern Republicans finally joined northern Democrats to stop the southern Democrats' filibuster and pass the bill. It seems that Kennedy's death aided the movement more than Kennedy ever did while in office. Kennedy is still remembered as a "civil rights" president, but his influential opposition to direct nonviolent action had convinced organizers to make the March on Washington a one-day, nonconfrontational affair and, thus, a missed opportunity, as King eventually acknowledged. [22]

Unholy Alliance

In 1965, the SCLC organized a far more rigorous march—54 miles, from Selma, Alabama, to Montgomery—taking their demand for black voting rights to the state capital. Many came from outside Alabama, including a sizeable contingent of church workers, but the majority of the marchers were locals.[23] John Lewis later recalled that, despite lousy weather and four long days on the road, "No one complained. No one got tired." In the preceding years, Lewis had marched through the streets of Nashville, suffered a terrible beating on the Freedom Ride, and addressed the masses on the Mall, but Selma-to-Montgomery was, he said, "more than an ordinary march."

> To me, there was never a march like this one before, and there hasn't been one since. The incredible sense of community—of *communing*—was overwhelming. We felt bonded with one another, with the people we passed, with the entire nation.[24]

SNCC member Stokely Carmichael, who was critical of the SCLC for just marching through rural Lowndes County rather than organizing there, used the opportunity to recruit bystanders for later actions. On the fifth day, with the television networks providing live coverage, some twenty-five thousand joined the parade through Montgomery to the capitol building. On the capitol steps, King gave one of his finest speeches. In it, he quoted an elderly woman from the 1955 bus boycott who had declined a ride, saying, "My feets is tired, but my soul is rested."[25] This was the culmination of the Selma campaign—a campaign that led, four months later, to passage of the Voting Rights Act, which led to the registration of hundreds of thousands of black voters across the South. Still, the Montgomery march, like the March on Washington, was marked by compromise that muted the movement's revolutionary potential.

The Selma campaign grew out of events in Birmingham. In September 1963, in response to the SCLC's ongoing efforts to desegregate that city, Klan members dynamited the church where the Children's March had originated, killing four little girls. In their rage, Diane Nash and James Bevel discussed hunting down and killing the bombers—nonviolent discipline can be difficult in the face of cowardly, vicious violence. Knowing that revenge would not further movement goals or honor the victims, the couple instead turned their righteous anger toward planning a wider campaign that would build to a mass occupation of Montgomery to demand black enfranchisement in Alabama. Like so many nonviolent strategists before and since, they had come to understand that a nonviolent army—columns of trained satyagrahis—was necessary to challenge the entrenched state. The dilemma posed by nonviolent occupation—concession or crackdown?—would diminish state authority and delegitimize state violence.[26] Nash typed a summary of their plan, which included "Marching and drills in command and coordination of battle groups....Practice in blocking runways, train tracks, etc." She proposed "severing communication from state capitol bldg. and from city of Montgomery" by overwhelming the phone lines with calls and shutting down transportation arteries with parked cars and nonviolent occupiers. The Nash-Bevel plan received mixed reviews from King's inner circle, but, fifteen months later, with the Civil Rights Act passed and its signatory, President Johnson, securely reelected, the SCLC leadership endorsed Bevel's suggestion for a campaign in Selma to redirect the movement from civil rights to voting rights. In other words, King wanted the push for electoral reform in Alabama, but not the potentially revolutionary siege of Montgomery.[27]

The primary issue for the joint SNCC-SCLC Selma campaign was that blacks were unable to register to vote. In 1962, SNCC member Bernard "Little Gandhi" Lafayette had, almost singlehandedly, started a registration drive in Selma, but the registrar's office in the county courthouse was only open two days per month, the clerks were obstructive, and those few blacks who applied to vote were rejected on technicalities and faced retaliation from segregationists. In January 1965, Bevel and Nash began recruiting ward and block captains to canvass Selma neighborhoods, and held youth rallies, nonviolence workshops, and mass church meetings. Then, with leadership from King and other ministers, they daily sent marchers to the county courthouse to be arrested for violating a local judge's injunction against such gatherings. The injunction specifically named SCLC and SNCC, and was enforced by a cruel sheriff and his deputies armed with electric cattle prods.

In the first week, one hundred schoolteachers marched—a remarkable and inspiring event because black professionals generally chose job security over movement participation, and black teachers, as employees of white school boards, were particularly vulnerable to retaliatory dismissals. In the second week of marches, daily participation exceeded five hundred, and at the end of the fourth week, the sheriff collapsed and was hospitalized—sadism can be exhausting. Meanwhile, the Johnson administration had announced interest in federal legislation to ensure voting rights, and a US district judge in Mobile had overturned the ban on assembly in Selma, suspended the Alabama literacy test for voters, and ordered the Selma registrar to speed up the application process.[28]

Six weeks into the campaign, the registrar was still not enrolling black voters, but Alabama segregationists, including the governor, knew they had to stop the daily marches. For decades, whites had intimidated black voters and then claimed blacks didn't want to vote, but now Selma blacks were voting with their feet and drawing federal support. The Selma police chief, a decent man in an indecent situation, was following the Albany model of outlasting rather than crushing protests. He released prisoners to avoid overcrowding jails, and was able to rein in the sheriff and white vigilantes within city limits, but he had no authority in surrounding areas where blacks were also mobilizing. In nearby Marion, hundreds of students had marched to the courthouse, and were being held in horrible conditions in jail cells and prison farms. On the night of February 18, four hundred Marion blacks started to walk from a church to a nearby jail where SCLC youth organizer James Orange was confined. Under cover of darkness, a white mob—local police, deputies from surrounding counties, Alabama state troopers, civilians— attacked with clubs and drove the demonstrators back into the church. A young voting rights activist named Jimmy Lee Jackson tried to pull his bloodied grandfather and mother to safety, and was shot by a trooper.

Never let violence stop the movement: Jackson's death, eight days later, moved Bevel to call for an SCLC march to Montgomery. On Sunday, March 7, six hundred marchers, led by John Lewis and Hosea Williams, headed out.[29] They didn't get far. Ordered by the governor to prevent the march, state troopers attacked with clubs and tear gas, and mounted troopers chased the marchers off the Edmund Pettus Bridge and back into Selma. Fifty marchers, including Lewis, were hospitalized. ABC broke into its broadcast of *Judgment at Nuremburg*—irony too rich for words—to show footage from the bridge. The Selma mayor later admitted, "The wrath of the nation came down on us."[30] With national sympathy on his side, King announced he would lead a second attempt, on Tuesday, and the SCLC petitioned a US district judge in Montgomery to enjoin the governor not to interfere. At a rally that night, King said, "We've gone too far to turn back now. We must let them know that nothing can stop us—not even death itself." But King had a problem: At his request, an estimated eight hundred out-of-state supporters were arriving for Tuesday's march, yet the district judge, with White House encouragement, ordered no marching until he heard the SCLC complaint on Thursday.[31]

King's dilemma in Selma was years in the making. Historians typically point out that King had never violated a federal injunction, and now the SCLC's choice was either cancel the Tuesday march and risk making a mockery of King's unyielding words and losing campaign momentum, or disobey the very judge they had asked to intervene on their behalf and who they fully expected to take their side. But the contradiction ran deeper than that. From the beginning, movement strategy had assumed federal cooperation—NAACP lawyers sued in federal court, SCLC leaders negotiated with the White House—but federal officials had no commitment to nonviolence. National government is, by definition, a system of power relations. Put broadly, federal officials exert exchange power when negotiating deals and spending money, exert persuasive power through rhetoric and propaganda, and exert integrative power when the human need for belonging is warped into allegiance to the state. The US government is also highly dependent on threat power, mostly obviously in its hundreds of violent interventions in foreign lands, but also in relations with US citizens: Political radicals will be persecuted! Whistleblowers will be prosecuted!! Pay taxes or else!!! Law enforcement is state threat power. When civil rights organizations requested that federal officials enforce court-ordered desegregation of schools and public transportation, when they demanded the arrest and prosecution of white terrorists, when they insisted on constitutional protections, they were asking armed men—US marshals and soldiers—to intervene on their behalf. Movement leaders wanted to harness federal authority to override southern state authority. Federal troops guarding black students in Little Rock, in 1957, represented the return of armed federal occupiers to a hostile white South eighty years after the Union Army stopped protecting Reconstruction-era freedmen.[32]

As movement activism spread across the Deep South, a grand contradiction emerged: civil rights activists employed nonviolent intervention and patient suffering to gain nationwide sympathy and support and, thus, federal action. In other words, integrative power to gain threat power. (Imagine Gandhi, once the Salt March had won international sympathy, calling for a Chinese military invasion to end British repression of Indians.) SNCC organizer James Forman described the dynamic in Selma: "Our strategy, as usual, was to force the U.S. government to intervene in case there were arrests—and if they did not intervene, that inaction would once again prove the government was not on our side and thus intensify the development of a mass consciousness among blacks."[33] An unholy alliance—the movement and the feds—but an effective reform strategy; the contradiction only existed if movement leaders claimed total commitment to nonviolence and if their goal was reduction of violence in all its forms. "It is true," Bob Moses told the 1963 SNCC national conference, "the Negroes are blackmailing the federal government to force other elements in the power structure to accept a compromise." Then he suggested that this was not enough: "Our job is to change the power structure."[34]

The varying degree of commitment to nonviolence, of refusal to cooperate with any violence, first became apparent within the movement in 1961, when Lawson's Nashville satyagrahis, including Nash, Bevel, and Lewis, hurried to Alabama to revive the Freedom Ride. After the first group of riders had been brutally thrashed, Shuttlesworth told Attorney General Kennedy that they needed police protection, i.e., armed intervention. Shuttlesworth's own nonviolent courage was beyond question, but he must have sensed the fear and fatigue of the battered out-of-towners, who soon abandoned the ride. When a Montgomery church rally for the Nashville reinforcements was surrounded by a white mob, King reluctantly called Kennedy and requested armed federal rescuers. Most in the church were not committed activists. It would have been wrong to sacrifice them to the cause, and, anyhow, many were preparing to fight back violently. King told Kennedy that if federal marshals "don't get here immediately, we're going to have a bloody confrontation." The media images of bloodied freedom riders and the requests from King and Shuttlesworth brought federal action, but the Kennedys' concern with maintaining order was an impediment to the employment of integrative power. When the Nashville group continued the Freedom Ride into Mississippi, they went with an armed motorcade, which Lawson said they did not want. Guarded by state policemen on the highway, then arrested in the bus terminal—that was Kennedy's solution—Lawson and company had to do their patient suffering in Parchman Penitentiary, away from the public eye.[35]

This contradiction—an indecisive King trying to prevent casualties by working with the Kennedys, who were primarily concerned with maintaining federal authority, and the Nashville satyagrahis willing to risk suffering rather than shrink back in the face of direct violence—reappeared in Birmingham. King asked Bevel to help him fill the jails, but balked when Bevel recruited children. While King ruminated on the morality of allowing youth participation and pursued telephone negotiations with the president, who sternly warned against using youngsters, Bevel unleashed the Children's March. In public, King always lauded those taking the greatest risks, but his reliance on federal support to achieve movement goals, and his understanding of his role as movement spokesman, compromised his own commitment to nonviolence—at least before 1967.[36]

King tried to finesse the issue in Selma. On that Tuesday—March 9—he and Ralph Abernathy appeared to be leading 1500 marchers to Montgomery, in violation of the judge's order. But when they encountered the same barricade of state troopers on Pettus Bridge, King turned the march around. It was scripted theater, negotiated in advance by King, a Justice Department official, and the governor and his state troopers. A few days later, in the judge's courtroom, King said that he had not intended to complete the Tuesday march, only to demonstrate the marchers' resolve by confronting the troopers. He later wrote that the short march had made its point by "revealing the continued presence of violence." In fact, the troopers had stepped aside on the bridge to make King's prearranged retreat even more embarrassing. The turnaround put the Selma campaign in jeopardy. Participants were disappointed and confused, the integrative power of Jimmy Lee Jackson's sacrifice, which had inspired the march to the capital, was dissipating, and SNCC members accused King of betrayal.[37] Rather than absorbing more state-sanctioned direct violence and relying on integrative power to draw sympathy and support, King had acquiesced to federal authority, essentially hoping federal threat power would overcome the Alabama governor's threat power. Meanwhile, the federal judge was in no hurry to render a decision on the proposed march.

King's caution and the judge's procrastination aside, the struggle in Selma between the forces of integrative power and the forces of threat power had its own momentum. Jackson's murder by a state trooper had led to the attempted march to Montgomery, which was broken up by more trooper violence, which had led King to ask prominent clergymen to fly in for the Tuesday march. After that march was aborted, local thugs caught up with three of the visiting ministers. (White bigots had a special hatred for compassionate whites who, by actively challenging Jim Crow, upended the racist cosmology.) One of the ministers, James Reeb, suffered a smashing blow to the head and died two days later, sparking demonstrations of outrage in northern cities and keeping the Johnson administration focused on crafting a voting rights law.[38] Reeb's death had more integrative power nationwide than Jackson's because, in general, the white majority, government officials, and newsmen put greater value on a white life—a racist reality that some organizers decried. But if that was the reality, recruiting whites to risk their lives was good strategy (just as Johnson's rhetoric had transformed Kennedy into a civil rights martyr). The Reeb story—white minister dies to further black freedom—had the John Brown effect of rehumanizing blacks in the eyes of northern whites. Orloff Miller, one of Reeb's companions that tragic night, later recalled that "people suddenly sat up and took notice and from then on things changed in the movement."

> Selma became a flood of demonstrators....When ministers went to the White House, Johnson rightly said, "Where have you been all these years?" And where had we been? We finally woke up, and it was Jim's death that woke us up.[39]

As Shuttlesworth had predicted during the Freedom Ride, "When white men and black men are beaten up together, the day is coming when they will walk together."[40]

The national outcry following Reeb's death suggests that "Turnaround Tuesday" was another missed opportunity. If King and Abernathy had refused to turn back, intentionally violating a federal order not to march, the troopers might have repeated their brutal frenzy on the bridge. The televised beatings of clergymen—white-skinned northerners, including Reeb and Miller, and the dark-skinned but internationally-known King—by Alabama cops at the behest of the state governor likely would have brought even greater national condemnation than did the unseen attack on Reeb by an anonymous hoodlum. The governor would have claimed that his troopers were enforcing the judge's injunction, thus placing the US attorney general in a bind. His job might require him to support the federal judge and indict King and Abernathy the way he had indicted the Albany Nine, but northern whites would be less interested in legal intricacies and more concerned with the images of police brutality against nonviolent ministers. If the federal government acted against the bloodied marchers, the anonymous white thug would have a familiar name: Uncle Sam. And what if, on Wednesday, as Selma "became a flood of demonstrators," Nash led one thousand more onto the bridge, defying the federal judge and heading for Montgomery? What if Shuttlesworth led another large group on Thursday? Like in the imagined nonviolent occupation of Washington, the federal government would be revealed as, first and foremost, a violent obstacle to human freedom, and the presidential administration would face the unhappy choice between concession or crackdown.

An interesting what-if, but the reality was quite different, as King's strategy of playing for federal support succeeded. President Johnson gave the Alabama governor a talking-to, then stood before Congress and network cameras to announce new voting rights legislation. "It's really all of us," he drawled, "who must overcome the crippling legacy of bigotry and injustice." C.T. Vivian, who watched the speech with King and other SCLC staffers, called it "a victory like none other. It was an affirmation of the movement." If Johnson's words were an affirmation of the movement's achievement in raising awareness regarding the cultural violence of racism, his proposed legislation was an affirmation of federal support for reform to forestall deeper political change.

The next day, though—March 16—brought another opening for radical action. In Montgomery, a small march to the capitol building, led by Forman, came under assault by mounted cops wielding whips and electric prods—a clear indication of how Alabama law officers would have responded to Nash's proposed occupation. That night, at a church meeting, Forman angrily formulated an almost perfect metaphor for the necessity of structural revolution: "If we can't sit at the table, let's knock the fucking legs off." King, too, spoke heatedly—"The cup of endurance has run over"—stoking the congregation's anger. Moments later, though, King received an urgent message, and announced that the federal judge had okayed the Selma-to-Montgomery march. On March 21, two full weeks after the initial attempt, thousands crossed the bridge and headed for the capital, marching with federal approval and the armed protection of US soldiers, federal marshals, and federalized Alabama National Guardsmen. Instead of challenging and undermining federal threat power, the march affirmed it.[41]

Purifying the Movement

Any acquiescence to violence weakens a nonviolent movement. Recall that Gandhi believed Indians had to develop fearlessness, self-reliance, and self-respect to become truly free. (See Ch. 4.) He hoped his nonviolent campaigns would cultivate these characteristics, would purify the participants, just as he fasted to purify himself. Gandhi also promoted Muslim-Hindu unity, women's rights, and the end of "Untouchability" because the subjugation of one group by another, he understood, is violence and an obstacle to *swaraj* (freedom)—for members of both groups. For satyagrahis, the greater their purity, meaning rejection of violence in all its forms, the greater their freedom to act with honesty and transparency—they don't run from suffering and have nothing to hide. Recall also that satyagraha means "holding firmly to Truth" and equates with "nonviolence of the strong." The impurities within a nonviolent movement—internal divisions, material dependency, personal ambitions, authoritarianism, secrecy and dishonesty, the willingness to compromise with violence—leave it vulnerable to exploitation by opponents. (For example, in negotiating British withdrawal from India, colonial officials played on all of the above, especially the Muslim-Hindu divide, thus contributing to the explosion of sectarian violence that ruined the nonviolent movement on the subcontinent.) In theory, the peace imperative is simple: if you want a radically nonviolent society, be radically nonviolent. The means become the end. Be the change you seek. Peace is the way. In practice, it's not so easy. True nonviolent purity being impossible, the struggle toward that ideal is endless. Even the majestic Civil Rights Movement was riddled with impurities that diminished its power to effect change.

Male chauvinism was conspicuous in the movement. Sexism was ubiquitous in pre-1970s US society, but came with a racialized twist for southern blacks. In general, during slavery and after, white males intimidated and terrorized black males, who they viewed as the greatest threat to white dominance.[42] Unable to protect the women they loved from white brutality, unable to gain influence and respect through economic success, unable to assert their own manhood, black men felt emasculated in the midst of an otherwise patriarchal society. One 20th-century legacy of slavery, then, was black male self-hatred, but also resentment of strong black women who, ironically, had more room to express themselves under Jim Crow. Southern black churches were often the only public place where black men could discard their submissiveness and wield power. Women did most of the church organizing, attending, teaching, and physical work, while male ministers and board members controlled the finances and spoke on behalf of the congregation—a situation accepted as normal, even desirable, by men and women alike. The biggest churches were able to offer middle-class salaries and social prominence, and thus attracted ministers who were highly educated and brilliant, eloquent and charismatic, and encouraged in them a sense of self-importance, entitlement, and chauvinism.

These characteristics were both a blessing and a curse for movement leadership, as became evident in Montgomery bus boycott, in 1955. Black women, far more than men, were the early organizers, but they needed the churches to promote the boycott and provide meeting space. Seeing a movement underway without them—and, in some cases, shamed into action—the ministers assumed official leadership roles and pushed Rosa Parks and other women aside. The blessing was that King, a reluctant participant at first, brought irresistible oratory and historical vision to a local action. The curse was that, once the buses were desegregated, the male leadership had no idea how to proceed, and the momentum generated by the female grassroots was lost. To put it crudely, the women organized and worked, the men took over, declared victory, and shut it down. The big-city ministers formed the SCLC as a community action alternative to NAACP legal strategies, agreed on a voter registration drive, then did little to promote it.[43] King grudgingly accepted Ella Baker, one of the original SCLC organizers, as "acting" director, but she found herself with little functional support. King believed that women belonged at home, not in the public eye, and he generally dismissed Baker's ideas and treated her like a secretary. Baker later observed,

> Because a person is called upon to give public statements and is acclaimed by the establishment, such a person gets to the point of believing he *is* the movement. Such people get so involved with playing the game of being important that they exhaust themselves and their time and they don't do the work of actually organizing people.[44]

The SCLC ministers—including King, Abernathy, Andrew Young, and Wyatt Walker—could preach and inspire, solicit money from wealthy northern men, play back-channel politics with the men in the White House, and attract the attention and respect of newsmen, but their authoritarian leadership style tended to make the movement dependent on their decision-making. In contrast, Baker, Septima Clark, Dorothy Cotton, and other women led by encouraging others to become leaders themselves. They tapped into the movement's greatest resource: poor black women. Clark, who developed her citizenship classes at the Highlander School, eventually needed SCLC support to expand the program, but she and Bernice Robinson succeeded in their educational work *despite* male oversight. While the SCLC ministers would sink or swim with one dramatic project at a time—Albany, Birmingham, Washington, Selma—the graduates of Clark's classes were quietly organizing across the South. Clark once wrote a letter to King suggesting he "develop leaders who could lead their own marches"—an idea King's circle found amusing.[45] Greater respect for female leadership and female leaders would have made the SCLC a stronger, more flexible organization, one better able to capitalize on the talents and energy of all its volunteers. But with the focus solely on the pursuit of racial equality, not total human equality, gender dynamics remained an obstacle to full emancipation.

The SNCC story provides an interesting counterpoint. If the chauvinism and self-importance of the SCLC ministers hobbled the movement in the late 1950s, the more egalitarian student uprising revived it. When student organizers, fresh from their sit-ins, attended an SCLC-sponsored conference, Baker strongly encouraged them to stay independent rather than become an SCLC youth branch. Following her advice, they created SNCC—more a loose coalition of far-flung activists than a tightly-structured organization—and Baker, who soon quit the SCLC, taught them how to build a decentralized mass movement. Even the most charismatic men in SNCC acknowledged Baker's indispensable leadership. Carmichael called her "the most powerful person in the struggle in the sixties." SNCC was not free from sexism—indeed, the patriarchal assumptions of the black power movement destroyed SNCC after 1966—but SNCC field secretaries, as they called themselves, would "Go where the spirit say go. Do what the spirit say do."[46] They were free to organize whenever and wherever they chose, which included Greenwood, Albany, and Selma. (Birmingham, alone, began as an SCLC project, and even that was built on a local movement of churchwomen.[47])

This independence allowed women to flourish in the movement, and allowed SNCC members, organized by Nash, to resuscitate CORE's Freedom Ride at practically a moment's notice. SNCC volunteers, on their own initiative, rushed to Birmingham to replace the original riders. In the besieged church in Memphis, Nash found herself ignored while King and other ministers maintained phone negotiations with Robert Kennedy. At the attorney general's urging, King asked James Farmer, the original CORE organizer, to stop the ride. Farmer was willing, but the SNCC riders accepted Nash as their lead strategist, and she didn't take marching orders. SNCC's informal structure and skepticism of authority made its leaders less vulnerable to federal pressure, and their commitment to nonviolent intervention, as taught to them by Lawson, made them stand firm in the face of violent reprisals. Nash told Farmer, "No, we can't stop it now, right after we've been clobbered."[48] To Kennedy's dismay, and without King on the bus, the Ride went forward, and a mass movement came to life in the Deep South. The freedom riders came out of Parchman steeled for movement. They organized across Mississippi, initiated campaigns in Albany and Selma, and recruited the children of Birmingham. Without Nash taking over the CORE project and standing up to Kennedy and King, the Freedom Ride would never have reached Mississippi, and the movement might never have reached Washington. That's the "glass half full" perspective. The "half empty" perspective asks what the movement might have accomplished if the SCLC leaders had fully respected female leadership, if they had absorbed Baker's wise counsel and learned from Nash's nonviolent integrity.[49]

One reason SNCC could resist federal officials was because no one person or elite inner circle had the authority to speak for all members. A SNCC organizer might be willing, for personal reasons, to compromise with federal demands, but that didn't mean the SNCC community would follow. At a meeting in the attorney general's office, Robert Kennedy told freedom riders that they were accomplishing nothing, that they should put their energy into conventional electoral politics (where they could be controlled by traditional party structures), not nonviolent intervention (where they couldn't). He promised that the government would arrange grants, tax exemptions, draft deferments, and Justice Department protection to support a voter registration drive. Nash had no interest in abandoning direct action. She knew what Kennedy did not: the suffering of the freedom riders was purifying them, preparing them to confront white terrorism. Also, she worried that accepting government largesse meant ceding control to federal authorities who had shown little commitment to black civil rights. But Nash couldn't speak for SNCC, the membership had to hash it out; authoritarianism is politically efficient, true democracy is messy. SNCC was usually short of funds, so federal aid was alluring to some members, and the internal debate over federally supported voter registration versus direct action turned hostile, almost destroying the coalition. It was Baker, of course, who reminded the rancorous SNCC leaders that nonviolence means "we listen to our brothers and sisters," and then pointed out that a voter registration campaign in the Deep South would inevitably provide opportunities for nonviolent intervention, for satyagraha. SNCC organizers divided into a direct action branch, headed by Nash, and a separate voter registration branch. Most energy went into recruiting voters in black-majority regions of Mississippi where white resistance was most ferocious, and SNCC members found out quickly that Nash was right when she warned that they couldn't depend on federal officials—not for protection, not for political backing.[50]

Which brings us to the indomitable Fannie Lou Hamer, a dirt-poor sharecropper who suffered childhood polio, miscarriages, and involuntary sterilization—and then things got worse. When Bevel and Forman came to town, in 1962, Hamer volunteered to try to register to vote, which got her family evicted from their farm and terrorized by nightriders. Undeterred, she undertook speaking tours for SNCC, describing her experiences and raising money. Many courageous Mississippi women, recruited by SNCC and trained by Septima Clark, were finding their voice in the movement, but Hamer, by all accounts, was a revelation—a powerful singer and an even more charismatic and inspiring orator than King; she had remarkable integrative power. In 1963, on their way home from one of Clark's training sessions, Hamer and several other women challenged the whites-only rules in a bus station. The police arrested them, took them to jail, and beat them nearly to death. Hamer never fully recovered from the beating, but, the following year, was a key organizer of the statewide voter registration and literacy drive known as Mississippi Freedom Summer. When some SNCC veterans opposed the recruitment of white college students for the campaign, Hamer offered a purifying response: "If we're trying to break down the barrier of segregation, we can't segregate ourselves." Bob Moses agreed, saying, "The one thing we can do for the country that no one else can do is be above the race issue." Like gender conflict, internal racial conflict weakened SNCC unity, but Hamer and other local women felt secure in their leadership roles, were profoundly inclusive, and had lived under Jim Crow long enough to know they needed all the committed activists they could find.[51]

Freedom Summer was a failure in officially registering black voters—the white terrorist backlash, including three murders, was too intense, and federal protection was an empty promise—but the campaign was an overwhelming success at awakening and empowering Mississippi blacks. Denied formal participation in two-party politics, they created the mixed-race Mississippi Freedom Democratic Party (MFDP) and sent a delegation—thirty-four men, thirty-four women—to the 1964 Democratic National Convention, in Atlantic City. With the MFDP challenging the legitimacy of the usual all-white Mississippi delegation, President Johnson faced a familiar Democratic dilemma: concede movement demands (seat the MFDP delegation) and alienate southern white voters, or cater to southern bigotry (seat the white delegation) and alienate the black voters he had pledged to support. The MFDP was doing what the March on Washington had not: challenging the status quo of national politics. Hamer's testimony before the Credentials Committee was so powerful—"If the Freedom Democratic Party is not seated now, I question America"—that Johnson called an impromptu press conference to interrupt her television coverage. He then put tremendous political pressure on moderate movement leaders and their white allies to convince the MFDP to settle for two at-large, nonvoting seats, even though the white Mississippi delegation had already walked out and never had any intention of supporting Johnson. Nash had been right: The Kennedy and Johnson administrations had told the movement to register voters, had said that electoral politics was the proper way to effect change, and now that same Democrat leadership was tossing black voters aside for fear of losing support from the Jim Crow South. Lewis later wrote that it "was a major letdown for hundreds and thousands of civil rights workers…who had given everything they had to prove that you could work through the system."[52] An old lesson relearned: A political network will ultimately protect its own; revolutionary work must be done outside the system. This is doubly true of a nonviolent revolution when the political structure is built on violence.

A meeting of Democratic power brokers, SCLC spokesmen, and the MFDP delegation epitomized the struggle for purity within the movement. Bayard Rustin insisted on the need for political alliance with the Johnson administration. King struggled between political pragmatism and moral conviction, saying, "So, being a Negro leader, I want you to take this, but if I were a Mississippi Negro, I would vote against it"—a telling remark about his view of leadership. The gentle scolding from Hamer that earlier had reduced Senator Hubert Humphrey to tears would have applied just as well to King: "The trouble is, you're afraid to do what you know is right." Humphrey, normally a civil rights advocate, was afraid that Johnson wouldn't choose him as vice presidential nominee if the compromise failed. King was afraid that a southern white backlash to the MFDP interruption would cost Johnson the presidential election and, thus, cost the movement a powerful ally in the White House. Rustin and King were angling for reform, not working for revolution; playing at politics, not holding firmly to Truth. It was Moses, though, who best articulated the difference between the MFDP and the SCLC: "We're not here to bring politics to our morality, but to bring morality to our politics." After the politicians left, the MFDP delegation voted to reject the Democrats' insulting offer, making it clear that the Mississippi activists were not interested in half measures and compromise with Jim Crow. As Hamer famously said, "We didn't come all this way for no two seats."[53]

If alliance with the federal government required the compromise of principles, it also meant entanglement in a web of deceit and cynicism—that being the nature of a political system that disproportionately benefits a small ruling class yet relies on the consent, rather than violent repression, of the masses. Today it reads like a soap opera, but the human stakes were enormous: The hate-filled FBI director, J. Edgar Hoover, who was immune from dismissal because he had the dirt on President Kennedy's extramarital affairs, was able to manipulate the Kennedys into pressuring King to distance himself from key advisors with old Communist Party ties. Because of incessant anti-communist propaganda in the United States, Communist Party affiliations were a political liability, even though party organizers had a long history of supporting blacks in the South. Attorney General Kennedy thought he could use this angle—communists in the movement—to rein in King, whose national influence after Birmingham was on the rise, to show him who was boss. King and his inner circle, fearing that the truth exposed could hurt them, cut off two movement stalwarts, effectively choosing political expediency over transparency, Cold War orthodoxy over Gandhian purity.[54] Throwing a few trusted friends under the bus, so to speak, would hardly hamper the movement, but ceding to the Kennedys final approval on King's associates was indicative of the compromising nature of the SCLC's relationship with the federal government. If you wanted the Kennedys' support, you had to abet Hoover's witch hunt.

The obsession with communist ties proved a slippery slope for the attorney general, who first approved FBI wiretaps on King associates, then signed off on almost constant FBI eavesdropping on King himself, which provided Hoover with evidence of King's extramarital dalliances. Like the Kennedys, King had something to hide, and Hoover saw an opportunity to ruin the man whose moral authority threatened the political status quo. The FBI sent the incriminating evidence to King's wife, encouraged King to commit suicide, and circulated a report claiming King had communist connections. After the assassination of John Kennedy, the duplicity of federal interaction with the movement became even more extreme. President Johnson, a more skilled political operator than his predecessor and more interested in helping poor folks, was able to steer major civil rights legislation through Congress, yet allowed Hoover to operate without oversight. Hoover continued sowing seeds of hatred for King and the movement among the more repressive elements of the federal government, which likely contributed to King's assassination, in 1968.[55]

The Enemy is Violence

In a decade of tragedies in the United States, perhaps the greatest tragedy—at least for those who strive for a less violent world—was that the nonviolent movement fractured just as it was finding a more radical voice. Part of that shift was King, who evolved from reluctant participant to cautious, compromising strategist to satyagrahi; the movement radicalized him. During the Selma campaign, while King was appealing for federal support, Nash had declared, "As far as I'm concerned, the federal government *is* the enemy." At the time, her structural critique was ahead of King's, but by 1968, he had reached a deeper insight, the same truth that animated Gandhi's Constructive Programme and Johan Galtung's systematic peace theory: "The enemy is violence," King told an advisor who didn't fully understand the concept, "violence begets violence." Ten long years of organizing and marching, absorbing segregationist violence and navigating through internal disputes, left many activists burnt out and bitter after Selma, but King, despite bouts of depression and fatigue, was just hitting his stride. Despite his human failings, he was fully committed to justice—for all people—and was willing to learn from his mistakes. King had long decried economic injustice and the direct violence of war, but racial segregation had been the primary target of most movement campaigns. With every success, though, King became more aware that desegregation wasn't enough, that US economic structures themselves brought the injustice of poverty, that first-class citizenship in such a violent system was not a satisfactory outcome. "We may be integrating into a burning house," he said.[56] In 1967, while the

SCLC leadership debated putting resources into antiwar demonstrations, voter education, or the economic opportunity program they called Operation Breadbasket, Marian Wright suggested an anti-poverty action in the nation's capital. Within weeks of the 1963 March on Washington, King had already understood that the compromise with the Kennedys might have been a mistake.[57] Now, inspired by Wright—perhaps King was learning to listen to women—he began organizing a return to Washington, recruiting Native Americans, Chicanos, and poor Appalachian whites for an open-ended occupation to demand government action on poverty issues. The 1968 plan for a "poor people's campaign" included freedom schools, daily demonstrations, and the relocation of an entire community of desperately poor Mississippians to the Mall by mule train—a real, extended march to Washington. King called it "traumatic nonviolent action."[58]

King also had become a forceful critic of the US military's escalating war against the people of Vietnam. In 1965, after King first publicly called for an end to the war, the SCLC lost the backing of many white liberals who supported civil rights efforts but still considered antiwar pronouncements unpatriotic and pro-communist—that's the power of cultural violence. King's advisors prevailed on him to stay quiet on foreign policy, but, on April 4, 1967, in Riverside Church, in New York City, King gave an entire speech denouncing the immorality of US militarism that was destroying a foreign land, undermining poverty programs at home, and teaching US citizens that killing was a legitimate way to resolve conflict: direct → cultural. "I knew that I could never again raise my voice against the violence of the oppressed in the ghettos without having first spoken clearly to the greatest purveyor of violence in the world today—my own government." Endemic poverty and the wartime draft affected blacks in disproportionate numbers, but King was addressing these as more than just racial issues. As a proponent of Christian nonviolence, Nobel Peace Prize laureate, the best-known civil rights leader, and a profoundly moving and unifying orator, King had become, for many, the voice of the nation's moral conscience—the awakening power of the movement embodied in one man. With the Riverside speech, that prophetic voice was offering a radical critique of the US political economy: "I knew that America would never invest the necessary funds or energies in rehabilitation of its poor so long as adventures like Vietnam continued to draw men and skills and money like some demoniacal destructive suction tube."[59] Hoover had called King "the most dangerous man in America," and finally it was true. King was the one man with the potential to unite the lower classes, previously divided by race, and lead them in nonviolent rebellion against the violent status quo.

Other black leaders were offering a radical critique, but lacked King's integrative power. In 1966, Carmichael replaced Lewis as SNCC chairman, and Floyd McKissick replaced Farmer as CORE national director. Where their predecessors had worked for inclusion within mainstream society, these new voices were rejecting it as hopelessly racist and corrupt. To their credit, they called for development of self-sufficiency and self-determination within black communities. That same year, the Black Panther Party for Self-Defense formed, in Oakland, California, to resist police harassment, but also initiated free health clinics and food programs.[60] Gandhi, too, had his Constructive Programme to develop a system of self-sufficient yet interconnected communities, but while Gandhi believed his nonviolent society would inevitably attract British participants—he wanted the "English people...not the civilization they represent"—and while King acknowledged "points at which I see the necessity for temporary segregation in order to get to the integrated society," Carmichael, McKissick, and the Panthers were adopting a black nationalism that often taught hatred and total exclusion of whites.[61] They traded Gandhian principles for racial segregation, male chauvinism, and violent rhetoric, which, for all their revolutionary fervor, limited their ability to offer a viable alternative to the dominant system, and made them remarkably similar to the ruling class they despised. Carmichael was a ready critic of King, and for six years had been a courageous nonviolent campaigner, but as SNCC chairman could offer little more than "Black Power!"—an empowering slogan, but hardly a revolutionary program.

This was the tragedy: Blacks had awakened to the problem of structural violence and to the power of mass resistance, but, in their frustration, many rejected the nonviolence that had achieved so much in the South, and turned to direct violence instead. From 1964 to 1968, hundreds of thousands rioted in cities across the country. These urban uprisings typically began in response to an incident of police brutality, but the underlying cause was deep resentment over a long history of police abuse, lack of economic opportunity, and substandard housing, transportation, medical facilities, and schools. The movement had raised the expectations of urban blacks, and Malcolm X and others had emboldened them with defiant language and symbols, but very few ghetto dwellers had received nonviolent training. In 1963, SCLC leaders had struggled to persuade angry young men not to riot in Birmingham, a relatively small city, and the much larger ghetto populations in the North and California were beyond their control. Belief in the efficacy of violent problem-solving was even more deeply entrenched in Western culture than was racism. "Violence," said H. Rap Brown, Carmichael's successor as SNCC chairman, "is as American as cherry pie"—which might have been an understatement.[62] A few years of successful nonviolent campaigning and eloquent preaching were insufficient to correct centuries of war worship. The battlefield residue of gunfighter mythology, equestrian statues, general-presidents, and militant hymns; manhood defined as dominance; and, after 1940, a permanent state of international belligerence carried an unavoidable message. If mass killing brought independence from English monarchy, ended slavery, defeated Hitler, and was now saving the world from communism, why shouldn't poor black men go to war against their oppressors? Angry and empowered, but lacking nonviolent discipline, they hurled bricks, looted stores, and burned buildings. The rioters constituted a very small percentage of the black population, but received almost all of the media coverage. Their anger and resistance were understandable, but rioting was a poor strategy; they accomplished little toward improving their lot. The police responded with tear gas and bullets. Far more blacks were injured or killed in riots in the North than in nonviolent actions in the South, and the rioters' main achievement was alienating the white support won by sit-ins, freedom rides, and marches. Impatient destruction had replaced patient suffering—the very dynamic that more than once caused Gandhi to halt large-scale noncooperation campaigns in India.

Warning: In destroying the legitimacy of an oppressive system, a nonviolent movement will awaken the oppressed masses, who may resort to violence, and their violence will restore the legitimacy of the violent state. Unlike the movement's nonviolent interventions, which created a moral dilemma for public officials, the rioting made it easier for mayors and governors to justify a police crackdown, easier to demonize poor blacks. The white majority, which might have condemned police attacks on Birmingham children and Selma marchers, didn't object when police shot down looters and arsonists and bystanders in Los Angeles and Newark. Now it was movement leaders in a moral quandary. They had repeatedly called for armed intervention against white rioters in Mississippi and Alabama, so how could they condemn a harsh police response to black rioters, even if the oppressors-oppressed dynamic was quite different? The FBI and local police departments could assassinate Black Panther members without fear of a popular backlash, without danger of triggering moral jujitsu. The Panthers, after all, carried guns and spouted violent rhetoric, seemingly affirming the deep white fear of dangerous black men coming to avenge centuries of racial oppression.[63] Whites tended to imagine a monolithic black community, and news reporters typically rushed to the sensation of broken windows and burning cities without investigating underlying causes, thus many now equated King's movement with spontaneous, arbitrary violence.

The loss of white sympathy came just when the movement needed it most. In 1967, King and the SCLC were trying to organize a new, deracialized, nonviolent majority—for economic justice, against war. In confronting the structural violence of capitalism shaped by centuries of white supremacy, the movement was asking middle-class whites to cede some of their unexamined privilege. The desegregation of restaurants, theaters, and other public venues had cost whites very little; in fact, it was good for profit margins.[64] But public spending for inner city development, increased hiring of blacks for public sector jobs, acceptance of black students in colleges and universities where seating might be limited, the arrival of black home-buyers in previously all-white neighborhoods—these were reforms, not revolution, but still meant asking whites to share with blacks for the greater good in a culture that otherwise celebrated individualism and self-interest, emphasized racial differences, and imagined economic struggle as a zero-sum game. We can apply the familiar peace triangle: direct, structural, cultural. From 1954 to 1965, sometimes referred to as the movement's "classic" phase, the nonviolent campaigns had opened minds to racial inclusion and the power of nonviolence: direct → cultural. Cultural peace (e.g., belief in human goodness, embrace of shared humanity) plus direct peace (nonviolent methods) are necessary to build structural peace, to replace institutions of exploitation and marginalization with institutions of cooperation and sharing. Nationwide support for the Selma marchers, in 1965, suggests that there was great potential for continued positive transformation of the movement, from civil rights to voting rights to economic rights, and from reformist to revolutionary. However, white backlash to modest reforms, reinforced by white perceptions of blacks as violent and criminal, rather than blacks as nonviolent and compassionate, was weakening the peace triangle, spoiling the barrel.

Like his career, King's last days were shaped by the nonviolent struggle against violence. On March 28, 1968, King was in Memphis, at James Lawson's invitation, to lead thousands of marchers in support of a trash collectors' strike—a labor action that had become a civil rights campaign after white police attacked an earlier march. Twenty-five minutes into the march, Lawson called it off, and King and Abernathy were evacuated, because black youths not associated with the strike were breaking windows and looting stores. Police rushed in and a riot ensued, leaving dozens of teenagers and nine officers injured, and one youth shot dead. The state governor sent in the National Guard, President Johnson promised to "stand behind local law enforcement agencies," and FBI agents seized the opportunity to intensify their smear campaign against King. With just weeks to go before the "poor people's" occupation of Washington, King's moral authority was under attack. "Memphis is the Washington campaign in miniature," he concluded, and began preparations for a "redemptive" march in Memphis to restore positive momentum because "nonviolence can be as contagious as violence."[65] But King didn't get to lead that march, or the march to Washington. He was shot and killed by a sniper on April 4, precisely one year after the Riverside antiwar speech.[66] Today, that speech is absent from popular discourse, at least compared to his speech at the 1963 March on Washington.[67] People might be aware that King said, "I have a dream," and they might know his "dream" was for interracial cooperation. That's the King trotted out by the ruling class as a positive symbol of national unity and racial tolerance, worthy of a Washington monument and a national holiday. The more radical King— the antiwar, anti-poverty King, who denounced any and all violence—has been largely forgotten. That forgetting is cultural violence. The study of King and the Civil Rights Movement, the recollection of their courageous examples, especially when it challenges the false doctrine of state violence as the most effective remedy to conflict, is cultural peace.

NOTES TO CHAPTER 9

[1] The War for Independence, 1775-1783, did not produce a political revolution. It was a separation, a coup of sorts—the rebels threw off British rule—and a counter-revolution against agrarian radicalism. The political and economic structures *within* the former colonies were fundamentally unchanged. The new US Constitution enfranchised a mere ten percent of the population—white, propertied males—and left slavery intact. If that was the "American Revolution," then the end of Jim Crow and the enfranchisement of blacks also constituted a "revolution."

[2] This reform was also the goal of "radical" Republicans, way back in 1865, who wanted a specific ban on discrimination by race written into the Constitution. Instead, the 14th Amendment required "equal protection" of the laws, an intentionally vague formulation that allowed for continued segregation of schools, bans on interracial marriage, and, eventually, the doctrine of "separate but equal."

[3] Some apologists for the US Constitution claim that the "genius" of the document is that it has allowed for expanded participation over the decades, but the small group of wealthy white men who formed the constitutional convention were not motivated by a desire for greater democracy. The real genius of American democracy, such as it is, can be found in the grand struggle by blacks, women, and other excluded groups to secure full rights *despite* the resistance of the ruling class.

[4] Clayborne Carson, et al., eds., *The Eyes on the Prize Civil Rights Reader* (Penguin, 1991), 284.

[5] For examples of peace systems, see Douglas Fry, *Beyond War: The Human Potential for Peace* (Oxford University Press, 2007), 21-32, 113-130.

[6] See Bart de Ligt, *The Conquest of Violence: An Essay on War and Revolution* (Pluto Press, 1989, originally published 1937), which warns, "The more violence, the less revolution."

[7] Quote from "God Part II," a song by U2: "Don't believe them when they tell me/there ain't no cure/the rich stay healthy/the sick stay poor/ Still I, I believe in love." *Rattle and Hum* , audio CD (Island, 1988).

[8] As an example, consider how the following bigotry, espoused by William Buckley Jr., in 1957, in *The National Review*, would be taken today: "The central question that emerges…is whether the White community in the South is entitled to take such measures as are necessary to prevail, politically and culturally, in areas in which it does not prevail numerically? The sobering answer is Yes—the White community is so entitled because, for the time being, it is the advanced race." Carl Bogus, *Buckley: William F. Buckley Jr. and the Rise of American Conservatism*

(Bloomsbury, 2011), 158-159.

[9] The organizers called it "The March on Washington for Jobs and Freedom." A. Philip Randolph, who first began organizing such a "march" back in 1942, was planning a labor rally in Washington for October 1963. He joined his labor action to the civil rights action, but, in the end, the "jobs" message was overshadowed. William Jones, *The March on Washington: Jobs, Freedom, and the Forgotten History of Civil Rights* (Norton, 2013).

[10] Unable to prove that picketers had conspired to target a grocery store in retaliation for the storeowner's jury service, the Justice Department turned to indicting the "Albany Nine" for perjury. The investigation was politically motivated from beginning to end. Taylor Branch, *Parting the Waters: America in the King Years, 1954-63* (Simon & Schuster, 1988), 866-869.

[11] Branch, *Parting the Waters*, 808, 823-824, 866-868. Kennedy's calculated support of the movement brings to mind T.S. Eliot's oft quoted line from *Murder in the Cathedral*: "The last temptation is the greatest treason:/to do the right deed for the wrong reason."

[12] Taylor Branch, *Pillar of Fire: America in the King Years, 1963-65* (Simon & Schuster, 1999), 102.

[13] Jones, *The March on Washington*, 166-168; John Lewis, *Walking with the Wind: A Memoir of the Movement* (Simon & Schuster, 1998), 203-204.

[14] In 1932, some forty thousand protestors—World War I veterans and their supporters—set up a well-organized tent city in Washington and demanded payment of bonuses promised to them. After several months, the US attorney general ordered police to drive out the veterans. When the police met resistance, President Hoover turned to the US Army. Gen. Douglas MacArthur ordered cavalry and infantry assaults on the encampment. The soldiers destroyed the tent city and injured dozens of its residents. Seemingly a failure, the occupation may have inspired progressive New Deal legislation for poverty relief. A second "Bonus March," the following year, encountered the more tolerant Roosevelt administration, and, in 1936, a Democratic Congress passed legislation to pay the bonuses. In 1963, the US military positioned thousands of soldiers in nearby suburbs for what they knew was a one-day rally on the Mall. One can only imagine the level of military deployment that would have preceded an announced nonviolent occupation of Washington by an army of civil rights activists.

[15] Jones, *The March on Washington*, 36-39.

[16] Branch, *Parting the Waters*, 839-840. The problem all along had been white violence against blacks and, far less frequently, black violence in response to

police assaults on black protestors. But, with deeply held racist assumptions, whites couldn't help but think blacks were somehow responsible for violent police actions. Indeed, in preparing for the appearance in Washington of thousands of "dangerous" blacks, federal officials banned the sale of alcohol, stationed thousands of troops nearby, put the hospitals on alert, and were prepared to shut off the public address system. Branch, *Pillar of Fire*, 131-132.

[17] David Dellinger, *From Yale to Jail: The Life Story of a Moral Dissenter* (Pantheon, 1993), 266-267.

[18] See, for example, Louis DeCaro Jr., *"Fire from the Midst of You": A Religious Life of John Brown* (New York University Press, 2002), 39.

[19] Judith Brown, *Gandhi: Prisoner of Hope* (Yale University Press, 1989), 236-238.

[20] In the short history of the United States before 1963, most large-scale marches were of the destructive sort, either armed forces marching to war, like Sherman's "March to the Sea," or Native communities forced to trudge into exile: "Trail of Tears," the Navajo "Long Walk," and other acts of ethnic cleansing. In 1894, Coxey's Army, led by businessman Joseph Coxey, introduced the idea of marching to Washington in support of federal policy changes. This was a real march, beginning with one hundred unemployed men in Ohio, and ending with five hundred arriving in the capital to demand the government create public works jobs. In 1913, leaders of the women's suffrage movement organized a large parade down Pennsylvania Avenue, knowing that the national media would be in town for a presidential inauguration the following day. Women came from around the country, an estimated five to eight thousand joined the parade, and two hundred were injured by male attackers. In January 1932, twenty-five thousand unemployed laborers marched in Cox's Army, led by Fr. James Cox, from Pennsylvania to Washington, to demonstrate for job creation. A few months later came the occupation by the Bonus Expeditionary Force, which the media called the "Bonus March." The American Indian Movement's "Trail of Broken Treaties," in 1972, was also a march to Washington. But the most powerful protest march in the 20th-century United States might have been the 340-mile trek from Delano to Sacramento, California, by Mexican American farm workers in 1966. The *peregrinación*, as they called it, began with dozens of participants, ended with thousands, and drew attention to their campaign for union recognition.

[21] Branch, *Parting the Waters*, 876-881; Jones, *The March on Washington*, 178-188.

[22] Jones, *The March on Washington*, 217-233. Quote on 218.

[23] Three or four thousand paraded out of Selma, then returned by car and train that

night. Some three hundred "designated marchers" continued the middle trek along a narrow two-lane highway, camping at night on black-owned farms. Various celebrities and organizers came and went. On the fifth day, thousands poured into Montgomery. Taylor Branch, *At Canaan's Edge: America in the King Years, 1965-68* (Simon & Schuster, 2006), 131, 140-170.

[24] Lewis, *Walking with the Wind*, 344-345.

[25] Carson, et al., *The Eyes on the Prize Civil Rights Reader*, 224.

[26] In 1961, after the Freedom Ride, James Lawson had called for creation of a nonviolent army. In 1963, when SNCC members prepared a speech for John Lewis to deliver on the Mall, they included lines that evoked images of an army: "We will march through the South, through the heart of Dixie, the way Sherman did. We shall pursue our own 'scorched earth' policy and burn Jim Crow to the ground—nonviolently." More moderate organizers pressured Lewis into omitting those lines. Branch, *Parting the Waters*, 869-870, 873-874, 879-880; Lewis, *Walking with the Wind*, 214-224. Gandhi and Ghaffar Khan also understood the need for a *shanti sena*.

[27] Branch, *Pillar of Fire*, 139-141, 145; Lewis, *Walking with the Wind*, 230-231. A copy of Nash's typescript made it to White House officials, giving them a vision of a march they wouldn't be able to control. According to Branch, Asst. Attorney General for Civil Rights Burke Marshall referred to Nash's plan as "revolutionary." Apparently, he understood the implications of mass, nonviolent intervention against state authority.

[28] Branch, *Pillar of Fire*, 391, 553-591.

[29] Branch, *Pillar of Fire*, 592-600; Lewis, *Walking with the Wind*, 307-331.

[30] Juan Williams, *Eyes on the Prize: America's Civil Rights Years, 1954-1965* (Viking Penguin, 1987), 273.

[31] Harvard Sitkoff, *The Struggle for Black Equality, 1954-1992* (Hill & Wang, 1993), 175-177; Branch, *At Canaan's Edge*, 68-74 .

[32] US troops occupied the postwar South from 1865 to 1877 to protect black rights. In 1877, a compromise allowed Republicans to retain control of the White House in exchange for withdrawing the troops, thus allowing southern Democrats to establish Jim Crow rule. Resolved: The Civil War led to the end of legalized slavery, but it took the nonviolent Civil Rights Movement, a full century later, to decrease white violence against blacks.

[33] Williams, *Eyes on the Prize*, 255.

[34] Jones, *The March on Washington*, 219.

[35] Branch, *Parting the Waters*, 426-430, 459-460, 472.

[36] The Nashville freedom riders were dismayed by King's refusal to join them on the journey from Montgomery to Jackson. King said he wanted to go, but his advisors discouraged it because he was already on probation and could easily end up serving six months. Still, Nash asked him to get on the bus, knowing that his participation in nonviolent intervention would be a powerful, inspiring example. "Where is your body?" was the refrain the Nashvillians used to encourage each other, but, faced with a reticent King, Lewis had to remind them of Lawson's dictum not to badger participants beyond their commitment level. Branch, *Parting the Waters*, 466-468.

[37] Sitkoff, *The Struggle for Black Equality*, 178-179.

[38] Branch, *At Canaan's Edge*, 75-85.

[39] Williams, *Eyes on the Prize*, 274-277.

[40] Branch, *Parting the Waters*, 423.

[41] Williams, *Eyes on the Prize*, 278-279; Branch, *At Canaan's Edge*, 109-123.

[42] White males assumed that a racially defined, oppressors-oppressed social structure was inevitable. Since white male rape of black females was common and done with impunity, it stood to (white) reason that black males, given the chance, would rape white females. White males used the specter of imagined black rapists as an argument for keeping blacks enslaved and, later, for rejecting anti-lynching laws.

[43] Jones, *The March on Washington*, 113-115.

[44] Lynne Olson, *Freedom's Daughters: The Unsung Heroines of the Civil Rights Movement from 1830 to 1970* (Scribner, 2001), 110-131, 141-146. Quote on 144. Dellinger, *From Yale to Jail*, 263, quotes Julian Bond of SNCC as saying that King "sold the concept that one man will come to your town and save you."

[45] Olson, *Freedom's Daughters*, 222.

[46] Lewis, *Walking with the Wind*, 101, 294.

[47] Diane McWhorter, *Carry Me Home: Birmingham, Alabama, the Climactic Battle of the Civil Rights Revolution* (Simon & Schuster, 2001), 111-112.

[48] Olson, *Freedom's Daughters*, 149-150, 160-161, 187-188.

[49] After getting married, Nash played more of a behind-the-scenes role, like a traditional minister's wife, while her husband, Bevel, emerged as an outspoken preacher and movement leader. Andrew Young has admitted, "It was not to our credit that we followed that model with Diane." After exposure to the 1970s women's movement, Nash realized she had been too tolerant of male chauvinism in the movement. Olson, *Freedom's Daughters*, 188, 341-342.

[50] Olson, *Freedom's Daughters*, 195-197; Lewis, *Walking with the Wind*, 180-182.

[51] Branch, *Pillar of Fire*, 50-74, 108-109, 164-165, 458-459; Lewis, *Walking with the Wind*, 243-245.

[52] Lewis, *Walking with the Wind*, 283.

[53] Branch, *Pillar of Fire*, 456-476. The MFDP changed Democratic Party politics. In 1968, as promised, the Democrats seated an interracial Mississippi delegation, and at future conventions, all state delegations were required to reflect the gender and racial make-up of their state populations. Olson, *Freedom's Daughters*, 324.

[54] The focus on reform and the appeal for federal help, ironically, made the movement more vulnerable to denunciation as "communists." Had they been committed to nonviolent revolution, SCLC leaders could have shaken off the "communist" slurs, which did not resonate among the poor masses as they did among middle-class voters.

[55] Branch, *Parting the Waters*, 835-862; Branch, *Pillar of Fire*, 148-154, 528-529, 556-557; Dellinger, *From Yale to Jail*, 275-277. Attorney General Kennedy bemoaned the fact that Hoover had ninety percent of his agents hunting for "communists" rather than investigating organized crime. The shameful career of Klan member Gary Rowe makes it clear that FBI agents were more interested in spying on any threat to the political status quo than in enforcing the law or protecting the civil rights of nonviolent activists. As an FBI informant, Rowe revealed that the Birmingham police and Klan were planning to attack the Freedom Riders. As FBI agents stood by, Rowe participated enthusiastically in the brutal onslaught. Though they rarely used his insider information to protect movement participants, the FBI allowed Rowe to continue his wicked ways with impunity, and he was more than a passive snitch. When a white woman named Viola Liuzzo was killed while shuttling marchers between Montgomery and Selma, the fatal shot came from a car carrying Rowe and three other Klansmen. McWhorter, *Carry Me Home*, 161-168, 177-178, 197-212, 572-573.

[56] Branch, *At Canaan's Edge*, 72, 690, 730.

[57] Just three weeks after the March, King was already deploring how the Kennedys actively obstructed the nonviolent movement while tolerating white violence, saying "They act to stop us. But they don't act when the whites do something. They just let us take another beating." Branch, *Pillar of Fire*, 144.

[58] Branch, *At Canaan's Edge*, 640-641, 715-716, 720-721, 746.

[59] Carson, et al., *The Eyes on the Prize Civil Rights Reader*, 389.

[60] Steve Wasserman, "Rage and Ruin: On the Black Panthers," *The Nation*, June 24-July 1, 2013.

[61] Louis Fischer, ed., *The Essential Gandhi: An Anthology of His Writings on His Life, Work, and Ideas* (Vintage, 2002), 104-109; Carson, et al., *The Eyes on the Prize Civil Rights Reader*, 401.

[62] Sitkoff, *The Struggle for Black Equality*, 203.

[63] Ward Churchill and James Vander Wall, *Agents of Repression: The FBI's Secret Wars Against the Black Panther Party and the American Indian Movement* (South End Press, 2001), 63-99.

[64] The exception would be those whites—typically southern and working class—whose fragile self-esteem hung on notions of racial superiority. As desegregation threatened to cost them social status, it's no wonder they resisted with violence.

[65] Branch, *At Canaan's Edge*, 738, 742.

[66] The conventional story says a small-time crook escaped from prison and shot King, but thanks to the investigative work of the indefatigable William Pepper, we now have a compelling picture of the participants in the plan to assassinate King. There is a good deal of evidence, much of it given under oath, implicating collaboration by Memphis police, organized crime figures, and federal agents. US special forces snipers were prepared to kill King at the start of the march out of Selma, and were also present in Memphis. Considering the FBI's smear campaign and general targeting of King, and its murderous actions against the Black Panther Party and the American Indian Movement, it would be surprising if the FBI did *not* plot to kill King. William Pepper, *An Act of State: The Execution of Martin Luther King* (Verso, 2003); *The 13th Juror: The Official Transcript of the Martin Luther King Assassination Conspiracy Trial* (MLK the Truth, 2009); Churchill and Vander Wall, *Agents of Repression*.

[67] The 1968 Poor People's Campaign went forward, but without the participation,

energy, moral authority, unity, nonviolent discipline, and media attention that would have come with King's leadership. The establishment of a shantytown on the Mall, and regular protest marches to government agencies, comprised a bold campaign of awareness-building. However, the few attempts at civil disobedience disintegrated into violent conflict between protestors and police, much of it sparked by federal agents provocateur. Gerald McKnight, *The Last Crusade: Martin Luther King, Jr., the FBI, and the Poor People's Campaign* (Westview, 1998), 112-139; Dellinger, *From Yale to Jail*, 288.

THE ARC OF THE MORAL UNIVERSE

—

THE ARC OF THE MORAL UNIVERSE

In his speech at the end of the Selma-to-Montgomery march, Martin Luther King Jr. proclaimed, "The arc of the moral universe is long, but it bends toward justice." Listening to a recording of a King speech, one can be mesmerized, moved to tears even, by the poetry of such a weighty, sorrowful voice delivering a message of hope, and not stop to consider the implications of what he is saying. "The arc of the moral universe" is marvelous language, but what does it mean?

If the "arc" is a timeline, an upward curve plotted on a time-justice graph, the phrase is readily understood as "justice always prevails in the end" or "you eventually get what you deserve" or "things will inevitably get better." The former appears to be the original meaning of the phrase, as constructed, in the 1850s, by Unitarian minister and abolitionist Theodore Parker. In predicting that the country would pay for the injustice of slavery, Parker wrote,

> Look at the facts of the world. You see a continual and progressive triumph of the right. I do not pretend to understand the moral universe, the arc is a long one....But from what I see I am sure it bends towards justice.

269

Deep in Western culture lies an assumption of progress, a belief that, despite ups and downs in the short term, the general trend is improvement. This notion grows out of a Judeo-Christian sense of linear time which, at least in Christian renditions, imagines a troubled beginning and a redemptive conclusion to earthly existence. An all-powerful, all-knowing, all-loving God surely wouldn't let the end be meaningless misery. The remarkable advances of science and human technology in recent centuries also contribute to belief in progress. Cell phones are getting smaller and smarter, space exploration is widening, and God is looking out for us—how can anyone be pessimistic about the future?

Certainly, there have been tremendous improvements in human society. Chattel slavery is no longer legal. Nonviolent movements against violent regimes have become almost commonplace. But there are also good reasons to be skeptical about human progress. Despite antislavery laws, millions still live in bondage. The wealth disparity between the richest few, who hoard wealth and use most of the world's resources, and the rest of the population is expanding. There exists a real and increasing threat of human extinction, either a quick, cruel end brought by nuclear annihilation or the slow, pathetic decline of a species methodically destroying its own habitat. It may be the case that the earliest and simplest form of human organization—the egalitarian, nomadic foraging band—was also the most sustainable and least violent; the adoption of agriculture was a catastrophic mistake, and it's been downhill ever since. Or maybe a collective understanding of the power of nonviolence will overtake our submission to violence, and together we will create a new way to exist. It's too early to say.

The language of Christian redemption flows through King's speech, but it's not a violent redemption. His philosophy of "creative nonviolence" suggests a different understanding of the moral arc. If morality is about the right way to act, then the sentence in question reminds us that righteous actions bring good results, even if the outcome is not readily apparent. Parker was expecting painful retribution for slavery: "Ere long all America will tremble." He was not the only one: "I John Brown am now quite certain that the crimes of this guilty, land: land will never be purged away; but with Blood." King, though, understood that violent punishment of evil-doers does not produce a better world. In a preceding line, King recited from Hebrew scripture that "you shall reap what you sow." Rather than promising punishment, he was assuring his audience that, even though "there are still some difficulties ahead," their suffering would not be in vain. In the same passage, quoting William Cullen Bryant and Thomas Carlyle, respectively, King insisted that "Truth, crushed to earth, will rise again," and "no Lie can live forever." He doesn't explain why this is so, but we know that threat power must be constantly reinforced, while integrative power builds on itself, making it stronger in the long term. The lie is that social or cultural differences are greater than biological interconnection. The truth is that humans need each other. "Like an idea whose time has come, not even the marching of mighty armies can halt us," King said earlier in the speech, and "we will go on with the faith that nonviolence and its power can transform dark yesterdays into bright tomorrows." Taken together, this is an affirmation of human goodness, and, coming from King, the great synthesizer of Christian agape (God is love) and radical nonviolence (violence is the enemy), the parallel to Mohandas Gandhi (holding firmly to Truth) is clear: ahimsa = non-harming = love = Truth = God. Despite their different religious contexts, that's the moral universe for both Gandhi and King. And the arc—not a two-dimensional timeline, but a three-dimensional framework—is shaped by a simple axiom: violence begets violence, nonviolence begets nonviolence.

In the midst of his own call-and-response, King continued to draw on the wisdom of 19th-century abolitionists. He sampled "The Present Crisis," a poem about slavery as a violation of human interconnection, written by James Russell Lowell, then concluded by breaking into the words of Julia Ward Howe's "The Battle Hymn of the Republic." The hymn was derived from the earlier marching song, "John Brown's Body," and ends with the stirring words "His truth is marching on." Here is King's passage:

> I know you are asking today, "How long will it take?" I come to say to you this afternoon, however difficult the moment, however frustrating the hour, it will not be long, because "Truth, crushed to earth, will rise again." How long? *Not* long, because "no Lie can live forever. How long? *Not* long, because "you shall reap what you sow." How long? *Not* long.
> "Truth forever on the scaffold,
> Wrong forever on the throne, —
> Yet that scaffold sways the future, and, behind the
> dim unknown,
> Standeth God within the shadow, keeping watch
> above his own."
> How long? *Not* long, because "the arc of the moral universe is long but it bends toward justice." How long? *Not* long, because "Mine eyes have seen the glory of the coming of the Lord."

King's message was empowering. He wouldn't have told his audience, "We can sit back and relax now, things will get better, they always do, that's God's plan." Smug complacency might resonate for people raised in privilege, who pray to a god of entitlement and personal material gain, but it wouldn't ring true for those coming out from under centuries of slavery and Jim Crow. And it shouldn't ring true for people honestly confronting the 21st-century terrors of a militarized, despoiled planet. The message was, and is, that nonviolence is holiness, it will make the world less violent, it's the only thing that can, but it requires patience, commitment, the willingness to suffer, and the refusal to cause harm. Choose your path wisely.

Today, the study and practice of nonviolence is of greatest urgency. Privileged voices in US society continue to insist that warfare and other forms of violence will lead to a safer, less violent world—despite centuries of evidence to the contrary. Theirs is a road paved with fear and cynicism and leading to extinction. Fortunately, we now have at least a century's worth of thought and evidence acknowledging human goodness and revealing the power of nonviolence to reduce violence. As this book has argued, if we're serious about creating a more peaceful world, we must systematically address direct and structural violence and pay careful attention to the deep assumptions that constitute cultural violence. Teaching, developing, and promoting aspects of cultural peace are imperatives, not luxuries, because the survival of our species appears to hang in the balance.

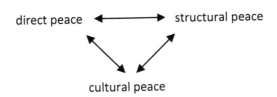

If you're asking where to begin, remember the lesson from the students who challenged racist discrimination in their schools and started a movement: find like-minded people, identify a *local* problem, and together, using nonviolent means, try to fix it. If everyone does that, we'll be fine.

APPENDIX

APPENDIX A

SHAKE OR STAB?

The Game

The game "Shake or Stab?" is based on "Prisoner's Dilemma," a puzzle developed by 20th-century game theorists to understand better the nuclear weapons standoff between the Soviet and US governments. In a typical version of Prisoner's Dilemma, two people have been arrested for armed bank robbery. The prosecutor places them in separate isolation cells so they cannot communicate, then offers them each the same bargain: If you confess and your accomplice remains silent, I'll release you and use your confession to ensure a thirty-year prison term for your accomplice. Conversely, if you remain silent and your partner confesses, your partner goes free and you'll get the thirty-year sentence. If you both confess, you'll both go to prison, but after ten years will get out early on parole. If you both opt for silence, I'll have to drop the armed robbery charges, and you'll both get only one-year sentences for weapons possession. The dilemma for each prisoner is that, no matter what the other does, the best option is to confess. The prosecutor is giving them both the incentive to confess. However, if they both confess, as seems likely, the punishment is far worse than if they both remain silent. The basic question seems to be, will a person put group interest ahead of self-interest, knowing that this will only pay off if the other member(s) of the group can be trusted to make the same choice.

	You confess	You stay silent
Partner confesses	You = 10 years Partner = 10 years	You = 30 years Partner = Freed
Partner stays silent	You = freed Partner = 30 years	You = 1 year Partner = 1 year

The premise of Shake or Stab? is simpler. You and another person meet to settle a dispute. As you approach each other, you both begin to extend a hand. Do you offer an empty palm for a friendly handshake, or do you produce a knife and stab the other person? Two players (A and B) and two options (shake or stab). The basic assumption behind the game scoring is that when people fight, at least one side gets hurts, but when people cooperate they all benefit. So if both players stab, both get hurt, both get minus five points (-5). If one shakes and the other stabs, the shaker dies and receives minus ten points (-10), while the uninjured stabber earns ten points (+10), perhaps because the stabber steals the deceased shaker's wallet. If both players shake, they become friends, share some conversation, and each gets five points (+5). Both have an incentive to stab, but mutual shaking is far more rewarding than mutual stabbing.

	A stabs	A shakes
B stabs	A hurt (-5) B hurt (-5)	A dead (-10) B unhurt, richer (+10)
B shakes	A unhurt, richer (+10) B dead (-10)	A unhurt, befriended (+5) B unhurt, befriended (+5)

While the action is between two players, Shake or Stab? is designed for a classroom of twenty to fifty participants. The basic instructions are as follows:

Part One

(1) Participants arrange themselves in small groups. The ideal group size may be four or six members, but it is best to have all groups contain the same number of players. (When this isn't possible, a group with an unusual number of players will have to make adjustments in play.)

(2) Within each small group, players pair up and decide how they will simultaneously reveal whether they have decided to shake or stab. They might write "shake" or "stab" on scraps of paper and show them to each other, or they might agree on a simultaneous hand signal, as in "rock-paper-scissors."

(3) The two contestants in each pair begin play, simultaneously declaring "shake" or "stab" in the agreed upon method, then recording their individual scores (+5, -5, +10, or -10). Then they do it again. Each and every pair repeats the encounter (shake or stab?) the same set number of times—three times is a fine choice. Players keep track of their own individual scores.

(4) After each pair in the small group has played the set number of times, players form new pairs *within* their group and repeat the process. In this fashion, each player will play the same number of times with every other player *within* the small group, keeping track of individual score all the while.

(5) A round is complete when each player has played against all fellow group members. (A group with an unusual number of players will have to make adjustments so that the individual players in that group will have the same number of scoring opportunities as all other participants.) One round may be sufficient, but depending on time and enthusiasm, more rounds may be played, each player facing off against all others *within* the same group, so long as all groups play the same number of rounds. (The number of rounds, like the set number of plays within a round, is not critical, so long as all participants end up having played the game the same number of times, thus having the same number of scoring opportunities.)

(6) After the agreed upon number of rounds is complete, each group votes on which player they want to remove from their group. The expelled player is considered an outcast.

(7) After the vote-out, individuals add up their individual scores, and the highest-scoring player among all participants, including outcasts, is determined. Each group then adds up the individual scores of the group members, including outcasts, and the highest-scoring group is determined, declared the winner, and properly rewarded. (The lesson of the game is most effective if participants are not told in advance that group scores will be considered.)

(8) The next step is to discuss the game. Which individuals had the most points? What was their strategy? Which group had the most points? Why did some groups score higher than others? Who was voted out of a group, and why? Did players develop and adjust strategies during play? What was their logic? Did players assume individual scoring was paramount? If so, why? Would they have employed a different strategy had they known group scoring mattered?

Part Two

(9) Select two participants to play against each other under new guidelines. Two known stabbers—perhaps two outcasts—may be best. Give them each 10 one-dollar bills, and explain the scoring: If both stab, they each surrender 1 dollar. If one stabs and the other shakes, the shaker gives 2 dollars to the stabber. If both shake, no money changes hands.

	A stabs	A shakes
B stabs	A = -$1 B = -$1	A = -$2 B = +$2
B shakes	A = +$2 B = -$2	No change

(10) The pair plays until one player has no money left, or until they reach a point of continuous, mutual shaking.

(11) Repeat the game with a different pair—perhaps a known shaker against a known stabber. (Two known shakers may not be very interesting.)

(12) Again, the final step is to discuss the play, strategies, outcomes, and implications.

Discussion

The game is designed to dramatize, albeit in simplistic fashion, the evolutionary value and liability of both pacifism and violence (as discussed in Ch. 1). In Part One, typically the highest-scoring individual will have employed a strategy of only or mostly stabbing. This violent strategy is particularly effective among a group of shakers—so far as individual scoring is concerned. But stabbers are typically voted out of their groups. They are rejected because they are too dangerous to have around. The highest-scoring group, of course, will be noted for its shakers. In fact, mutual shaking (cooperation) is the only way a group gains points, as any stabbing garners either 0 (+10 plus -10) or -10 (-5 plus -5) points for the group total. The reward for cooperation—acceptance in a successful group—fits what we know about human evolution.

By raising the stakes, Part Two of Shake or Stab? illuminates the advantages and disadvantages of human aggression. No longer competing for meaningless points, the two players can see their unexpected windfall ($10) decreasing as they stab each other, and they can also find a way out: if they trust each other to shake, no more money will be lost. But if they do agree to shake and then one breaks the agreement and stabs, the trust will disappear along with the money as mutual stabbing resumes.

Computer modeling has found that in such a game of repeated interaction, the best strategy is the *retaliator* approach, also called "Tit for Tat," meaning you start with cooperation (shaking), and then in every subsequent encounter you mirror your opponent's previous move (e.g., if your opponent stabs in the first encounter, you will stab in the second encounter). Once your opponent identifies your Tit for Tat pattern and trusts your consistency, your opponent can safely cooperate (shake), knowing you will continue to do likewise. Also, your opponent has a disincentive to defect (stab), knowing that stabbing will bring stabbing in return. In contrast, if you are a *dove*, if all you do is shake, your opponent is free to stab you every time, and you will lose badly. If you are a *hawk*, if all you do is stab, your opponent will have to stab in self-defense, and you will both lose. Thus, one lesson of Shake or Stab? is that to survive and pass down their genes, early humans had to be somewhat aggressive—in self-defense, in retaliation—but mostly they were cooperative and found ways to avoid violence.

APPENDIX B

WHAT WOULD YOU DO IF...?

The Setup

What would you do if a crazed gunman broke into your house and tried to rape your grandmother?

This question, which places the problem of the "ruthless opponent" at the interpersonal (one-on-one) level, is usually intended to discredit nonviolence. Because the gunman is "crazed"—lacks moral conscience, has no concern for his own well-being, cannot listen to reason—there is no way to dissuade him. In some renditions, he is "on PCP," giving him superhuman strength. Thus, a nonviolent response appears hopeless, and violent intervention is necessary to save poor Grandma.

The question is a setup alright, and probably shouldn't be dignified with solemn consideration. But using it as the basis for a game can, besides highlighting its absurdity, provide insights into how best to respond to rhetorical traps—which, by imposing a single conclusion, are violent in spirit. Also, the "Crazed Gunman" does invite evaluation of any notions of nonviolent action as a fail-proof panacea—deeply dehumanized killers, though not ubiquitous in the way Hollywood screenwriters imagine, do exist.

Instructions

The game probably works best if the question is first introduced as an individual writing assignment and/or topic for small group discussion. An instructor might ask students (1) to create their own "what would you do if...?" scenario—use your imagination, make the attacker ruthless—and then (2) to figure out a way to respond to the scenario. In small groups, students could discuss their responses and see if new ideas arise. After this preparation, it's time for some fun.

Tag Team

Two contestants sit facing each other in front of the class. One plays the interrogator, creatively and insistently posing a "crazed attacker" scenario. The other responds, trying to defend nonviolence or maybe not—it's a free-flowing debate, see where it goes. However, at any time, anyone can "tag in," meaning they can take the place of the interrogator or the defender and continue the dialogue. A quick "tag in" is helpful if a participant gets stuck or runs out of words. Creativity and humor are encouraged; absurdity may be appropriate.

Discussion

Which responses were most effective, and why? A well-played game will probably reveal the futility of responding to the "crazed attacker" scenario on its own terms, and thus lead to a discussion of other strategies.

Short of ending the conversation, the way to avoid a rhetorical trap is through redirection; don't let your opponent dictate the terms of debate. For example, rather than take the setup seriously, give a hypothetical answer—it's a hypothetical question after all.

One can also redirect the conversation by responding to the intent behind the scenario, rather than to the scenario itself. Why are you trying to trap me with an imaginary scenario? Why are you so eager to discredit nonviolence? Since the spirit of the rhetorical trap is violent—imposing an acceptance of violence by discrediting nonviolence—it shouldn't be left unchallenged. Respond with questions, not answers, and see if the questions can lead to a discussion of real, not imaginary, violence.

For a marvelous response to a "Crazed Gunman" scenario, see Joan Baez, *Daybreak* (Dial Press, 1968), 131-138.

APPENDIX C

___

TWO GUYS IN A BAR

The Setup

Guy B (Mr. Bumper) accidentally bumps Guy A (Mr. Aggressive). They are in a bar, they don't know each other, and Guy A takes offense. He says to Guy B, "I'm gonna kick your ass." If you could temporarily freeze time, stop all the action in the bar for a few moments, and have a quiet word with Guy B, how would you advise him to respond to Guy A's threat?

"Two Guys in a Bar" can be used as a classroom exercise to introduce the concept and dynamics of nonviolence and to make the important distinction between active nonviolence and passivity. US culture typically offers violent solutions—personal handguns, martial arts, armed police, capital punishment—to the problem of violent crime, perpetuating the belief that violence and the threat of violence must be countered with more of the same. In their calls for war-making, prominent opinion-makers insist (with no intended irony) that foreign enemies "only understand force." The heroic figure meting out well-deserved physical punishment to the dastardly villain is a staple of television dramas and Hollywood films. Such revenge fantasies are immensely popular because they allow some temporary emotional satisfaction to voters and viewers trapped in their own victor/victim psychologies. And when violence is considered the only effective response, not responding with violence is equated with doing nothing; pacifism is equated with passivism.

This oppressive cultural violence has caused many people to forget, bury, or not recognize the effectiveness of nonviolent responses. Yet, somehow, when asked to apply disinterested analysis to a violent scenario, when freed from the emotional pressures of in-group identity and out-group threat, people are quick to see the legitimacy of nonviolence. Two Guys in a Bar provides an opportunity to do just that.

Instructions

An open discussion of the bar scenario, before an instructor (or Ch. 3) offers potential answers, will deepen student engagement by encouraging them to think through the problem for themselves.

Begin by presenting **The Scenario**: Guy B bumps Guy A, who then threatens violent retaliation. Guy B steps "out of time," dials your number on his cell phone, and asks for advice on how to respond.

Then present **The Question**: What advice do you give Guy B? Students might entertain this question as an individual writing assignment, in small groups, or collectively as a class. Perhaps all three, in that order.

Before the question is considered, ask students what more they would like to know about the scenario. They will probably request **Specific Details** about Guy A and Guy B. How big are they? Are they armed? Are they drunk? Are they with friends? Also, they might ask about the bar—the size, the exits, the class of clientele.

It's probably best to make **Guy B** as average as possible—average height and weight, not carrying a weapon, not trained in martial arts, not rich, he's in a bar with a friend or two, he's consumed a beer or two. This information is available because, during his "timeout," Guy B can answer questions.

For details on **Guy A**, Guy B can only tell you that this aggressive stranger is average height and weight. About other pertinent information—weapons? friends? drunk?—Guy B cannot be sure. Simply put, Guy B is familiar, a friend on the phone, while Guy A is unknown, a random guy in some random bar.

Discussion

Identifying the Options

While you may find reason to add to this chart, most advice for Guy B will include one or more of the following categories:

Avoidance: Walk away, leave the immediate area, leave the bar.

Appeasement: Apologize for the bump, offer to buy a drink for Guy A.

Passivity: Stand still, curl up in a ball, say "please don't hurt me."

Distraction: Commence odd behavior, sing loudly, undress, play the fool.

Violent Resistance: Get ready to fight, look for a weapon, mock Guy A, strike the first blow.

Another category of advice is often overlooked:

Direct Nonviolence: Look Guy A in the eyes and tell him that if
he needs to hit you that's his business,
but you reject violence and won't fight
back, you won't hurt another human.

Did anyone suggest a direct nonviolence response? Do the discussants understand how it can work? Do they believe it? For many, this will be their first time considering nonviolence as something other than passivity, so it's worth discussing.

Identifying the Goal

One common consideration will be avoiding injury, so a chart can be drawn to outline the likelihood of someone getting physically hurt with each potential response employed by Guy B, assuming he employs no other response. For example, if Guy B attempts to hit Guy A (Violent Resistance), there is a good chance one or both of them will get hurt. If, instead, Guy B walks away and leaves the bar (Avoidance), Guy A won't get hurt, and it's unlikely Guy B will get hurt, though Guy A could throw something at Guy B or follow him out the door and hit him over the head. In fact, any response could lead to Guy B getting hurt. When confronted with a violent threat, there are no guarantees of physical safety.

	Guy A hurt?	Guy B hurt?
Avoidance	No	Unlikely
Appeasement	No	Unlikely
Passivity	No	Maybe
Distraction	No	Maybe
Violent Resistance	Probably	Probably
Direct Nonviolence	No	Maybe

The value of this chart is it reveals how little value it has. With the exception of Violent Resistance, the possible responses seem to offer similar results, suggesting that the potential for injury to Guy B may not be the key determinant in advising a course of action. Since there may be other considerations, an important question must be asked—perhaps the fundamental question in any decision-making: *What's the goal?* Your advice to Guy B is more likely to be useful if you first ask him, "What is your goal in this situation?" Guy B's primary concern might be to avoid physical injury, or maybe he's more worried about injury to his pride and doesn't want to appear cowardly, or perhaps most of all he wants to teach Guy A a lesson by punishing him for being a bully.

Emphasize this: *What's the goal?* It will come in handy.

Matching Options to Goals

The following paragraphs (extracted from Ch. 3), are offered to instructors as a guide for discussion of the final step: determining which strategy offers the best chance of attaining the desired goal. These scenarios, likely outcomes, and interpretations are open to debate and intended to encourage greater exploration of these themes, but the emphasis is on introducing and analyzing the potential of direct nonviolence as a response to violence.

If Guy B just wants to avoid physical injury, the best advice may be walk away and leave the bar. If he's concerned about his pride and thinks a hasty retreat will be shameful, you might recommend he offer to buy a beer for Guy A—no shame in that, and they might become friends. However, such appeasement, like avoidance, probably won't dissuade Guy A from future bullying, as his boorish behavior earned him a free drink. So how about teaching him a lesson? If Guy B feels up to it, he could punch Guy A in the mouth, knock him down, kick him in the ribs. That'll teach him! It's a high-risk strategy because Guy A might be armed, or be a more skilled fighter, or have five friends with him, and Guy B might end up on the ground. Also, if Guy B does give Guy A a beating, what lesson will Guy A learn? Guy B is hoping Guy A will conclude that bullying is unhealthy behavior as it gets you hurt, but a more likely message is that Guy A needs to get better at fighting or carry a weapon so that next time he comes out on top. This suggests a more extensive chart might be useful.

	Damage to Guy B's self-esteem?	Best likely outcome	Worst likely outcome	Lesson on violence
Avoidance	Maybe	Nobody hurt	B hurt	Bullying rewarded
Appeasement	Unlikely	Nobody hurt, mutual respect	B hurt	Bullying rewarded
Passivity	Probably	Nobody hurt	B hurt	Bullying rewarded
Distraction	Maybe	Nobody hurt	B hurt	Bullying rewarded
Violence	Maybe	Nobody seriously hurt, mutual respect	Serious injury to A/B, escalation into brawl	Be a skilled fighter

What about nonviolence—what can it accomplish that avoidance and appeasement cannot? If Guy B stands up to Guy A, but with compassion not hostility—if he says, "I won't fight you because I don't believe in violence, and I'd rather we were friends"—how will Guy A respond? You can imagine for yourself how the scenario plays out, but consider a few possibilities. Guy A may realize that Guy B is not a threat and leave him alone, maybe even shake his hand. If so, Guy B has avoided injury, rejected violence, and boosted his self-esteem. Alternatively, Guy A might physically attack Guy B, maybe punch him in the mouth. If Guy B resists the urge to run or hit back, if instead he wipes the blood off his lip and says, "I still won't fight you. I care about you as a human being," what then? Onlookers in the bar are likely to view Guy A's violence as inappropriate and disgraceful. Female onlookers especially, due to gender differences in socialization, are likely to think, "What a jerk!" Guy B's nonviolence exposes Guy A's violence as illegitimate. If, by comparison, Guy B fights back with violence, Guy A's violence is less likely delegitimized in the eyes of onlookers because both participants agreed to use violence. Yet another result may develop if Guy B responds with nonviolence and Guy A still assaults him. It may take some time, but Guy A, unless he is deeply dehumanized, is likely to experience some remorse for having hurt someone who was trying to help him. This is the power of nonviolence: to reach a would-be opponent at a deeper level, to touch his heart.

	Damage to Guy B's self-esteem?	Best likely outcome	Worst likely outcome	Lesson on violence
Nonviolence	Self-esteem boosted	Mutual respect, A/B transformed	B hurt	Violence delegitimized

While probably not the safest choice in the short term, only a direct nonviolence response to direct violence carries a real possibility of interrupting the mutually reinforcing triangle of violence. The other tactics either avoid violence without challenging it or lead to increased violence. They offer little hope of transforming the cultural violence, whatever it might be, which caused Guy A to think that inviting combat is an appropriate, perhaps necessary, response to incidental contact. In this sense, Guy A has presented Guy B with an opportunity—conflict equals opportunity—to reduce, however slightly, the level of cultural violence in his world. With a few brief words and some courage, he may be able to show Guy A, and any onlookers, that physical violence is unacceptable and unnecessary, and that direct nonviolence can be an effective antidote. That's a lesson worth teaching! The entire chart looks like this:

	Guy A hurt?	Guy B hurt?	Damage to Guy B's self-esteem?	Best likely outcome	Worst likely outcome	Lesson on violence
Avoidance	No	Unlikely	Maybe	Nobody hurt	B hurt	Bullying rewarded
Appeasement	No	Unlikely	Unlikely	Nobody hurt, mutual respect	B hurt	Bullying rewarded
Passivity	No	Maybe	Probably	Nobody hurt	B hurt	Bullying rewarded
Distraction	No	Maybe	Maybe	Nobody hurt	B hurt	Bullying rewarded
Violence	Probably	Probably	Maybe	Nobody seriously hurt, mutual respect	Serious injury to A/B, escalation into brawl	Be a skilled fighter
Nonviolence	No	Maybe	Self-esteem boosted	Mutual respect, A/B transformed	B hurt	Violence delegitimized

But before you go advising Guy B, or anyone else, to respond to direct violence with direct nonviolence rather than with avoidance, you may want to inquire if he has the discipline to stay nonviolent and the will to risk physical injury. Remember, reducing cultural violence may not be his immediate goal. Guy B may mean well, but doubt that standing up to a barroom bully will have much effect in the grand scheme of things. "Thanks for the advice, I see your point, but is it really worth the trouble?"

One answer is that with violence so pervasive, every tiny bit of active nonviolence helps. A big peace is made up of lots of little pieces. A second answer is that the person most affected by a nonviolent act usually is the nonviolent actor. If, when threatened by Guy A, Guy B responds with nonviolence, imagine the boost to his self-esteem. He didn't back down, didn't resort to violence, didn't give in to a desire to punish Guy A, and likely discovered courage and strength he didn't know he had. Even if he comes away with a bloody mouth, even if he never finds out what affect he had on Guy A and any onlookers, he will know he did the right thing.

NONVIOLENCE BIBLIOGRAPHY

Ackerman, Peter, and Jack Duvall. *A Force More Powerful: A Century of Nonviolent Conflict.* Palgrave, 2000.

Arsenault, Raymond. *Freedom Riders: 1961 and the Struggle for Racial Justice.* Oxford University Press, 2007.

Banerjee, Mukulika. *The Pathan Unarmed: Opposition and Memory in the North West Frontier.* School of American Research Press, 2000.

Boulding, Kenneth. *Three Faces of Power.* Sage Publications, 1989.

Brown, Judith. *Gandhi: Prisoner of Hope.* Yale University Press, 1989.

_____, ed. *Mahatma Gandhi: The Essential Writings.* Oxford University Press, 2008.

Burrowes, Robert. *The Strategy of Nonviolent Defense: A Gandhian Approach.* State University of New York Press, 1996.

Chenowith, Erica, and Maria Stephan. *Why Civil Resistance Works: The Strategic Logic of Nonviolent Conflict.* Columbia University Press, 2012.

Chernus, Ira. *American Nonviolence: The History of an Idea.* Orbis Books, 2004.

Dalton, Dennis, ed. *Mahatma Gandhi: Nonviolent Power in Action.* Columbia University Press, 1993.

De Ligt, Bart. *The Conquest of Violence: An Essay on War and Revolution.* Pluto Press, 1989 (1937).

Dellinger, David. *From Yale to Jail: The Life Story of a Moral Dissenter.* Pantheon, 1993.

Dumont, Rhea, Tom Hastings, and Emiko Noma, eds. *Conflict Transformation: Essays on Methods of Nonviolence.* McFarland & Co., 2013.

Easwaran, Eknath. *Nonviolent Soldier of Islam: Badshah Khan, A Man to Match His Mountains*. Nilgiri Press, 1999.

Fischer, Louis, ed. *The Essential Gandhi: An Anthology of His Writings on His Life, Work, and Ideas*. Vintage, 2002 (1962).

Friere, Paolo. *Pegagogy of the Oppressed*. Continuum, 2006 (1968).

Fry, Douglas. *Beyond War: The Human Potential for Peace*. Oxford University Press, 2007.

_____, ed. *War, Peace, and Human Nature: The Convergence of Evolutionary and Cultural Views*. Oxford University Press, 2013.

Galtung, Johan. *Peace by Peaceful Means: Peace and Conflict, Development and Civilization*. Sage Publications, 1996.

Gregg, Richard. *The Power of Non-Violence*. Navajivan Publishing, 1938.

Grossman, Dave. *On Killing: The Psychological Cost of Learning to Kill in War and Society*. Back Bay Books, 1995.

Halberstam, David. *The Children*. Fawcett, 1999.

Hallie, Philip. *Lest Innocent Blood Be Shed: The Story of the Village of Le Chambon and How Goodness Happened There*. Harper Perennial, 1994.

Iyer, Raghaven, ed. *The Essential Writings of Mahatma Gandhi*. Oxford University Press, 1991.

Lewis, John. *Walking with the Wind: A Memoir of the Movement*. Simon & Schuster, 1998.

Liyanage, Gunadasa. *Revolution Under the Breadfruit Tree: The Story of Sarvodaya Shramadana Movement and its Founder Dr. A.T. Ariyaratne*. Sinha Publishers, 1988.

Lynd, Staughton, and Alice Lynd, eds. *Nonviolence in America: A Documentary History*. Orbis Books, 1995.

Mahony, Liam. *Unarmed Bodyguards: International Accompaniment for the Protection of Human Rights.* Kumarian Press, 1997.

McWhorter, Diane. *Carry Me Home: Birmingham, Alabama, the Climactic Battle of the Civil Rights Revolution.* Simon & Schuster, 2001.

Nagler, Michael. *The Search for a Nonviolent Future: A Promise of Peace for Ourselves, Our Families, and Our World.* Inner Ocean Publishing, 2004.

Nepstad, Sharon. *Nonviolent Revolutions: Civil Resistance in the Late 20th Century.* Oxford University Press, 2011.

Olson, Lynne. *Freedom's Daughters: The Unsung Heroines of the Civil Rights Movement from 1830 to 1970.* Scribner, 2001.

Parkman, Patricia. *Nonviolent Insurrection in El Salvador: The Fall of Maximiliano Hernández Martínez.* University of Arizona Press, 1988.

Roberts, Adam, ed. *Civilian Resistance as a National Defense: Nonviolent Action against Aggression.* Stackpole Books, 1968.

Roberts, Adam, and Timothy Ash, eds. *Civil Resistance and Power Politics: The Experience of Non-violent Action from Gandhi to the Present.* Oxford University Press, 2011.

Rosenberg, Marshall. *Nonviolent Communication: A Language of Life.* PuddleDancer Press, 2003.

Schock, Kurt. *Unarmed Insurrections: People Power Movements in Nondemocracies.* University of Minnesota Press, 2004.

Semelin, Jacques. *Unarmed Against Hitler: Civilian Resistance in Europe, 1939-1943.* Praeger, 1993.

Sharp, Gene. *Gandhi as a Political Strategist.* Porter Sargent, 1979.

_____. *The Politics of Nonviolent Struggle.* Porter Sargent, 1973.

_____. *Waging Nonviolent Struggle: 20th Century Practice and 21st Century Potential.* Porter Sargent, 2005.

Shridharani, Krishnalal. *War Without Violence: A Study of Gandhi's Method and Its Accomplishments*. Harcourt Brace, 1939.

Slate, Nico. *Colored Cosmopolitanism: The Shared Struggle for Freedom in the United States and India*. Harvard University Press, 2012.

Stokes, Gail. *The Walls Came Tumbling Down: The Collapse of Communism in Eastern Europe*. Oxford University Press, 1993.

Tolstoy, Leo. *The Kingdom of God is Within You*. Wilder, 2009 (1894).

Unsworth, Richard. *A Portrait of Pacifists: Le Chambon, the Holocaust, and the Lives of André and Magda Trocmé*. Syracuse University Press, 2012.

Watson, Bruce. *Freedom Summer: The Savage Season of 1964 that Made Mississippi Burn and Made America a Democracy*. Penguin, 2010.

Weber, Thomas. *Gandhi's Peace Army: The Shanti Sena and Unarmed Peacekeeping*. Syracuse University Press, 1996.

Williams, Juan. *Eyes on the Prize: America's Civil Rights Years, 1954-1965*. Viking Penguin, 1987.

INDEX

ABOUT THE PHOTOGRAPHS

Front Cover   Democratic Convention, Los Angeles, 2000, in author's possession.

Chapter 1   March on Pentagon, Washington DC, 1967, Frank Wolfe, National Archives and Records Administration.

Chapter 2   Indian Memorial, Little Bighorn Battlefield National Monument, in author's possession.

Chapter 3   A.T. Ariyaratne, Colombo, Sri Lanka, Wikimedia Commons.

Chapter 4   John Brown, Wikimedia Commons.

Chapter 5   Wenceslas Square, Prague, Czechoslovakia, 1989, ŠJů, Creative Commons.

Chapter 6   Solidarity marchers, Warsaw, Poland, 1989, Wikimedia Commons.

Chapter 7   Daniel Trocmé (back row, center) and Jewish children, Le Chambon, France, 1941-42, US Holocaust Memorial Museum, used with permission.

Chapter 8   Diane Nash (third from left), Post House restaurant, Nashville, 1960, Gerald Holly, Creative Commons.

Chapter 9   Selma to Montgomery, 1965, Peter Pettus, Library of Congress.

Conclusion   Martin Luther King Jr., Montgomery, 1965, National Archives and Records Administration.

ABOUT THE AUTHOR

Timothy Braatz is a professor of history and peace studies at Saddleback College in Mission Viejo, California. His historical writings including *Surviving Conquest: A History of the Yavapai Peoples* and *From Ghetto to Death Camp: A Memoir of Privilege and Luck* (with Anatol Chari). He is also the author of numerous plays, including *The Devil and the Wedding Dress*, *Helena Handbasket*, and *One Was Assaulted*, and a novel, *Grisham's Juror*.

ABOUT THE PRESS

The Disproportionate Press, a curated publishing arm of Luny Crab LLC, helps connect authors with their audiences. Our first two titles tell the story: *Grisham's Juror,* a fun and witty tale about jury duty in Laguna Beach, California; and *From Ghetto to Death Camp: A Memoir of Privilege and Luck,* a first-hand account of the how one man made his way through the tragedy of war. Two stories disproportionate in scope (one fiction, one nonfiction), but similar in the quality of writing and storytelling.